DATE DUE

S0-ARX-626

8 JUN 1971 G X E G

8 FEB 1972 H W B

Latin America:
Internal Conflict
and International Peace

Peter Calvert

St Martin's Press

New York

© Peter Calvert 1969

Published by
ST MARTIN'S PRESS INC
175 Fifth Avenue New York N. Y. 10010
MACMILLAN AND CO LTD
Little Essex Street London WC2
and also at Bombay Calcutta and Madras
Macmillan South Africa (Publishers) Pty Ltd Johannesburg
The Macmillan Company of Australia Pty Ltd Melbourne
The Macmillan Company of Canada Ltd Toronto
Gill and Macmillan Ltd Dublin

Library of Congress catalog card no. 77–75263

Manufactured in the United States of America

F
1414
C16

For Di

7 7 Ja 71

5L

Contents

Maps and Tables

MAPS

TABLES

Abbreviations

AD	Acción Democrática, Venezuela
APRA	Alianza Popular Revolucionaria Americana, Peru
A.P.S.R.	*American Political Science Review*
CACM	Central American Common Market
CIA	Central Intelligence Agency, U.S.
ECLA	United Nations Economic Commission for Latin America
GOU	Grupo de Oficiales Unidos, Argentina
H.A.H.R.	*Hispanic American Historical Review*
J.I.A.S.	*Journal of Inter-American Studies*
LAFTA	Latin American Free Trade Area
MNR	Movimiento Nacional Revolucionario, Bolivia
OAS	Organisation of American States
P.H.R.	*Pacific Historical Review*
UNEF	United Nations Emergency Force at Suez
UNFICYP	United Nations Force in Cyprus

Preface

THE aim of this book is an unpretentious one: to present a succinct outline of the political and diplomatic history of Latin America in this century. It presents it with a continuous theme: the fact that the preoccupation of Latin American politicians with the politics of violent internal conflict – something of importance in itself in a world increasingly conscious of revolutions or *coups d'état* – has been attended by notable efforts to achieve that stable framework of international relations which could make their skills obsolete. I should like to hope that it could inspire others more favoured by nature and history to take note, and to do better than they do.

One word of warning seems necessary. Since much of the tension in recent Latin American diplomacy has arisen from the interaction of the Caribbean system and the continental system of South America, this in turn means that in describing it the development of United States involvement in the area must be taken into account. This though, is not a diplomatic history of the United States nor a history of United States – Latin American relations as such.

For this reason, as it would have been inappropriate to give too much prominence to any one country, I have chosen to present the material needed to understand each, by chronological treatment within defined areas. I believe this is not only convenient for reference purposes, but necessary if the analytical concepts that underly the treatment are to be of any real use to the reader.

The sources for such an outline are many and various. No one can hope personally to be a student of more than a small part of two continents' history in any given time span. I am much indebted to the research of many experts whose works I have given credit in the references and in the bibliography. They are much broader and much deeper than I can indicate here, given the space available, and the reader is urged to consult those that interest him for himself. If he does, he will find that I have not necessarily agreed in all cases with their interpretations of the facts or have phrased them differently, and throughout any errors of fact or interpretation are my own.

It is pleasant to have the opportunity to thank Professor Alexander DeConde, from whom I first learnt about the diplomatic history of the United States. In dealing with its crucial role in modern Latin America I have tried to appraise it fairly. I should also like to thank Professor David Joslin, who encouraged me to write this book; Christopher Platt, Christopher Thorne and Michael Shaw, who read it in manuscript and made helpful and constructive comments; my colleagues at the University of Southampton, who have at different times discussed with me theoretical approaches to politics; and Miss Gillian Boyle, who volunteered to help out with the typing of the manuscript at a critical time. I am grateful too, to my wife for her encouragement, and to my son for his forbearance.

South America

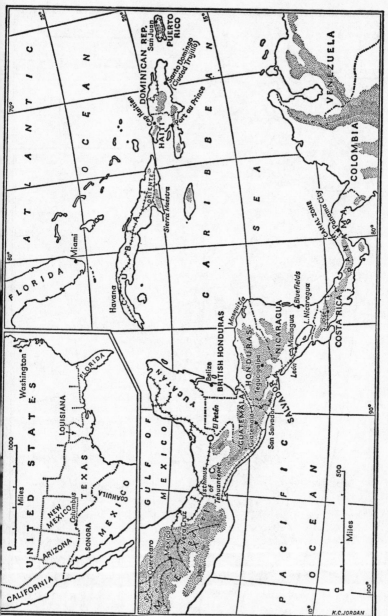

The Caribbean

K.C.JORDAN

1 The New Century

IN 1900 there were twenty-one self-governing states in the Americas. By an odd fiction three of them, Canada, New-foundland and the United States, all of them former British colonies, were (and are) regarded as being in some way different from the rest, which are collectively known in the English language under the generic term of 'Latin America'. 'Latin America' is a purely artificial concept. The Latin Americans themselves do not often use the term.

Eighteen states in Latin America had, in 1900, been independent from their former colonial powers for seventy years or more. As entities they had then had a longer history than Italy or Germany, and as independent entities they had had a longer existence then, than say, Norway, Ireland or Egypt have today. Of the eighteen, sixteen are Spanish speaking, one Portuguese and one French. Other territories in the same region were under the control of foreign powers and some have remained so to the present day. This fact gave those powers an interest in the affairs of the independent states which otherwise they might not have had.

The countries with which this survey is concerned, then, were almost all in existence as mature states over sixty years ago. The basic factors which have formed their national identities had already long since had time to operate. Of these, of course, the most important were the physical, topographical and climatic factors.[1] Most of the states lie within the tropics and have very severe regional differences in climate and altitude which act as impediments to relations of all kinds not only with each other but also within each state. The division between high mountain, upland plateau and coastal plain, with its accompanying differences in social and economic organisation, is repeated again and again throughout the republics. In the north, in Mexico, the division is between the northern desert, the high plateau (the so-called 'Core' region around Mexico city), and the swamp and jungle of the south. The same pattern, on a smaller scale, is repeated in Central America, complicated by volcanic and seismic activity which in geological terms is still forming the link between North and South America. In fact, however, the fault that runs from Alaska to Cape Horn has had no less drastic effects on life in Mexico and Chile.

To the south again, the Andean countries exhibit the sharpest contrasts. In Colombia, Ecuador, Peru and Bolivia the coastal strip is very narrow and its foothills carry a disproportionate percentage of the population. Behind it the mountains rise to an average of 14,000 feet. On the *altiplano* soil is thin, and on the *páramo* (*puna*) snow and sleet are common, and breathing itself difficult. Yet the dweller on the *altiplano* is spared many of the dangers and diseases that attack the dweller in the humid Amazonian region that lies beyond, much of it still unexplored; a virtual 'inland sea' to the countries that border it, for it is navigable by ocean-going vessels as far as Iquitos in Peru.

Brazil is the master of this Amazonian region and the largest country in Latin America, with an area greater than that of the United States less Alaska. The most favoured region lies south, around the river Plate, where Uruguay, Paraguay and Argentina share common boundaries and temperate climate with Brazil's southern states. The majority of the Brazilian population, despite every encouragement, has stayed close to the coast. This has not been from choice. Apart from the Amazon, other rivers in Brazil rise close to the coast, but are cut off from it by an escarpment of mountains and so flow inland. Communication between the coast and the Amazon region thus had to await the age of air transport. Rivers and mountains serve as the most formidable of many barriers to inter-American trade and commerce.

The historical foundations are no less important than the geographic. The most significant moment in time for many parts of Latin America remains the moment of independence. It was at that point that the relationship was formalised

Table 1

Population and Ethnic Composition, c. 1900

Country	Date	Population	Eur	Mes	Ind	Neg	Other
Argentina	1904[e]	5,410,028	99[1]	—	tr	—	—
Bolivia	1900[c]	1,816,271	13	27	50	tr	9
Brazil	1900[c]	17,318,556	44	32	9	15	—
Chile	1902[e]	2,983,359	39	60	1	—	—
Colombia	1899[e]	3,917,000	10	40	15	35[2]	—
Costa Rica	1904	331,340	14	77	9	—	—
Cuba	1907	2,048,980	70	—	—	30	tr
Dominican Republic	1900[e]	500,000	Insufficient data available				
Ecuador	1900[e]	1,500,000	8	30	62	—	—
El Salvador	1906	1,116,253	10	50	40	tr	—
Guatemala	1903	1,842,134	tr	40	60	—	—
Haiti	1900[e]	1,500,000	—	—	—	90	10[3]
Honduras	1905[o]	500,136	tr	98	2	—	—
Mexico	1900[c]	13,607,259	19	43	38	—	—
Nicaragua	1905[e]	550,000	5	40	55	tr	—
Panama	1909	361,000	13	57	14	15	7[4]
Paraguay	1905[e]	631,347	50	30	20	—	tr
Peru	1906[o]	3,547,829	14	25	58	2	2
Uruguay	1908[c]	1,042,668	99[1]	—	tr	—	—
Venezuela	1904[o]	2,663,671	10	70	—	—	20[3]

[c] = census. [o] = official estimate. [e] = estimate.
[1] incl. *mestizo*. [3] mulatto.
[2] incl. mulatto. [4] mainly Chinese.
SOURCES: *Whitaker's Almanack* (1901); *Encyclopaedia Britannica*, 13th edition; *The Statesman's Year Book* (1911).

between the descendants of Spanish (or Portuguese) settlers (or creoles) and the indigenous populations with whom many of them intermarried. The product of that inter-marriage is the *mestizo* – the dominant racial type in Latin America, a mixture of races with the problems of both and lacking acceptance, historically speaking, as part of either (Table 1).[2]

Some Latin American countries, such as Argentina, Uruguay and Costa Rica, are very largely creole. In the first two, and in Brazil, the creole element has been reinforced by immigration in the late nineteenth and early twentieth centuries. Others, such as Paraguay, Guatemala, Mexico, Ecuador and El Salvador are very largely either Indian or mestizo. Most lie in between, an exception being Haiti, which is entirely negro or mulatto, of African descent. The present century has been the century of the emergence of the mestizo.

Interestingly enough, although this has had profound effects on the pattern of social life, its political consequences are both vague and uncertain. Power has been transferred from one set of hands to another, but the style of politics, more often than not, has not changed. Any attempt to construct a theory of political behaviour in Latin America on the basis of racial composition is doomed to failure.

Before tackling these, and other problems, therefore, it is necessary to have some idea of the history of Latin America before 1900, and the factors which influenced the development and emergence of these interesting countries.[3] The lessons which they have to yield are the more valuable since the heritage of common colonial background and culture make them much more comparable than any other selection of countries of the modern world.

From the standpoint of the international community the story begins in a year in the 1480s, in the climate of exploration and discovery which had already taken the Portuguese to southern Africa and may well, on the long dog-leg run to clear the Azores, have taken a Portuguese navigator to the coast of Brazil. At all accounts, it was in these years that the concept of land across the Western Ocean was accepted, though it was believed then that that land was in fact a continuation of the Asian mainland.

The discovery by Columbus of Hispaniola in 1492 confirmed the existence of land. But it was not until after 1510
that the explorations of Amerigo Vespucci proved that
behind it lay a continent which was not part of the Indies.
By then, however, the name had stuck and America remained
the Indies throughout the period of Spanish rule, and its
inhabitants 'Indians' to this day.

It was the observation of gold ornaments on the inhabitants of the islands that brought into play a second
reason for exploration, the desire for gold. It was this
pressure that brought about the expansion of activity that
disclosed the great civilisations of the Americas. Accounts of
this have too often failed to take account of the nature of the
times. Three points are of special importance to the kind of
society that emerged.

The Spanish colonisation of the Americas preceded British
colonisation of New England and Virginia by more than a
century. Indeed, it was a prime factor determining the
nature of that colonisation. It therefore took place in a very
different atmosphere of religious, cultural and economic life.

In general, Spanish colonisation followed the earlier
pattern of colonisation based on 'trading posts' and was of
the 'exploitation' rather than the 'settlement' type. But
there was nevertheless extensive Spanish settlement in the
less inhabited areas. Where they met advanced civilisations,
however, they were very much in the minority, and in self-
defence adopted a system of control of the indigenous
population which was geared primarily to the interest of
their own survival. Three of these civilisations were of special
interest and have contributed extensively to the diversity of
the Latin American cultural heritage.

These were, from north to south; the Aztec-Toltec, the
Maya and the Inca civilisations. The Aztec-Toltec civilisation of the Valley of Mexico flourished in two stages from
about A.D. 1000 and succeeded in unifying much of the
Core. It was characterised by a high level of bloodshed, both

by war and by human sacrifice; by the raising of crops and working of gold, silver and semi-precious stones.[4]

The Mayas lived in Central America, in the area of the Petén in Guatemala and the Yucatán peninsula of Mexico, where their descendants still live and their language is still spoken. Their civilisation at the time of conquest was, however, already in decline, probably owing to the failure of its means of 'slash and burn' cultivation. It was characterised by megalithic building regulated by a complex and extremely accurate calendar, whose correspondence with the Christian Era is still disputed. It flourished in the south from A.D. 60 to 630, and in the north down to 1300.[5]

The Incas lived in the highlands of Peru. Some observers have called its form of state organisation a 'socialist empire', because everyone was equal except the Inca himself. It was characterised by solar religion, coupled with megalithic building at high altitudes and the creation of mysterious, patterns probably of astronomical significance, and community of lands, which were redistributed at the end of a fifty-year cycle.[6]

Over each of these civilisations the Spanish conquerors had technical, if not technological, superiority to offset their minute numbers. Above all, they had steel weapons and the horse as a means of transport. The most developed civilisations of the New World lacked the wheel, were still essentially a stone age culture, and had no animal capable of bearing burdens in excess of 100 lb. other than man himself. Yet both in Mexico under Cortés in 1519, and in Peru under Pizarro in 1528, the success of the conquerors owed more to surprise, ruthlessness and the certainty of being right than to the technical advantages they possessed.[7] It was by near-magical prestige that they secured the acceptance of the majority of the populations that surrounded them, aided by their political feel for the divisions in their enemies which made their recovery hopeless.

Spain itself was in a position to extend its effort only

because of the fortunate coincidence of its own unification on the eve of the discovery of the Indies. The dominant position of Castile in united Spain, however, allied to the fact that it was Castile rather than Spain that had chartered the voyage of discovery, meant that in the new colonies the forces of Castilian centralism were dominant to the exclusion of the mediaeval tradition of liberty represented by Aragon and Barcelona.

The system of administration that was imposed on the Indies was, in short, the one developed in the seven-century long reconquest of Spain from the Moors. Naturally the attitudes of the *conquistadores* were influenced by the resemblance. In each case those conquered were infidels and their conversion to Christianity the principal object of a devout monarchy.[8] For both spiritual and secular reasons the Crown was concerned to establish its authority at the earliest possible date.

The *conquistadores*, the men of the sword, were authorised to establish their own pattern of interim government following the first acquisition of new territory – dignified, as was Columbus himself, with the title of *adelantado*, the man who goes in front. This form of concession, however, being potentially dangerous to the Crown and its pretensions to equal authority in all its dominions was supplanted as soon as possible by the development of a regular pattern of rule from Spain. The Council of the Indies at Seville acted as the royal council, making decisions on policy and transmitting orders to the Viceroys. Below the Viceroys stretched a hierarchy of Governors and lesser officials, each checked, in the Spanish tradition, both by a local council and by roving commissions of inquiry. There was little latitude left for local initiative by the codification of the elaborate body of law known as the *Recopilación de las Leyes de las Indias*. Once developed in a few brief years, this pattern was to remain substantially unchanged throughout the three centuries of Spanish rule, though during the Seven Years war a significant modification was made in allowing the colonists to establish their own militia for their defence from other colonial powers.[9]

Spanish colonisation was mostly conducted by scions of wealthy or at least aristocratic families in the search for wealth, land or status. The rule of the Indies, however, did not pass into their hands, but remained firmly in the hands of those born in Spain (*peninsulares*) until the last years of the Empire. Not only did the colonies not attract vigorous elements of a reforming society, as did the United States or later Australia, but if they produced any they could not make use of them except in one special field.

Secondly, of all Spaniards, Castilians tended to have the most fanatical devotion to the delimitation of race. Castilian society had for generations been most seriously threatened by the attraction of the superior Moorish culture from which they had borrowed so much, and which they had transmitted to a not very grateful Europe. To resist this attraction they went to great lengths to stress their racial superiority. This racial superiority, however, was also cultural, for it found its fullest expression in an uncompromising concept of religious faith. The Castilian rulers of the Indies, spontaneously as well as by deliberation, brought with them the parallel structure of mediaeval church organisation which to them was still a vital part of every aspect of administration. It was this organisation that offered the creole the sole avenue to preferment in political questions. By the time of the later Habsburgs, the Archbishops of Mexico regularly acted as Viceroys of New Spain on the death or recall of the secular incumbent.

There were other, broader social consequences. The first Mexican bishopric was created in the year of the conquest (1519); the Archbishoprics of Mexico, Lima and Santo Domingo were set up in 1545. By the end of the colonial period there were no fewer than ten ecclesiastical provinces and thirty-eight dioceses in Latin America. Clergy both secular and regular were multiplied in proportion. By 1574 there were 200 monasteries in New Spain alone. Incidentally it was not until 1618 that creoles were admitted to the ranks of the clergy in New Spain, by the Franciscans. The size of this ecclesiastical establishment was a heavy burden on the indigenous population which was subject to forced labour in lieu of taxes like the Spaniards themselves, but in addition was racked and ravaged by the strange European diseases the conquerors had brought, and which in places reduced the population by more than half.[10]

In Peru and Mexico an additional burden on the Indians was forced labour in the mines, whose produce was dispersed in the wars of Charles V (Carlos I) among Italian and Dutch bankers, producing on the way a steady inflation which aided the emergence of new political forces both there and in such unlikely places as England and Scandinavia.[11] Much more general was the partly legal dispossession of the Indians as landowners by secular owners who often left their land in mortmain to the Church, until in places it owned more than four-fifths of the land in areas as big as a modern European state. In return, the Church did through missionary activity open up substantial tracts of country. Paraguay, Venezuela and California owed their first contact with Western ideas to these missionaries, and their journeys remain a permanent influence on the map of those areas. When this is coupled with the role of the Church in education, it is not so surprising to find Venezuela and Paraguay in the vanguard of the movement for independence.

Such structure as was created by the Portuguese Empire in Brazil was in the first instance largely a consequence of the acquisition of Portugal itself by Philip II and its rule by Spanish monarchs between 1582 and 1640. But during the eighteenth century, particularly under the dictatorship of Pombal, the Portuguese went far further than the Spaniards in developing a modern system of colonial rule through a

Minister for Brazil. In consequence, the development of Brazil approximated much more closely to the ideal of growth of the mother country.[12]

The attainment of independence by the Spanish colonies forms in itself the clearest evidence of the appalling problem of communications before recent times. Its political lesson, however, was that however remote the colonial power, colonial rule did serve one useful purpose which was much missed in the years following independence. This was the function of impartial arbitration between local interests. The Crown, in particular, did much to mitigate the harshness with which colonists treated the indigenous races. A final judgement, taking into account every aspect of the question, might fairly be that the Spanish colonial empire, for better or for worse, conferred on its new subjects as far as lay within its power every aspect of its culture which it considered to be beneficial; its shortcomings were those of its own nature and no more.

The course of liberation began in a place and in a manner which were to be far from typical of its final outcome.[13] The movement, so far as the Spanish Empire was concerned, arose from the cession by Spain to France of part of the island of Hispaniola, the colony of Santo Domingo, by the Treaty of Basle in 1795. This cession, which was an act of alliance between the two countries in the French Revolutionary Wars, had unexpected consequences. The French had hoped to round off their possession of the other part of the island, Haiti. But already since 1791 the island's vast population of Negro slaves, under their leader Toussaint L'Ouverture, had been in a state of revolt. Oppressive conditions and the influence of the doctrines of the French Revolution made for an explosive mixture.

Cession meant that the revolt spread to the Spanish-speaking part of the island. Attempts to recapture the island and to reintroduce slavery following the Treaty of Amiens were foiled by the retreat of the army of Toussaint's

successor, Dessalines, into the Spanish half, and ended by
the resumption of the war in Europe. Haiti became independent in 1804. The tradition of violence in its relations
with Santo Domingo survives to this day.[14]

The Treaty had a more serious consequence for the
security of the Empire. The territory of Louisiana had also
been ceded to France, and Napoleon took advantage of the
peace to transfer it to the United States, though his right to
do so was invalidated by the terms on which Spain had
ceded it.[15] This substantial loss of territory was hurtful to
Spanish prestige, but the loss of the combined French and
Spanish fleets at Trafalgar in 1805 was even more so, and it
vitally damaged communications between Spain and the
Indies. The opportunity for independence had come. Who
would take advantage of it? Since there was no general
consensus on grievances, no united action was likely.

The impetus came first from the region of the river Plate,
at the end of the long line of communications that stretched
from Cádiz to Panamá, and thence via Lima and overland
to Buenos Aires. An enthusiastic British sea-captain attacked
and captured that port in 1806. The Royal Spanish Army
was conspicuously defeated, but the British expedition was
dislodged by the spontaneous rising of the creoles. Their
success gave them confidence. Moreover the British settled
down across the river mouth in Montevideo and gave them
a taste for free trade in Birmingham ware and Bolton
textiles. Free trade meant free transit of ideas between ports,
too.[16]

At this point, Napoleon knocked away the symbolic
foundation of Spanish unity. In his pursuit of the embargo
against England known as the Continental System his
armies demanded and received passage through Spain for
the invasion of Portugal. Arriving at Lisbon the day after
the Royal Family had sailed from it for Brazil on a British
ship, their pride demanded retribution and their safety
required guaranteed lines of communication. On 18 March

1808 a French military *coup* deposed Carlos IV and at Bayonne both he and his son Fernando were forced to resign their claim to the Spanish throne, subsequently assigned to Napoleon's brother. An incident in which French forces opened fire on civilians in Madrid stretched nerves to snapping point, and on 2 May a spontaneous rising of the citizens inaugurated the great Spanish War of Independence.[17]

Since there was no central authority to co-ordinate the effort against the French it was at first erratic and not very effective, despite such aid as could be lent to it from outside. The great French armies were able to keep Wellesley's army bottled up in Portugal, and did not have to face a major battle. Slowly guerrillas began to wear down their communications and their morale, but it took a long time to do so. It followed, quite logically, that the individual provinces, both in the Peninsula and in the Indies, attempted to make good the deficiency of authority by setting up interim régimes.

Traditionally, under the monarchy, the provinces were all regarded as co-equal kingdoms under the monarch. In the absence of the monarch there was no general agreement from what authority the interim governments were derived.

The name of Fernando, the heir to the throne, was certainly freely used to legitimise the general maintenance of existing personnel. As he was in French custody the actual making of decisions necessarily fell to others. After 1810 this for Spain itself meant the Spanish parliament or Cortes, meeting in Cádiz. The Cortes, however, contained a large number of men of radical views, not necessarily sympathetically received in the outer provinces, and the less so because of their tendency to regard those provinces as being inferior, subject to them as the representatives of the Spanish people. They were the *liberales*, or Liberals; a name first applied to them in derision by their opponents.

The Constitution of 1812 which was drawn up by these

men was of fundamental importance as the last political contribution by Spain to the colonies in their period of dependence.[18] Because of its origins it was not effective in the Indies, although it was proclaimed there, and the provinces overseas were invited to send delegates to the Cortes. In brief, therefore, the further course of separation was accomplished, though in different ways in different places, by this ideological division between Liberals and Conservatives, and Spanish colonies entered on independent life with these two parties.

Some, in fact, had already done so. 1810 itself had been a year of creole revolts. That of Caracas proclaimed the independence of Venezuela for the first time. It lasted about a year. Its example spread to the province of New Granada (modern Colombia) and the series of risings which followed made the name and reputation of Simón Bolívar, 'the Liberator'.[19] Meanwhile a priest, Miguel Hidalgo in Mexico had touched off an Indian revolt in the name of the patroness of the Americas, the Virgin of Guadalupe. Calling for death to the Spaniards and the reconquest of lands for the Indian, Hidalgo's summons led to the sack of Querétaro and Guanajuato and the outbreak of race war. Hidalgo was executed in 1811, but Morelos took over the cause of independence, and by 1815 had liberated most of the territory of modern Mexico. The end of the Napoleonic Wars in 1815 enabled Spain to reconquer on all fronts, and in 1816 Morelos too was executed. With the simultaneous failure of Bolívar's campaign of liberation it appeared that the greater part of the Spanish Empire had been saved.

But not all of it. On independence, Santo Domingo had immediately been annexed by Haiti. Independent once more in 1844, it returned to Spain in 1861 and only finally became independent in 1865. There was also no success for Spain in the area of the river Plate. The revolt of Buenos Aires in 1810 was leaderless. Despite this apparently major handicap, it was successful because its people were more united, more confident than their fellows, and secured firm control over the then relatively compact area of Argentine settlement.

The attempt, however, of Buenos Aires to retain its traditional rule over the up-river territory of Asunción – modern Paraguay – broke down in 1811, when Paraguay seceded from it and from the Empire under Dr Francia, subsequently its first dictator.[20] Simultaneously the hero of Uruguayan independence, Artigas, led the first fight for secession in Uruguay, the territory then known as the Banda Oriental. He was successful insofar as he attained its liberation from both Spain and Buenos Aires, with British help, but he was unsuccessful in that, when that aid came to an end, Uruguay was annexed to Brazil and remained part of that Empire from 1817 to 1830.[21]

There was, lastly, no unity between the Platine provinces of modern Argentina and the port on which they were dependent. Almost thirty years went by before Argentina attained the semblance of a modern state.

The second wave of independence was to reinforce the lessons of the first. It originated in the Andine province of Cuyo in Argentina, where between 1814 and 1817 San Martín built up, as Governor, an army with which to attempt the incredible feat of liberating Chile by a campaign across the Andes. Once over the Andes his courage proved justified and Chile secured its independence in 1818 by the combined efforts of San Martín, its own leader O'Higgins, and the fleet trained by Lord Cochrane.[22] The combined forces then set out to secure their position by striking at the heart of Spanish power in Peru.

On the day they landed on the coast of Peru, news was received by the Royal Government in Lima of the Spanish Revolution of 1820. The Liberals were once more in power and the forces of conservative Europe were faced with simultaneous revolts in Portugal, Naples, Piedmont and Greece. It was at this juncture that the conservative creoles of New Spain attained independence largely peacefully. The former Viceroyalty remained united briefly under the short lived Empire of Iturbide and then split into Mexico and Central America. Similarly it was this transformation that ended resistance to the latest campaign of Bolívar, who in turn advanced on Peru. The Spanish Revolution was already a memory when the decisive battle was fought for the liberation of Peru under its hero of independence, Sucre. San Martín had retired from the field to leave the glory to Bolívar who himself had already returned to his native territory. This, the area of modern Venezuela and Colombia, was organised as one state briefly under the name of Gran Colombia, but already the Liberator's name was becoming associated with his last battleground, the territory of Upper Peru since known as Bolivia.

The liberal revolution in Portugal also played its part in turning loose the co-equal kingdom of Brazil. The fact that the heir to the Portuguese throne was still living there meant that it attained its independence under a monarchy (1822), and one, furthermore – for there were other attempts at monarchies which did not survive – which lasted until 1889.[23]

For all these territories the last battle was fought out not on the military but on the diplomatic field. It did not involve the forces of independence at all. This was the battle between the British, who desired to trade with the new states, and the French under Louis XVIII, who were prepared at first to aid Spanish reconquest. The position of the British looked weak; they even asked the United States to support their pressure on France, but were snubbed by the verbal broadside known later as the Monroe doctrine. The facts of sea power, however, were overwhelmingly on their side, and the British statesman Canning was successful in causing France to believe that it doomed any expedition to failure. In the Polignac Memorandum (1823) the French Government undertook to abstain from aiding the Spaniards.[24]

Understandably, the Spanish themselves did not accept the position as final, and there is little doubt that Monroe himself would not have expected them to. Until late in the nineteenth century they continued to take all reasonable opportunities of recovering their lost territories. Expeditions to Mexico (1829) and to Peru were sent in vain, the latter leading to war between Spain on the one hand and Peru, Ecuador, Bolivia and Chile on the other, which lasted from 1864 to 1871. It ended only amid the ruins of Spain's own political order in the period of the First Republic. Spain recognised the independence of a Latin American state for the first time in 1836 in the case of Mexico. But Paraguay was only recognised in 1880, Colombia in 1881, Uruguay in 1882 and Honduras not until 1894.

Several points about the general pattern of independence were to have a marked effect upon the course of nineteenth-century history.

To begin with the role of leadership was important. The number of leaders was few and their relation to affairs was largely military.

Complications of internal dissent, moreover, were very marked. For this as well as for topographical and strategic reasons, the Spanish Empire fragmented on independence, all four of its component Viceroyalties being dismembered.

Unfortunately the heroes of independence, being military, were relatively uninterested in civil government, and in the course of the long war – three times as long as that of the United States for independence – the civil government fell into the hands of the second-raters. Short periods of rule by outstanding men increased rather than decreased the tensions that resulted.

In Mexico and Peru, since the immediate cause of the Spanish fall was the revolution in Spain, independence was in itself a sign of the failure of traditionalism to form a stable government. The irony was that it was revolutionary Spain that initiated the theory of regarding colonists as equals and hence Indians as inferior, and it was this that widened the scope of hostility to Hispanic values in these two countries, with significant results. A contributory consideration was that Spanish efforts to reconquer the Indies were naturally directed first at the traditional centres of rule. However strategic considerations affected others besides the Spanish. It was no coincidence that it was Mexico where Napoleon tried to plant a puppet Empire, where the Kaiser sought to outflank the United States, and where De Gaulle sought to invoke Latin America against the supposed hegemony of the 'Anglo-Saxons'.

The legacy of independence, therefore, was the rule of military leaders, or at least of the leader who ruled because of outstanding personal qualities: in Spanish, the *caudillo*.[25] Some have even claimed that the *caudillo*, as the military leader of independence, inherited the legitimacy of the Crown. It was then his to transmit to the civil government of his choice, and also his to take away. Certainly this was how the *caudillo* looked at it.

More importantly the *caudillo* was the man who displayed actual power. When the Royal power had gone, his remained, and if it was accepted it was because power was envisaged as a physical attribute of a commander. Authority was shown by the exercise of power. Other qualifications for positions of leadership were relatively insignificant, and the history of the early years of the new Republics is the story of how such men came to realise their human limitations, freely or otherwise. It is therefore doubly important to sound a warning against easy acceptance of the idea that the existence of such outstanding personal characteristics actually gave their possessors power, without relation to the wishes of those they ruled. Power demands at least the tacit consent of the ruled if it is to be effective. The remarkable men serve to date events, and do so most effectively because events are made by men and they were the men principally evolved in the shaping of those events. But they ruled only with the help of a great many who were prepared to implement, and even more who were prepared to obey.

With this in mind we can now attempt, very widely, to summarise the main trends of Latin American development in the nineteenth century. Five features of particular importance can be dealt with in turn.

Common as a problem to the outlying portions of the former Spanish, Portuguese – and British – Empires in America was the need to occupy the national territory. So in the early years of the nineteenth century the newly independent Chilean government waged war against the Araucanian Indians south of the Bío-Bío river, and gradually extended their power southward from there to the Strait of Magellan. The dictator of Buenos Aires, Juan Manuel de Rosas (1833–52) established his authority with the Platine states by his successful wars against Indians and the great consequent extension of the cattle country of the savannah. In Yucatán, successive Mexican governments strove with the autonomous governments of that peninsula until in the savage conflict known as the Caste War (1847–8) it was forcibly incorporated. Unfortunately for Mexico this was only achieved after Mexico itself had lost more than half its territory to the United States, first by the secession of Texas (1836) and then through the war of 1845–8 after which the United States annexed California, New Mexico and Arizona together with other territory less clearly delimited.[26]

Only in the case of Texas did these conflicts involve areas with much settlement, and that was very recent. But in others simultaneous expansion by two otherwise friendly countries led to long term strife. For example, the northward expansion of the Chileans came into collision with the southward expansion of Peru. This was one of the causes of the great War of the Pacific (1879–83).[27] It resulted in Bolivia losing to Peru and Chile respectively its coastal provinces of Tacna and Arica, and the diversion of its expansion in the direction of the east and Paraguay, with important consequences for the course of events in the twentieth century. The expansion of Argentina on the one hand and Brazil on the other led to constant war between them, much of it over the question of Uruguay, until the common interests of both powers in resisting the pretensions of Francisco Solano López of Paraguay led to the War of the Triple Alliance (1865–70).[28] In this war half the population of Paraguay perished, barely 150,000 men being left alive.

To the desire for expansion as a cause of conflict, however, must be added divergent interests and wishes between central governments and peripheral, provincial areas. In most of the countries this took the form of constant struggle between so called 'Centralists' and 'Federalists', generally assimilated to the pattern of Liberal-Conservative conflict and attended by changes of constitutional organisation symbolic of the aims of the contending parties.

In many ways, the most striking example is that of New Granada or, as it is now known, Colombia, where the present strong centralist form was not imposed until 1886.[29] In Mexico the influence of the United States helped the retention of federal forms, but the great Liberal Constitution of 1857 did not stand in the way of, and in some ways even assisted, the long dictatorship of Porfirio Díaz (1877–80, 1884–1911). In the twentieth century the conflict was resumed in a different form in each case.

Mexico was more fortunate at least than its neighbour to the south, the Central American Republic, which simply dissolved into its five constituent states in 1838–9.[30] Despite sporadic attempts, and a definite desire for reunification which has latterly resulted in more than symbolic efforts at co-operation, all these moves have come to nothing. The dissolution of the Bolivarian union of Gran Colombia in 1830 into Venezuela, New Granada and Ecuador similarly did not end centre-periphery conflict. But where in Central American states this conflict took the form of armed expeditions to impose unity on the others, in northern South

America it simply continued within the new boundaries. In Venezuela it remained a live issue until the anti-clerical dictatorship of Guzmán Blanco (1872–88); in Ecuador until the Catholic dictatorship of García Moreno (1861–5, 1869–1875). Nor was conflict ended there. Long after the Constitution of 1886 secessionist feeling in one part of Colombia was still strong enough to inspire the creation of independent Panama.

Also of interest are the unsuccessful attempt at confederation between Bolivia (former Upper Peru) and Peru between 1865 and 1869, and the fact that disunity persisted in Argentina after the fall of Rosas, and was only reduced to a tolerable level by the powerful presidencies of Mitre (1862–8) and Sarmiento (1868–74).

Mention has already been made of the ideological content of liberalism, and of some of its associations in Latin America with the forces of centralism. Much of this revolved round the liberal antipathy to clericalism and to clerical domination. The figure of Juárez in Mexico stands out as the example of a ruler who could not attain civil control over the national territory until he had broken the power of a Church that was even prepared to ally itself with foreigners to keep its rights and powers.[31] The attack on clericalism was, after all, an attack on the organisation that had been co-equal with the Spanish colonial administration at all times, and therefore partook of a crusade for the maintenance of the state itself. This makes it less surprising that liberalism in the Americas should so often have been associated with highly centralised government, even where, as in the Chilean case, for example, it was also associated with *laissez-faire* economic policy and free trade.[32] But in Chile, as in Colombia, the conflict with clericalism was postponed and in close alliance with the Church a conservative oligarchy developed that was able to maintain uninterrupted rule into the late years of the century.

Elsewhere, again, the last thirty years of the century saw

an additional cause of conflict in the influx of foreign capital and the development of private business interests. At the time of independence the declared interest of Europe in Latin America was mainly focused on trade and mining. Europeans were looking for markets in new places. Investment in these early years was otherwise limited to loans made through private bankers by the governments of the new states, in order to finance their administrative needs. In view of the instability and short life of these governments, and their tendency to divert funds into civil strife, most of the states were saddled with heavy foreign debts within the first ten or fifteen years of their existence. These they were not then in a position to repay, since economic liberalism frowned on taxation, and tax collectors' lives were short.[33] Money for mining gold could still be had many times over, but only the share promoters seemed to have any gold to show for it.

It became difficult, therefore, for Latin Americans to raise capital for any other purpose, unless very high dividends were to be expected. In the mid-years of the century the discovery of the guano beds – natural fertiliser – in the territories of Bolivia claimed by Peru and Chile offered just such another set of opportunities, with the consequences for international conflict already seen.

The need to move larger quantities of raw materials to the point of export led to Latin America's late boom in railway construction (Tables 2 and 3). The natural difficulties were formidable, and many companies crashed. It was one thing to link Mexico to the United States across the northern deserts; it was another matter to open up the Andes, and, but for the reckless daring of Henry Meiggs, the American railroad engineer, the feats of the 1880s and 1890s, culminating in the Trans-Andine Railway, would not have been achieved.[34] During the slump of 1890 huge areas still lay remote from all likely forms of transport. But the great states of Brazil – São Paulo and Minas Gerais – had begun to yield their vast wealth, the former in coffee and the latter in minerals, and the invention of the refrigerated ship turned Argentina into a vast meat-producing and exporting nation.

It was coffee that was to rescue the Brazilian economy from the consequences of its dependence on the boom in

Table 2

Area and Communications, c. 1900

Country	Date	Rly 1900s	Area 1900s	Date
Argentina	1901	10,304	1,083,596	1902
Bolivia	1903	430	515,156	1904[e1]
Brazil	1905	10,600	3,228,452	1900[e1]
Chile	1906	2,950	307,774	1900[o]
Colombia	1906	383	481,979	1904[o]
Costa Rica	1901	147	18,500	1904[o]
Cuba	1900	2,097	44,164	1904[o]
Dominican Republic	1901	100	18,045	1908[e]
Ecuador	1908[2]	290	116,000	1900[o]
El Salvador	1901	34	7,225	1906
Guatemala	1901	350	48,250	1903
Haiti	1900	43	10,204	1900
Honduras	1905	57	46,500	1905
Mexico	1909	14,857	757,907	1909
Nicaragua	1905	180	49,200	1905
Panama	1900	47	31,500	1909[e]
Paraguay	1906	154	97,700	1905[e]
Peru	1893	849	439,014	1900[e]
Uruguay	1900	1,002	72,210	1908[o]
Venezuela	1908	540	599,538	1906[o]

[e] =estimate   [o] =official
[1] Gotha estimate.
[2] Railway opened in 1908.
SOURCES: *Whitaker's Almanack* (1901); *Encyclopaedia Brittanica*, 13th edition.

natural rubber in the Amazon basin. But it was achieved only at the expense of increasing already great disparities in the distribution of land. In the Brazilian case the existence of vast unexplored territories relieved the impact of this to some extent. Similar developments in the Caribbean area, where boundaries were tightly drawn, were to create greater resistance.

In the last years of the century, as the tide of 'progress' rolled on, entrepreneurs turned their attention to the

Table 3

Urbanisation, 1900–1960

Country	Capital	Altd (ft)	Pop 1900	Pop 1960
Argentina	Buenos Aires	0	950,891^m	6,735,000^e
Bolivia	La Paz	12,400	54,713	347,394^e
Brazil	Rio de Janeiro	0	691,565^m	3,288,000^e
	Brasília[1]	3,000	—	142,000
Chile	Santiago	1,950	332,059^e	1,627,962
Colombia	Bogotá	8,661	120,000	1,406,230
Costa Rica	San José	3,700	24,500	167,573
Cuba	La Habana	0	297,159	783,162
Dominican Republic	Santo Domingo	0	25,000	367,053
Ecuador	Quito	9,375	50,841	384,151
El Salvador	San Salvador	2,237	60,000	248,100
Guatemala	Guatemala	4,897	97,000	417,218
Haiti	Port au Prince	0	75,000	250,000
Honduras	Tegucigalpa	3,200	35,000	134,075
Mexico	Mexico, D.F.	7,434	344,721	4,829,402
Nicaragua	Managua	180	30,000	276,016
Panama	Panama	0	30,000	294,539
Paraguay	Asunción	235	60,259	300,000^e
Peru	Lima	480	140,000	1,715,971
Uruguay	Montevideo	0	309,231^c	1,173,114
Venezuela	Caracas	3,025	60,000	1,500,000^e

^{c} = census. ^{e} = estimate. ^{m} = municipal census.
[1] Capital transferred to Brasília 21 April 1960.
SOURCES: *Whitaker's Almanack* (1901); *Encyclopaedia Brittanica*, 13th edition; *South American Handbook*.

ancillary structures of economic life, to factories to supply consumer products – textiles, paper, soap – and civic improvements such as paving, tramways, electric light and power, gas and sewage undertakings. Indeed, asphalt paving virtually originated in Mexico as a byproduct of the conditions of oil competition at the turn of the century.

Wise after the event, modern writers and critics have often pointed out that many of these developments were inspired in the first instance by the interests of European or United States trade.[35] Thus the railways of Argentina were centred on Buenos Aires, since their prime function was to move the meat out to the port. What is less clear is how else they could have been built or operated. Communications and trade are inseparable, and communications cannot of themselves promote trade where the other conditions for trade do not exist. A more just criticism is that development inspired by external factors left the Argentine economy vulnerable to world recessions to an alarming extent. What must not be forgotten, however, is that states as well as private individuals tend to centre trade on the capital city, and in Argentina the capital was also a port. By contrast, where Mexican national pride was hurt it was largely due to the physical obstacles to such a centralization. The mountain ranges in Mexico run north and south, so that it was easy to build a line from the capital to the United States border but took years to build one a fraction of the length from the capital to the port of Vera Cruz.

Nevertheless the sentiment in both countries that the national territory was becoming economically speaking a virtual colony was one which was to provoke profound political consequences later.

Lastly, the nineteenth century saw, following the short-term shift of power from the *peninsulares* to the creoles, a long-term shift of power from the creoles to the mestizos, who outnumbered them. This meant that with the exception of Argentina, Uruguay, Chile and Costa Rica, the broadening of participation in government was also reflected in the altered composition of government leadership. The role of the *caudillo* accelerated this change. Mestizos made as good soldiers as creoles. The army to which the *caudillo* looked for the defence of his interests was itself concerned first with its own power. This meant promoting the able man, whatever his origins.

Latin America participated in the general movement for the abolition of slavery and the liberation of indigenous races. Brazil, most tolerant of racial mixture, was the last area to free its slaves. Their liberation in 1888 was the last act of the liberal monarchy and brought about its fall. It was replaced by a conservative republic, but one which did not dare to attempt to restore the institution. It was a great achievement to secure at such a small price a humanitarian reform that had cost the lives of millions in the United States just over twenty years before.

Abolitionism, however, also represented another aspect of unification. The freeing of Negro slaves went together with the subjection of Indian races and their forcible enrolment in the national community. Furthermore, the abolition of actual slavery was often the occasion for an acceleration of the development of bondage based on debt. Because of its association with regional independence, the attempt in turn to eradicate this bondage often came into conflict with the interests of ruling oligarchies, whose power depended on their regulation of the regional balance. Where these regional interests became identified with the new wave of plantations under the ownership of foreign companies a further set of obstacles to change was set up.

The foreign companies moved into a vacuum left by the distrust of the oligarchs in the future of their own countries. They preferred to invest their money, or even to deposit it, in Europe or the United States, rather than to plough it back into the national economy. The capital lost was often sufficient in quantity to counter balance the entire value of foreign investment. The intellectual *élite* criticised the shortcomings of the country but, conditioned by traditional respect for non-manual values, confined their criticism to words. They would not themselves turn entrepreneur.

The intellectual preoccupation with grand designs, or *proyectismo*, has continued to the present. But it is not in itself wholly unusual, or peculiar to Latin America. What did accentuate it there was political instability, which meant that many intellectuals were forced to spend substantial portions of their prime of life in exile or in gaol.

With all these factors taken into account we must return to the picture of Latin America in 1900. The states that made it up then formed a substantial proportion – almost half – of the world's independent states. The invitation to Mexico in 1899 to take part in the First Peace Conference symbolised the coming acceptance of their role in the international community which was to replace the imperial domination that then seemed unshakeable. The imperial powers, of course, stood apart. But the development, in absolute terms, of Mexico, Argentina, Brazil, Chile and Peru, in contrast to the lesser European powers was already very great.[36]

Even among the smaller Latin American states the experience of settled and ordered government which they had compared favourably with that of turbulent Italy or disunited Germany. If the Latin American powers did not play a greater part in the world at an earlier date it was simply because their fortunate geographical isolation placed them somewhat apart from the world of the international community. The rise of the United States to the north and of Japan to the west was to alter this substantially. From then on, Latin America could not be disregarded in any future calculation of the world's balance of power, particularly since in those latter years of the last century the area's increasing importance as a source of all sorts of modern raw materials was just beginning to be appreciated.

The development of world-wide press agencies meant that already Latin Americans were not less aware than their neighbours in the United States of what went on in the world outside. They were, if anything, more in touch with the mainstream of French, Italian and German culture. Many of the *élite* sent their sons to France for their education or to Germany for their military training. The outside world might not seem particularly interested in them, but they were affected, and deeply affected, by its perturbations, particularly by the contributions to political thought which the nineteenth century threw up in such profusion.

Comte, Saint-Simon and Herbert Spencer were among the prophets of the future to whom they looked.[37] Of these Spencer was probably the most influential, though positivism left an indelible mark on the history of both Brazil and Mexico. The Mexicans stimulated capital investment, encouraged immigration to fill the desert north, and forbade the Indians to enter the capital unless they wore European dress. The Brazilian leaders of the Old Republic, more gentle in their methods, did certainly take as their motto 'Order and Progress' (without the 'Love' prefixed by Comte himself).

Nor did foreign political tracts go unread. Socialism, at least in its Marxist form, seemed alien as yet, since it demanded a degree of economic organisation which Latin America had not yet attained. But no future seemed too remote to be considered seriously. Socialism reached Latin America, therefore, before there were the workers' movements it envisaged, and it could be accepted as perfect by men knowing little of the reality of European industrial conflicts.

Authority in everyday life still lay with the landowner. The landowner was an individual member of the local oligarchy, and the oligarchs regulated the distribution of power among themselves by their own rules. These rules, the 'real constitution' of so many states, recognised the 'right' of military rebellion and military tutelage; also the more definite right of asylum for deposed rulers and some degree of concurrence in the limits of 'arbitrary' power. These conflicts were professional ones.

The landowners controlled the land, and with it the Indians. This was the key to their power. Some basic rights had, however, to be alienated in the interests of the oligarchy as a whole. Colonial tradition made mineral and water rights the common property of the state. Infringement of this tradition by permitting unrestrained private exploitation was to be the sin of nineteenth-century Mexican reformers that the twentieth century found hardest to atone for.

To sum up, therefore: the nineteenth century was for Latin America a period in which a colonial system gave way to an international one. The states that comprised the system found their national identities defined principally by their conscious differences from one another. These differences were marginal; often less significant than differences within individual countries. Because they occurred in states that shared a common language and culture, they could readily be transferred from the national to the international plane according to the need and desire of individual political actors.

But these political actors were not necessarily politicians in the sense that they would have been recognised as such in Western Europe. As in the contemporary United States, but generally in a higher degree, interests were expressed in Latin America through the politics of violence. Revolutions and *coups d'état*, then, are not, as many still think, a tiresome irrelevance in the social reality of Latin American public life, but the institutional expression of its most fundamental divisions, and of the pattern of dominance and loyalty between territorial magnate or officer and peasant or private soldier. For this reason such conflicts have been given due prominence here in the story of the making of the twentieth century.

What distinguishes the twentieth century from the nineteenth in Latin America (apart from those factors common to the whole world) is the fact that in the Caribbean area, outside Mexico, the United States entered the Latin American system as an active participant, and rapidly developed into the dominant one. This entry, as will be seen, was facilitated by the politics of violence, to the extent that on the one hand all participants in armed internal conflict tried to invoke United States aid, or at least neutrality, while on the other, the growth of United States financial interest in the region to some extent comprised its ability to pursue a wholly independent policy. In the second half of the period, this involvement was extended to the great states of South America, with consequences that are yet to be resolved.

In 1900, though, this still lay in the future. For much of South America it seemed that the dream of 'order and progress' might be on the point of coming true. It is therefore with South America that this study begins.

1. For a geography of Latin America see Preston E. James, *Latin America*, 2nd ed. (New York, Odyssey Press, 1950).

2. C. E. Marshall, 'The Birth of the Mestizo in New Spain', *H.A.H.R.* xix (May 1939) 161.

3. See in particular the valuable Donald M. Dozer, *Latin America, an Interpretive History* (New York, McGraw-Hill, 1962). George Pendle, *A History of Latin America* (London, Penguin Books, 1964) is a good short introduction.

4. George C. Vaillant, *The Aztecs of Mexico: Origin, Rise and Fall of the Aztec Nation* (London, Penguin Books, 1950).

5. Sylvanus G. Morley, *The Ancient Maya*, 3rd ed. rev. (Stanford, Stanford University Press, 1956).

6. J. A. Mason, *The Ancient Civilizations of Peru* (London, Penguin Books, 1957).

7. Now old, but still of great literary merit are William Hickling Prescott, *History of the Conquest of Mexico with a preliminary view of the ancient Mexican Civilisation and the life of the conqueror Hernando Cortez* (London, Allen & Unwin, 1949) and *History of the Conquest of Peru* (London, Everyman's Library, 1908).

30   LATIN AMERICA

8. Lewis H. Hanke, *Aristotle and the American Indians; A Study in Race Prejudice in the Modern World* (London, Hollis & Carter, 1959).

9. C. H. Haring, *The Spanish Empire in America*, rev. ed. (New York, Oxford University Press, 1952).

10. Lesley Byrd Simpson, *The Encomienda in New Spain: the beginning of Spanish Mexico* (Berkeley, University of California Press, 1966) pp. 210–11.

11. John Lynch, *Spain under the Habsburgs*, 2 vols (Oxford, Blackwell, 1964).

12. H. V. Livermore, *A New History of Portugal* (Cambridge, Cambridge University Press, 1966).

13. R. A. Humphreys, *The Evolution of Modern Latin America* (Oxford, Clarendon Press, 1946).

14. Wendell G. Schaeffer, 'The Delayed Cession of Spanish Santo Domingo to France, 1795–1801', *H.A.H.R.* xxix, 1 (February 1949) 46.

15. F.-P. Renaut, *La question de la Louisiane, 1796–1806* (Paris, Édouard Champion, n.d.).

16. R. A. Humphreys, *Liberation in South America, 1806–1827; the career of James Paroissien* (London, Athlone Press, 1952).

17. Raymond Carr, *Spain 1808–1939* (Oxford, Clarendon Press, 1966).

18. Ironically, one of the few easily accessible statements is Karl Marx in *New York Daily Tribune*, 24 November 1854, quoted in Karl Marx and Friedrich Engels, *Revolution in Spain* (London, Lawrence & Wishart, 1939).

19. Gerhard Masur, *Simón Bolívar* (Albuquerque, University of New Mexico Press, 1948).

20. H. G. Warren, *Paraguay, An Informal History* (Norman, University of Oklahoma Press, 1949) pp. 142–56.

21. John Street, *Artigas and the Independence of Uruguay* (Cambridge, Cambridge University Press, 1959).

22. Simon Collier, *Ideas and Politics of Chilean Independence 1808–1833* (Cambridge, Cambridge University Press, 1967).

23. Oliveira Lima, *O Movimento da Independência, O Imperio Brasiliero (1821–1889)*, 2nd ed. (São Paulo, Ediçoes Melhoramentos, 1928).

24. H. W. V. Temperley, *The Foreign Policy of Canning, 1822–1827; England, the neo-holy alliance and the new world* (London, Bell, 1925) p. 131–37. Dexter Perkins, *A History of the Monroe Doctrine*, rev. ed. (London, Longmans, 1960) gives the principal United States interpretation.

25. R. A. Humphreys, 'Latin America, The Caudillo Tradition', in Michael Howard, ed., *Soldiers and Governments. Nine Studies in civil-military relations* (London, Eyre & Spottiswoode, 1957) p. 151.

26. Luis Galdames, *A history of Chile*, trans. and ed. I. J. Cox (New York, Russell & Russell, 1964). L. W. Bealer, 'Juan Manuel de Rosas', in A. Curtis Wilgus, ed., *South American Dictators during the First Century of Independence* (New York, Russell & Russell, 1963). Otis A. Singletary, *The Mexican War* (Chicago, University of Chicago Press, 1960).

27. Clements R. Markham, *The War between Peru and Chile, 1879–1882* (London, Sampson Low, Marston & Co., n.d.).

28. P. H. Box, *The Origins of the Paraguayan War* (Urbana, University of Illinois Press, 1929, Studies in the Social Sciences 15).

29. J. M. Henao and G. Arrubla, *History of Colombia*, trans. and ed. J. F. Rippy (Chapel Hill, University of North Carolina Press 1938) is the most complete account in English.

30. Franklin D. Parker *The Central American Republics* (London, Oxford University Press for Royal Institute of International Affairs, 1964).

31. Charles Allen Smart, *Viva Juárez, a biography* (London, Eyre & Spottiswoode, 1964); Ralph Roeder, *Juárez and his Mexico*, 2 vols (New York, Viking Press, 1947).

32. Aníbal Pinto Santa Cruz, *Chile, un caso de desarrollo frustrado* (Santiago, Editorial Universitaria, 1962) pp. 14 ff.

33. Leland Hamilton Jenks, *The Migration of British Capital to 1875* (New York, Knopf, 1927) pp. 44–9, 63.

34. Watt Stewart, *Henry Meiggs, Yankee Pizarro* (Durham, N.C., Duke University Press, 1946).

35. e.g. Arthur P. Whitaker, *Argentina* (Englewood Cliffs, N.J., Prentice-Hall, 1964); George Pendle, *Argentina*, 2nd ed. (London, Oxford University Press for Royal Institute of International Affairs, 1961).

36. Frederick B. Pike, *Chile and the United States, 1880–1962; the emergence of Chile's social crisis and the challenge to United States diplomacy* (Notre Dame, University of Notre Dame Press, 1963) pp. 34–8, cf. pp. 81–5.

37. Stephen Clissold, *Latin America, A cultural outline* (London, Hutchinson University Library, 1965).

2 Order and Progress

In 1900 the great countries of Latin America seemed to have attained an almost unprecedented degree of stability. If there was revolution in Colombia and the future of Peru without Piérola was still uncertain, the fact remained that other countries were relatively quiet. If new and strange political doctrines were on the increase and the domestic state of both Spain and Portugal (to say nothing of France) left much to be desired, their former colonies seemed to be on the point of coming into their own.

Five of them may be taken as typifying in different ways aspects of the interaction between economic betterment and political progress, the type of progress most striking to the general observer.

Above all there was the development of Argentina. Since 1880, Argentina had been under strong centralised rule of a conservative character. It had developed beyond all recognition as a meat producing country, and its transport and town planning, basic to a modern society, were second to none in the Western Hemisphere. The regular presidential succession had not been broken since the foundation of the Republic in 1853. And the stability of the régime continued, despite the unparalleled degree of immigration, mostly from Italy and Spain. The flow of immigrants has been more than twice that of the United States, in proportion to the existing population, in all periods from that time down to the present.[1]

The consequent turbulence of new ideas which the immigrants brought with them was, however, no less significant than their work. Furthermore, dependence on European ideas was paralleled by that dependence on the world market (previously noted) brought about by the development of the trading economy of Argentina. Of all Latin American countries it was most seriously shaken by the great recession of 1890. In the climate of unrest brought on by hard times, Argentina, alone among Latin American states, became distinguished for the prevalence of Spanish anarchism. Like Spain it even had a strong, organised anarchist movement.[2]

But even this turbulence, and the rise of the Radical Party which followed it, did not at once challenge the dominance of conservative rule. Rather, by dividing the forces of the Liberals and their supporters, it reduced their cohesion. At the same time, the actual policy of the Radicals of 'abstention and revolution' made them singularly ineffective as a force in the parliamentary arena where they could have secured concessions and made propaganda. Worst of all, it meant that their leaders lacked training in operating the political process. Even with the disadvantage of limited franchise and public ballot they could at least have secured something of a voice.

Against this, the Conservatives would have had to admit that the quality of men that they were producing as leaders was in general no longer that of the early days of the Republic. Economic development proceeded headlong without them.

General Julio A. Roca, who was President from 1880 to 1886 and from 1898 to 1904, was certainly more distinguished than the majority of his contemporaries. The conqueror of the southern desert and Patagonia, he had set bounds to the national expansion which in its time had given Argentina its distinctive *gaucho* (cowboy) culture. In his first term (1880–6) Roca had carried out measures of anti-clerical legislation including the provision of secular marriage and the prohibition of religious education in state schools. His control over national politics had been shown in his sensitive handling of the so-called 'Revolution of 1890' –

actually an unsuccessful revolt – and Argentina entered the new century under his guidance and that of his colleague and predecessor Carlos Pellegrini.

Roca's second term, however, was distinguished less in internal affairs than for the part played by his Foreign Minister, Luis Drago, in establishing the Latin American position on debt collecting by European powers. This was one of firm opposition, justified in terms of legal argument. It was one, however, which because of the lack of strength and cohesion among the smaller states of Latin America, they were not able to make good, and the coming intervention of the United States to regulate debt collection in its own interests was actually to make the situation worse by making the pressure more effective.[3]

Roca's Finance Minister stabilised the currency and placed Argentina on the gold standard. This too had external rather than internal significance, for it was the final act in linking the economy to that of the European world. But as elsewhere it did lead to rising pressures at home and the exacerbation of labour agitation. The administration responded to these pressures, instituting a reasonably progressive labour code which to a considerable extent cut the ground from under the feet of the Radicals. These years also saw the final establishment of Argentina's boundary with Chile, subsequently commemorated by setting up the famous statue of Christ which watches over the principal pass joining the two countries.

Two points about this settlement merit further attention. The limitations of arbitration in general were shown by the fact that the boundary was not wholly delimited in the region of Tierra del Fuego and the off-shore islands. Some problems there have lingered on for later discussion, though happily without causing any great hostility. And both countries retained, from their very size and importance, undefined and indefinable spheres of influence among their neighbours which were to be of continuing significance.

Thus while Bolivia during these years was rigidly tied to Chile by the expectation of a settlement for her grievances resulting from the War of the Pacific, Paraguay and Uruguay, voluntarily or involuntarily, looked to their large Hispanic neighbour first for a degree of support in the international community.

Under Roca's successor, Dr Manuel Quintana (1904–6) the combination of irritation and anarchist propaganda culminated in an actual revolt by a section of the Radicals. It was suppressed without difficulty. Quintana died in office. In the same year, 1906, both Roca and Pellegrini died also. A new generation was coming to the fore. Quintana's successor, Dr José Figueroa Alcorta, continued the tradition of encouraging and developing education which had been implanted in the Argentine Republic before the years of conservative dominance. But the very enlightenment of the new generation was to bring about its downfall, though contemporaries saw in it the only hope of long-term stability. It was in this spirit that Alcorta's successor, Roque Sáenz Peña (1910–14), himself a son of a member of the oligarchy and former President of the Republic, passed the famous law that bears his name which at a stroke widened the franchise, reformed the electoral procedure, and even encouraged the representation of the 'proletarian' parties. It was, in short, a reform in the grand Hispanic tradition: magnificent, wholesale, just and dangerous.

Sáenz Peña lived just long enough to see the law amended. For the last year of his presidency he was incapacitated, and it was greatly to the credit of his successor, Victorino de la Plaza, that the law was honestly administered at the elections of 1916. The Radicals showed their weakness by their slow response to the new opportunity. Despite this, the term of de la Plaza was the last of the old régime. With the personality of Hipólito Irigoyen as their leader the Radicals secured a narrow victory and entered office peacefully.[4]

It was ironical therefore that in almost every respect the

administrations of the Radicals, between 1916 and 1930, fell short even of reasonable expectation. They lacked cohesion, it is true, but still more important, they lacked a leadership as efficient as it was inspired. Irigoyen was a striking personality with a messianic fervour and turn of phrase, and a devotion to the public good which few could deny. But he almost entirely lacked any concept of active policy which could be put into practice, and like his contemporaries Wilson and Lloyd George too often considered that if a thing were well said then it was well done.

Only in the field of public education, where the old régime was least vulnerable to criticism, did Irigoyen really make a solid contribution of enduring effect. Neither he, in his first term (1916–22), nor his successor Marcelo T. de Alvear (1922–8), did more in the economic field than swim with that tide of prosperity that washed over the Western Hemisphere in those years. The triumphant recall of Irigoyen to a second term in 1928 was almost immediately followed by the Great Depression.

The sensitive economy of Argentina did not long withstand the shock, and the Radicals took the blame. An attempt on the President's life in 1929 was the prelude to an upsurge of disillusion and riots in the towns. The spell was broken. On 5 September 1930 Irigoyen was deposed by a military *coup* and Argentina entered on a new and less happy era.

Argentina had chosen to progress with the world. When the world ceased to progress, it did so too. But there seemed to be nothing to put in the place of progress, unless Europe had something new to offer.

The experience of Uruguay in the same period was remarkably similar, though of course there were great differences between the two countries which made exact parallelism improbable. The smallest of the South American states, Uruguay had had an exceptionally turbulent history in the nineteenth century, even for Latin America. It was involved not only in the great War of the Triple Alliance against President Solano López of Paraguay (1865–70), but also, previously, in a series of foreign interventions and war between Argentina and Brazil. The stalemate between these two guaranteed its independence. But this did not mean that it settled down to an orderly form of political succession. Its two political parties, the Blancos and Colorados, fought out the issues of Uruguayan politics on the battlefield. Revolt followed revolt, and dictator followed dictator, even when, after the defeat of the Blancos in 1864, the supremacy of one party became a permanent part of national life.

No one in 1900 could reasonably have predicted that transformation of Uruguayan politics which was already in the making.[5] It was largely due to the role of one outstanding man, José Batlle y Ordóñez,[6] who became President in 1903 and by patient negotiation with the Blancos finally succeeded in securing peace with them, by treaty, on 20 September 1904. This put an end to the military conflict of the nineteenth century at one stroke. It was another question to create the orderly twentieth-century constitutionalism which was to receive its crowning justification when after 93 years in opposition the Blancos returned to power by peaceful means.

Batlle (pronounced Bah'zhay) was the great educator of Uruguay, as Sarmiento was the educator of Argentina. In his two presidential terms (1903–7, 1911–15), and under Dr Claudio Williman (1907–11), a wide range of measures designed to promote social and economic development was carried out. Schools were founded, public works (especially harbours and railways) were undertaken, and the foundations laid for the development of a modern economy based as in Argentina on beef. Indeed the favourable climate and soil of the Banda Oriental ensured that in time its stock-raising was to become even more intensive than that of its larger neighbour.[7]

Batlle, however, was not just concerned with the physical condition of the country, but with the moral and spiritual regeneration of it. It was not a unique aim, but its appropriateness to the intellectual climate of the time does not detract from its success. As in Argentina where Sarmiento had built on the work of Alberdi, whose great rallying cry was 'to govern is to populate', so had the 'Generation of Eighty' built on the bases left by Sarmiento in considering, more deeply than he, just what was to be taught to the new inhabitants of a new nation, and why. Now it was a contemporary of Batlle, José Enrique Rodó (1872–1917), who in his *Ariel* (1900) cast doubts on the trends hitherto unquestioned.[8] Was it, he asked, the true end of Latin Americans to pursue the goal of economic development for its own sake? Ought they not to seek their own destiny, a destiny they would find in the things of the mind?

To Batlle it became axiomatic that no true foundation for democratic government would exist in his country until its government was truly representative of the will of the people. The fact that his party was in power did not detract from the conclusion that the monopoly of power, by one party just as much as by one man, contained the seeds of its own destruction.

To secure true representation, he argued, what was needed was a reduction in the power of the presidency and the inclusion of the opposition in the executive process by the establishment of conciliar government, on the model of the Confederal Government of Switzerland. Under Dr Feliciano Viera (1915–19) extensive constitutional changes were in fact realised, including the establishment of a nine-man Council of State under the President, and the reduction of the presidential powers. This went far to realise Batlle's aims, for in the Council provision was made for representation of the minority party by three out of the nine members.[9]

Such a course was not without its hazards. After all, until relatively recently, the two parties had been in open conflict with one another. The Colorados had every reason to suppose that the traditional conservative party, the Blancos, would undo their gains if they succeeded in getting into power. The effects of the conciliar system might well be to give them the chance to do so. At first, this was not apparent, but under Dr Baltasar Brum (1919-23) it became clear that the system gave the Blancos the chance they needed to speak directly to the country from a platform of authority.

The administration of José Benigno Serrato (1923-7) therefore outflanked them by a further constitutional reform. In 1924 Uruguay adopted a new electoral system both conspicuously democratic and strikingly complicated. This was the system known as the 'double simultaneous vote', devised by a Belgian named Borély. In brief, this system provided for the separation of individual factions within parties under separate 'tickets' (lemas). The votes for each faction having been counted, they were credited as a total to the leading ticket, thus in a sense combining the functions of two ballots, and undoubtedly it gave (and gives) the individual voter much more confidence and power in voting for an individual member of a party than most other systems. A by-product is, however, that it enables a less divided party to maintain its supremacy over a more divided one, regardless of the total number of votes cast for each party.

The Colorados stayed in power. Led by Juan Campísteguy (1927-31) they had to meet the forces of the Depression that struck Uruguay no less heavily than they struck Argentina. Undoubtedly the fact that development was more recent, and therefore to some extent continuing, lessened the shock. It remained to be seen, however, what means would be used to counter the Depression when as time wore on it showed no sign of coming to an end.

The largest republic of South America, Brazil, was of course of very recent creation in 1900, and its first few years had been marked by considerable faction fighting among the leaders of the revolution of 1889.[10] The two traditional parties of the monarchy had given way to four, resulting in additional problems. Nevertheless, it was then already true that Brazil had entered upon a period of oligarchical stability, the system nostalgically known after 1930 as the 'Old Republic'.

The early years of the century were marked by little that was more dramatic but nothing less important than the establishment of boundary settlements with neighbouring powers, for these settlements secured the gains of the period of Imperial expansion. For Brazil too had advanced under the Empire far beyond the narrow coastal strip it had inherited; heading the advance were the *bandeirantes*, pirates of the 'inland sea', whose campaigns in the 1890s were imperishably recorded in Da Cunha's *Os Sertões*. Behind them came a powerful, though indolent, government and army. Thus the term of Francisco de Paula Rodrigues Alves (1902–6) was marked by agreement with Bolivia (1903) and settlement with Britain and the Netherlands over the boundaries of the Guianas. Under Afonso Augusto Moreira Pena (1906–9) Brazil reappeared on a world stage at the Second Peace Conference, adopted the gold standard and enjoyed fortunes at the height of the rubber boom. His successor, Nilo Peçanha (1909–10), who held office for only one year, nevertheless by the fact of his presence exemplified the degree of the Brazilian achievement, for he was largely of Negro blood. His presidency was also distinguished by its deeds: protection was extended to the Indians, both on and beyond the great plantations (*fazendas*), and a generous boundary settlement was negotiated with Uruguay.

The rubber boom, however, meant more to Brazil than just the creation of an unprecedented number of million-aires.[11] It marked a real displacement of national interest towards the interior, towards the Amazon basin. The rise of the great city of Manaus, with its vast Opera House where Jenny Lind appeared at the height of her fame, seemed for a glittering moment to realise the dreams of the Empire. Now however the end of that moment was in sight, for the seeds of the rubber tree, stolen by an Englishman, propagated at Kew and planted in the Malay States, were no longer the monopoly of the Brazilians. Vigorous competition ruined the new owners as effectively as the old.

Marshal Hermes Rodrigues da Fonseca (1910–14) was the President who had to meet the challenge of the slump that rocked Brazil. Regrettably, he was particularly badly placed to do so, since he was personally antipathetic to many because of his association with the military element behind the Revolution of 1889. The election of 1910, in consequence, was fought out on the issue of military versus civilian rule, and when the military element won, civilians were not reassured by the arbitrary style and authoritarian temperament of their new President. It was therefore indicative of the pressures of the slump that the civil candidate withdrew in 1914 in the cause of national unity in face of disaster. Much of Manaus fell into ruins and the cause of development of the interior was set back for an entire generation.

In the fortunate way Brazilian history has had of redressing the mistakes of humanity by revealing new, hitherto undeveloped resources, a new crop was at hand to which its inhabitants could turn their attention. This was coffee, the demand for which was stimulated by the Great War; coincident with the term of Venceslau Brás Pereira Gomes (1914–18), this great export crop advanced to first place in the national economy. Under Epitácio da Silva Pessoa (1919–22) successor to Delfim Moreira da Costa (1918–19) Brazil celebrated its centenary of independence in good heart.[12] Alone of the South American states it had played a real part in the war, when submarine attacks on Brazilian ships had led to involvement with Germany and a declaration of war in 1917. Brazilian forces served in Flanders and the Ardennes on the Entente side, and Brazil became a founder member of the League of Nations.

The centenary had a greater significance, too, in that it closed the link with the days of the Empire which had meant so much to Brazil. The bones of the last Emperor, Pedro II, were brought back for honourable interment in the Cathedral at Petrópolis. Brazilian nationalism was not, however, synonymous with the Republic, however successful it had proved itself to be, and new strains resulting from the increase of population and the emergence of new regional interests were to provide an immediate challenge to the system.

The compromise within the oligarchy that ruled Brazil at that time depended on the fact of the ascendancy of the two great States of São Paulo and Minas Gerais: thus the presidency alternated between them, though the régime had been secure enough to depart from this arrangement in 1918. Now under Artur da Silva Bernardes (1922–6) the small states demanded a share in government, and in alliance with Paulistas a revolt broke out in the southern state of Rio Grande do Sul which was suppressed only with difficulty.

What was not clear to the régime, it appears, was that this revolt was the product and not the cause of a long-term shift of power southward. Since 1900 this area had been the object of intense immigration. The fact that much of it came from the modern, developed countries of northern Europe – especially Germany – meant that there would be a particular bite in the campaign they were prepared to wage. In 1926 Washington Luis Pereira de Souza (1926–30) became President for the last term of the Old Republic. By the end of it, in 1930, his administration was already undergoing the ferocious stresses of the new Depression. His intervention on the behalf of his chosen successor, Dr Julio Prestes, led to the second revolt from Rio Grande do Sul – and this time it was successful.[13] From it a new Brazilian hero emerged, who was prepared to channel into one powerful movement discontent with economic collapse, big state domination, the old oligarchy and every form of dependence on anything other than Brazilian initiative.

Chile during the nineteenth century had been the leading

exemplar of stable government in Latin America. The autocratic régime of Joaquín Prieto, Manuel Bulnes and Manuel
Montt had given way as early as 1861 to thirty years of
Liberal rule. The Liberals had bound the country closely to
the classic principles of free trade and in time of prosperity
this had resulted in vast economic growth.

This period came to an end with the term of José Manuel
Balmaceda, which though successful in some respects, ended
in collision between the President and the Congress, which
under Liberal rule had by convention taken on many of the
characteristics of a parliament. When his opponents ob-
structed the budget, Balmaceda declared it in force by
decree, and the Congress and the Navy proclaimed revolt
against the President and the army. In the special circumstances of Chile, they were successful, and the Civil War of
1891 gave Chile a parliamentary constitution that clearly
subordinated the executive to the will of the congressional
majority.[14]

The result was that following the rule of Jorge Montt, the
presidents of the next thirty years were not on the whole men
of outstanding calibre. It is still convenient, however, to use
their names as delimiting periods of time in which further
developments took place.[15]

Thus, for example, it was in the time of Germán Riesco
(1901–6) that the long awaited Treaty of boundary settlement with Bolivia was finally signed. Bolivia had had to give
up her access to the sea immediately after the War of the
Pacific and so far had enjoyed right of access to the sea only
by informal agreement. Chile's hold over the nitrate fields
was thus consolidated. But already it was clear that the
nitrate fields, along with the general dependence of Chile on
mineral resources, brought with it special considerations of
the place of labour in society.[16] The very concentration of
Chile's labour interests, and the absolute dependence of the
country on their good will, gave them unique bargaining
power.

Chile's social legislation was therefore already well advanced. A series of strikes, however, kept the government of Riesco, and that of his successor, Pedro Montt (1906–10) fully occupied. A consequence of the Civil War of 1891 was that both the traditional political parties had split, and the parliamentary system needed considerable nursing if it were to continue to work. The majorities for labour legislation were achieved by the governments of Ramón Barros Luco (1910–15) and Juan Luis Sanfuentes (1915–20), and these administrations were also associated with the development of new kinds of industry. But the parliamentary republic received little credit for it, because of what followed.[17]

Chile, with its nitrate-based economy, benefited inordinately from the market for explosives created by the Great War. It was the wealth of this second 'nitrate boom' that made the wartime programme of social and economic legislation. But the war, too, brought artificial substitutes and so the slump of 1919–21. The last years of the parliamentary régime were overshadowed by the dispute over counter measures, especially the claim by one formidable personality, Arturo Alessandri ('The Lion of Tarapacá') that he was indispensable to the restoration of sound finances.[18]

The choice of Alessandri as President (1920–4) was made by congressional compromise after a hotly disputed election. He represented the new middle class in the so-called Liberal Alliance with the workers' interests, and was an advocate of extensive social reforms. But he lacked the money to carry them out, and his Budget proposals were held up for months on end by conservative opposition while the country drifted. In the end, the military felt it necessary to intervene to achieve something, and pressed the President to devalue in order to stabilise the currency and end inflation. Alessandri's reply was to leave the country in 1924, refusing to resign.

Certainly he hoped to be recalled, but his methods only succeeded in adding political to economic chaos. After a few months, his supporters in the lower ranks of the army, under

Colonel Carlos Ibáñez del Campo, overthrew the conservative military junta under General Luis Altamirano (1924–
1925) which had been maintaining the administration, and
recalled Alessandri, who demanded and received the restoration of the presidential system of the days of Balmaceda.[19]

The Constitution of 1925 still survives as the basis of
Chilean politics. But first men were needed to make it work,
and it was clear that Alessandri was not capable of the action
his supporters demanded. In face of the hostility of Ibáñez,
he resigned after less than six months in his second term
(1925) and an election held by the interim President Luis
Barros Borgoño installed a very capable lawyer, Emiliano
Figueroa Larráin (1925–7) in his place. The new administration, however, was not allowed to operate. By the fact of
its existence the position of Ibáñez had been enhanced to the
point at which military elements demanded that he take
over full power.

As President and dictator (1927–31) Ibáñez suppressed
plots ruthlessly and enjoyed the strength to carry out many
of the reforms that Alessandri had advocated. The boom of
the late twenties lent the administration the brittle prestige
of momentary prosperity based on the rise in the world
commodity market and the resumption of investment. The
administration was even strong enough to settle the question
of boundaries with Peru by the Treaty of Lima, 1929 by
which Peru received Tacna together with an indemnity for
Arica. Development of public works, and above all the
establishment of the state nitrate monopoly (COSACH)
dramatised the new involvement of government with the
national economic life.

But the administration made heavy weather of the Great
Depression. Chile was no longer first choice for foreign
investors, who distrusted its new governmental instability as
much as the trend towards state intervention. Riots became
endemic. The fission of political ideologies, begun under the
parliamentary régime, was resumed, and extremist solutions

enjoyed a vogue, extending into the ranks of the army itself. In July 1931 Ibáñez was forced by a combination of popular unrest and military dissension to transfer authority to the President of the Senate, Pedro Opazo Letelier (1931) who then resigned.[20] The Minister of the Interior, Juan Esteban Montero, came forward to take over the task of governing, but he was overthrown by a military *coup* in mid-1932 and was succeeded by a radical military junta proclaiming Chile a 'socialist republic'.

The switch from parliamentary to presidential régime seemed to have failed at the most elementary level to solve the problems of the country. Yet in material terms Chile was still in a great many ways Latin America's most advanced state.

Finally, among the major countries of South America that enjoyed a period of progress during these three decades, Colombia must be singled out because of the peculiar difficulties which that progress encountered.

As we have seen, in 1900 Colombia had for many years been under the control of the Conservatives, an ascendancy maintained down to 1930.[21] But this was not achieved without persistent hostility from the Liberals. The fall of Antonio Sanclemente in 1900 gave rise to the so-called War of 1000 Days and left the country even more divided and much weaker than she had been since the ascendancy of Rafael Núñez. Yet the war was an internal conflict for the Conservatives too, the opposition to Sanclemente being initiated by his Vice-President, José Manuel Marroquín, proclaiming himself President (1900–4).

Unfortunately for Colombia, the effect of the war was less for the country as a whole than for one part of it. Regional separatism in the territory of Panama was stimulated by the fact that for much of the time the isthmus had been the scene of the fighting. It was this irritation that led to the combination between the forces of separatism and United States interest in obtaining the right of transit across the isthmus. This in turn resulted in the secession of Panama in 1903.[22]

The loss of national territory, an appalling disgrace, was blamed on the United States alone; it does not seem to have occurred to the Conservatives that they might have contributed to it. Secure in their self-righteousness and the knowledge that the Liberals were weak, they began the long search for an apology and indemnity. The unifying effect of hostility to a common enemy played into their hands. Marroquín was succeeded as President by Rafael Reyes (1904–9), an autocratic ruler who subordinated all other interests to this one end. In 1907 he even relinquished to Brazil Colombian claims over the ownership of the Caquetá and Río Negro, and proceeded in the following year to secure his own re-election.

But Colombian constitutionalism was not dead, and Congress remained a forum for national sentiment. When Reyes attempted to conclude a treaty with the United States which did *not* include an apology for its predecessor's role in Panama from the Republican administration of President Taft, he was ejected from office.

The administration of Carlos Restrepo (1910–14) was marked by governmental reforms. Minority representation in Congress was encouraged, and even extended to the Cabinet, so the administration was able to carry out educational improvements as well as to present a united front to the outside world. Meanwhile the expectation of future benefits from the United States paradoxically led to the development of involvement with that country in the investment field.[23] This was to lead in 1914 to the appearance of American oil companies and in 1919 to the signing of the contract that made Colombia in time the second-largest oil-producing country in Latin America. In fact, this development might have been greatly accelerated had circumstances not given United States interests a powerful weapon to crush possible European competition.[24]

The coming to power of a Democratic administration in the United States in 1913 then gave the Colombians the chance they had been waiting for. The two countries negotiated the Thomson–Urrutia Treaty. The United States expressed its 'regret', offered an indemnity of $25 million and accorded 'most favoured nation' treatment to Colombian ships in the Panama Canal. Colombia recognised the independence of Panama. But the treaty was not ratified by the United States Senate, where the Republicans were able to prevent it receiving the necessary two-thirds majority.

Under the presidencies of José V. Concha (1914–18) and Marco Fidel Suárez (1918–21) Colombia stayed neutral in the Great War but accepted the invitation to become a founder member of the League in 1920. The United States Senate that again considered the Thomson–Urrutia Treaty in 1921 was a very different body from that of 1913, and its Republican majority made no bones about the indemnity. They refused once more to admit regret, but this time the Colombians were willing, reluctantly, to yield, as they had nothing further to hope for in the new age of 'normalcy'. Under General Pedro Nel Ospina (1922–6) relations with the United States were much improved. Nel Ospina visited the United States and an American mission aided Colombia to stabilise its currency.

Meanwhile, however, the cautious policy of mild social reform had given way to a policy aimed much more frankly at the encouragement of business interests. Though it was covered for the moment by the enthusiasm for prosperity, in fact the conservative position was a weak one. The issue that had so long cemented national unity in face of the United States had disappeared. Labour unrest became noticeable, and the term of Miguel Abadía Méndez (1926–30) was marked by a wave of strikes. The considerable differences among the Conservatives as to how these disturbances should be handled, and at the election of 1930 the combination of middle-class dissension, internal division and unrest, left the way open for the election of the moderate Liberal, Enrique Olaya Herrera.[25]

In this way the rule of the Conservatives in Colombia came to an end, at least for the time being. But the experience of Colombia was not that of the Andean countries to the south, nor that of its neighbour Venezuela to the west, which, with Peru and Ecuador, showed that the traditional form of rule by *caudillo* was by no means dead.

This was particularly unlucky in the case of Peru. It had been fortunate just before the turn of the century to obtain an enlightened ruler in the person of Nicolas Piérola. His distinction was that he had the strength to maintain his government against military competition while promoting the development of a democratic party to allow institutional support and expression of opinion.[26] His own withdrawal from the scene, at the end of his term (1899), cost Peru the chance of also obtaining a full spectrum of social reforms. But he did show that no man was indispensable.

His two successors followed his lead, and when the second, Manuel Candamo (1903–4) died in office, a rival political party, the Civilistas, had developed. They elected their candidate, José Pardo (1904–8). Unfortunately, however, this peaceful transition of power between civilian parties was not accompanied by a similar trend towards more able men in the presidency. Pardo fell short of the qualities of political leadership needed to give coherence to a new, inexperienced party, and his successor, Augusto Leguía (1908–12), accentuated rather than reduced the new party's tendency to become the personal expression of one individual's ambition, a regression to the traditional pattern of *caudillo* government.

Indeed, it was clearly Leguía's intention to go further and to impose a docile successor, but his plans were upset by the emergence of a new and outstanding personality in the Civilista ranks. The challenge came from none other than his Vice-President, Guillermo Billinghurst, descendant of an

English naval officer who had fought for Peru in the war of independence. Billinghurst's conversion to the democratic party meant that the campaign of 1912 was a display of his personal brilliance and his choice was ratified by the electorate, despite the fact that the Civilistas had won considerable popularity with their encouragement of education, establishment of labour laws and reform of the finances, all measures that Pardo should have got credit for promoting.

Billinghurst's task was to be more successful in making these ambitions real, and the fact that Peru was enjoying an economic boom gave him little excuse for failure. But he was dominated by a messianic desire to 'put Peru on the map', and this in turn involved the raising of substantial loans abroad and heavy government expenditure at home. The scale of this gave rise to traditional military concern, and the revolt of 1914 which deposed Billinghurst was a sharp reminder that the maintenance of the democratic régime was conditional on good behaviour.

The leader of the military *coup*, General Oscar Benavides, held office briefly while fresh elections were prepared. The popularity of José Pardo made him a favourable choice, while the policy of military preparedness associated with his first term (when rubber cultivation in the Peruvian Amazon region had threatened conflict over boundaries with Colombia) made him an attractive candidate to the Army. The long-term emergence of a young military officer, the hero of the *coup*, named Luis Sánchez Cerro, should not be overlooked. He was the man actually instrumental in forcing the entrance to the Presidential Palace, though himself critically wounded in the first engagement.

Pardo was not well equipped to deal with the emergence of militarism which this *coup* represented, and he was too honest to ally himself with it, as did his rival Leguía. Leguía was elected to succeed him, but overthrew his predecessor before the end of his term of office on the improbable grounds that Pardo was trying to stop him from assuming office.

Leguía (1919–30), though notionally elected only for the term 1919–23, was able with this support to impose a form of personal rule which made him dictator of Peru. He had complete control over internal political life. All forms of radical groups were suppressed and the Press subject to strict censorship. Many Peruvians went into exile, voluntarily or involuntarily. This was of particular significance, since it was just in these years that the main challenge to the traditional order in Peru was being prepared.

Peru is, after all, the successor of the old Inca empire, and the speech of the Incas is still used among the Indian majority of its population. The rule of a handful of creoles at Lima, or the prosperity of the copper mines of Cerro de Pasco, are similarly foreign to the great majority of its citizens. This basic fact was transmuted into a political ideology in the person of a young, Marxist-inspired intellectual, in exile in Mexico in the early twenties, by the name of Víctor Raúl Haya de la Torre. Haya was influenced by the writings of the Peruvian Marxist Mariátegui and the Mexican visionary José Vasconcelos. He spoke and wrote and dreamt of an alliance of 'Indoamerica' to recover the American states for their original inhabitants. His philosophy, muddled and unclear as far as its pan-American aspect was concerned, was however sharp enough in the radical nature of its 'minimum programme' for Peru itself.[27]

When Leguía's rigid dictatorship tottered to a close under the stresses of the Depression, Aprismo – as Haya's movement was called – was in a formidable position to make a bid for power. It was however the hero of the 1914 *coup*, the now Colonel Sánchez Cerro, who actually emerged as Peru's new ruler. His personal courage and daring was to make him a strong ruler and a formidable opponent to proposals for radical reform.

To the North, in Ecuador, no such radical movement

appeared at this time. Throughout the first thirty years of the century Ecuadorian politics and society were 'out on a limb', as far as the mainstream of Latin American development was concerned. By 1900 they had only just reached the stage of Liberal success and the secularisation of the Church.[28]

The rule of Eloy Alfaro (1897–1901), Leónidas Plaza Gutiérrez (1901–5) and their followers was in fact the point at which this transformation was carried out. The State assumed the properties of the Church and imposed the same forms of civil regulation on its actions which had been current elsewhere for many years. The strong personality of Alfaro was the crucial factor holding the Liberals together in these years. Once secularisation was an accomplished fact, Lizardo García (1905–6) tried to diverge from the Alfaro tradition, and was overthrown by him.

Alfaro then returned to the presidency for the term 1907–11, which was not in itself particularly notable. At the end of it, he withdrew formally from political life, though his disgust with renewed military intervention after his renunciation was to lead him to attempt an unsuccessful come-back. In the course of his attempt, he was assassinated by a political opponent.

Ecuador, therefore, unlike Peru, had not found a ruler who was prepared to renounce power come what may. The use of force for political purposes had, if anything, received added impetus from Alfaro's example, and at first it appeared that only the military had benefited. In the event, however, Plaza Gutiérrez had been able to retain sufficient support to re-establish stable oligarchy. He was succeeded in 1916 by Alfredo Baquerizo Moreno (1916–20), who made some progress in building schools and promoting education. This had little impact on the national life, though, compared with the substantial advances made in the same years towards the control of tropical disease in the coastal region, a direct product of the work of Colonel Gorgas in Panama.[29]

Stability, however, led to the alternative cause of military discontent, the blockage of promotion, and in 1925 Gonzalo Córdoba (1924–5) was overthrown by a military revolt and replaced by a military régime under Isidro Ayora (1926–31). But it was difficult to maintain it owing to the very stability of the situation. By 1929 the military had come to feel that it was again time they withdrew, and a new Constitution formally continued Ayora's rule, which had been accompanied by financial reorganisation and advanced social and labour reforms. Failure of credit meant his fall and the resumption of the traditional pattern of intervention and disengagement.

The fate of Ecuador in these years was certainly preferable to that of Colombia's eastern neighbour, Venezuela.[30] Venezuela's political history between 1899 and 1935 was spanned by the rule of two dictators. Cipriano Castro ruled from 1899 to 1908, and Juan Vicente Gómez (The Tyrant of the Andes)[31] from 1908 until 1935.

Castro became President through a military *coup*, the last of a century in which not one President of the land of Bolívar had completed a constitutionally elected term of office. Once Castro was in power the distinction was in any case meaningless. He was neither an attractive nor an intelligent ruler, but by force he succeeded in maintaining a minimum of order. In the process, the rights of foreign nationals to the protection of the law were persistently violated.

His refusal to admit these obligations brought about the intervention of three European Powers who in 1902, on German initiative, inaugurated a blockade of the Orinoco. The measures themselves were not new, though in scale they went beyond most preceding interventions. The difference was that this intervention occurred in the new age of 'spread-eagle' nationalism in the United States where it was wrongly thought the intervention was made to secure repayment for European bondholders. Pressure from the

Roosevelt Administration led to agreement to submit all claims to arbitration.[32] When in 1908 the United States found itself up against a similar refusal to pay compensation for injuries to foreign nationals (always a difficult question to put into precise monetary terms) the Roosevelt Administration itself blockaded the Orinoco. Venezuela under Castro, therefore, was seen in the United States as warning that local financial instability could threaten the Monroe doctrine. Castro himself, however, was to some Latin Americans a pathfinder in the search for Latin American independence that led to such unexpected and sometimes unwanted assistance from the United States (Table 4).[33]

For Venezuela itself, however, neither Castro nor Roosevelt represented much of positive value. The dictator's fall came in his absence in Europe for medical treatment in 1908, and in keeping with tradition it came at the instance of his Minister of the Interior. Gómez merely went out one morning, collected a column of troops from the nearby barracks, marched them round to the Presidential Palace and after a brief speech to the Presidential Guard, which was greeted by acclamation, announced that he had assumed office.[34]

As this might suggest, Gómez was personally courageous to the point of cold bloodness, and his policy of repression was correspondingly successful. Realism, too, suggested to him that he replace the policy of battling against the Powers by a policy of economic development, encouraging capital inflow and stimulating commercial and industrial growth. Like Díaz in Mexico, he achieved this largely through his ability to maintain order, at least in the first instance, and he was fortunate in the choice of able relatives with which he guarded the key offices in the state. He was more fortunate than Díaz, however, in that the vast economic potential of his country's oil reserves was realised while he was still at the height of his powers.

After the opening of the oil fields in 1918 the country in

Table 4

Revenue, Expenditure and Foreign Debt, 1900

Country	Year	Revenue	Expenditure	External Debt
		£000	£000	£000
Argentina	1899	19,075	24,427	316,999
Bolivia	1898	433	476	90
Brazil	1899	10,980	11,533	34,697
Chile	1899	7,543[1]	7,088[1]	8,070
Colombia	1899	2,493[2]	2,493[2]	3,514
Costa Rica	1899	587	532	2,000
Cuba		—	—	—
Dominican Republic	1898	680	680	8,000[3]
Ecuador	1898	909	1,100	690
El Salvador	1897	585	691	nil[4]
Guatemala	1899	234	1,744[5]	1,483
Haiti	1896–7	1,180[6]	1,105	2,750
Honduras	1897–8	217	215	5,985[7]
Mexico	1899–1900	5,491[8]	5,488[8]	22,700
Nicaragua	1898	267	322	276
Panama		—	—	—
Paraguay	1897	1,190[9]	1,650[9]	nil
Peru	1898	1,079[10]	1,149[10]	nil[11]
Uruguay	1899	1,179[12]	2,029[12]	[13]
Venezuela	1899	1,539	1,539	4,654

[1] Converted from Chilean currency.
[2] Converted from Colombian currency.
[3] National Debt.
[4] Extinguished 1899 when Internal Debt £8,650,000.
[5] 1896 figure.
[6] Customs Revenue only.
[7] No interest paid.
[8] Converted from Mexican currency.
[9] Converted from Paraguayan currency.
[10] Converted from Peruvian currency.
[11] Extinguished 1890.
[12] Converted from Uruguayan currency.
[13] Debt charge (1897) $9,120,000.

SOURCE: *Whitaker's Almanack* (1901).

international terms passed quickly into a state of sound economic management. The income from oil and other minerals was used to develop communications, particularly roads, primarily of course in an effort to unify the country. Incidentally, the problem of the national debt was solved by the simple process of paying it off. This was completed in 1930 to commemorate the centenary of the death of Bolívar. Alone of the major South American states, Venezuela was not substantially affected in political terms by the Depression, so essential by this time had petroleum become to the new age of the aeroplane and the Ford Model T. Gómez continued in power, though not necessarily in office, until he died peacefully in bed in 1935.

The rule of Gómez is therefore noteworthy. And it was fortunate that the economic gains made at such cost were not dissipated by civil strife after his death, as well as that, despite the repression of the intellectuals and in particular of student radicalism which was a feature of his rule, the spirit of Bolívar lived on in Venezuelan national life. As a result it was later to become possible to bring these two elements together in a way that was to extend the limited benefits of national wealth to a much larger number of people.

For the majority of the inhabitants of Latin America, therefore, the early years of the century were years in which, on the whole, their countries appeared to have reached a new plateau of maturity, and a condition of economic, social or political development which gave hope of better things in the future. In common, too, they found the end of the prosperity of the 1920s marked by sharp disillusionment at the reminder that, despite appearances to the contrary, their economies were bound closely to a world market. The consequences of this involvement could be bad as well as good.

The situation in two areas, however, was governed by special factors.

In the centre of the South American continent the two land-locked countries of Paraguay and Bolivia had followed a course of development largely independent of the outside world, and influenced primarily by considerations of power relationships within South America, particularly between the greater Latin American powers.

In the Caribbean, the process of change was governed in the first instance by the emergence of the United States both as a Latin American, and world power.

The importance of these developments transcends the period on which our attention has been concentrated so far, and requires special consideration in another chapter.

1. Whitaker, pp. 53–7.

2. S. Fanny Simon, 'Anarchism and Anarcho-Syndicalism in South America', *H.A.H.R.* xxvi, 1 (February 1946) 38.

3. Edwin M. Borchard, 'Calvo and Drago Doctrines', in *Encyclopedia of the Social Sciences* (New York, Macmillan, 1930); see also Thomas F. McGann, *Argentina, the United States, and the Inter-American System 1880–1914* (Cambridge, Mass., Harvard University Press, 1957); H. Edward Nettles, 'The Drago Doctrine in International Law and Politics', *H.A.H.R.* viii (May 1928) 204–23.

4. The critique of Irigoyen follows Whitaker, pp. 65 ff.; cf. Pendle, pp. 69–72

5. For the history of Uruguay in the twentieth century both Russell H. Fitzgibbon, *Uruguay, portrait of a democracy* (New Brunswick, N.J., Rutgers University Press, 1954) and George Pendle, *Uruguay* (London, Oxford University Press for Royal Institute of International Affairs, 1957), are indispensable.

6. Milton I. Vanger, *José Batlle y Ordóñez of Uruguay, The Creator of his Times, 1902–1907* (Cambridge, Mass., Harvard University Press, 1963). See also the brief biography of P. A. Martin, 'The Career of José Batlle y Ordóñez', *H.A.H.R.* x, 4 (November 1930) 413. For a view of Uruguay at this period see W. H. Koebel, *Uruguay* (London, Fisher Unwin, 1911).

7. Göran G. Lindahl, *Uruguay's New Path, a study in politics during the first colegiado, 1919–33* (Stockholm, Library and Institute of Ibero-American Studies, 1962). See also Simon G. Hanson, *Utopia in Uruguay* (New York, Oxford University Press, 1938).

8. José Enrique Rodó, *Ariel* (Cambridge, Cambridge University Press, 1967).

9. For a survey of the constitutional development of Uruguay see Philip B. Taylor, Jr., *Government and Politics of Uruguay* (New Orleans, Tulane University Press, 1960, Tulane Studies in Political Science, VII).

10. For Brazil in the twentieth century see José María Bello, *A History of Modern Brazil, 1889–1964* (Stanford, Stanford University Press, 1966). For its situation in the 1900s see Pierre Denis, *Brazil* (London, Fisher Unwin, 1911), and the most celebrated of Brazilian works, Euclides da Cunha, *Rebellion in the Backlands (Os Sertões)* trs. Samuel Putnam (Chicago, University of Chicago Press – Phoenix Books, 1944).

11. John Melby, 'Rubber River: An Account of the Rise and Collapse of the Amazon Boom', *H.A.H.R.* xxii, 3 (August 1942) 452.

12. H. G. James, *Brazil after a Century of Independence* (New York, Macmillan, 1925) illustrates this period.

13. John D. Wirth, 'Tenentismo in the Brazilian Revolution of 1930', *H.A.H.R.* xliv, 2 (May 1964) 161; Jordan Young, 'Military Aspects of the 1930 Brazilian Revolution', ibid., p. 180.

14. Harold Blakemore, 'The Chilean Revolution of 1891 and its historiography', *H.A.H.R* xlv, 2 (August 1965) 393.

15. For Chile in the twentieth century see Gilbert J. Butland, *Chile, An Outline of its Geography, Economics and Politics*, 3rd ed. (London, Oxford University Press for Royal Institute of International Affairs, 1956). For the situation in the early years of the century see W. H. Koebel, *Modern Chile* (London, Bell, 1913).

16. For the labour movement in Latin America generally see Víctor Alba, *Historia del movimiento obrero en América Latina* (Mexico, Libreros Mexicanos Unidos, 1964).

17. William S. Stokes, 'Parliamentary Government in Latin America', *A.P.S.R.* xxxix, 2 (June 1945) 522.

18. Clarence Henry Haring, 'Chilean Politics, 1920–1928', *H.A.H.R.* xi, 1 (February 1931) 1.

19. Frederick M. Nunn, 'Military Rule in Chile, The Revolutions of September 5, 1924, and January 23, 1925', *H.A.H.R.* xlvii, 1 (February 1967) 1.

20. Clarence Henry Haring, 'The Chilean Revolution of 1931', *H.A.H.R.* xiii, 2 (May 1933) 197.

21. For a brief study of Colombia in the twentieth century see W. O. Galbraith, *Colombia, A general survey* (London, Oxford University Press for Royal Institute of International Affairs, 1953). Of the major Latin American countries, Colombia is the one most noticeably lacking in historical documentation, either in English or Spanish.

22. D. C. Miner, *The Fight for the Panama Route, The story of the Spooner Act and the Hay-Herrán Treaty* (New York, Columbia University Press, 1940), is the classic study.

23. J. F. Rippy, *The Capitalists and Colombia* (New York, Vanguard Press, 1931).

24. Peter A. R. Calvert, 'The Murray Contract: An Episode in International Finance and Diplomacy', *P.H.R.* xxxv, 2 (May 1966) 203.

25. See also Vernon Lee Fluharty, *Dance of the Millions: Military Rule and the Social Revolution in Colombia, 1930–1956* (Pittsburgh, University of Pittsburgh Press, 1957), pp. 27–42.

26. This account follows Frederick B. Pike, *The Modern History of Peru* (London, Weidenfeld & Nicolson, 1967).

27. Harry Kantor, *The Ideology and Program of the Peruvian Aprista Movement* (Berkeley, University of California Press, 1953).

28. Oscar Efron Reyes, *Historia de la República; Esquema de ideas y hechos del Ecuador a partir de la Emancipación* (Quito, Imprenta Nacional, 1931) pp. 257–87 covers the period from the rise of Alfaro to the 1925 coup. George I. Blanksten, *Ecuador; Constitutions and Caudillos* (New York, Russell ; Russell, 1964) is detailed but episodic; it needs supplementing by Lilo Linke, *Ecuador, Country of Contrasts*, 2nd ed. (London, Oxford University Press for Royal Institute of International Affairs, 1955).

29. Lois F. Parks and Gustave A. Nueremberger, 'The Sanitation of Guayaquil', *H.A.H.R.* xxiii, 2 (May 1943) 197.

30. An excellent survey of Venezuelan history in this period in Edwin Lieuwen, *Venezuela* (London, Oxford University Press for Royal Institute of International Affairs, 1961), pp. 43–50. See also Guillermo Morón, *A History of Venezuela*, trs. John Street (London, Allen & Unwin, 1964) for a more detailed picture.

31. 'Thomas Rourke' (D. J. Clinton), *Gómez, Tyrant of the Andes* (London, Michael Joseph, 1937).

32. D. C. M. Platt, 'The Allied Coercion of Venezuela, 1902–3 – A Reassessment', *Inter-American Economic Affairs*, xv, 4, Spring 1962, p. 3.

33. Samuel Flagg Bemis, *The Latin American Policy of the United States, An Historical Interpretation* (New York, Harcourt Brace, 1943), pp. 151–9

34. Morón, p. 188.

3 Land and Liberty

THE history of the states of the Caribbean area between 1900 and 1930 was dominated by three factors. These were the emergence of the United States, the disintegration and reintegration of Mexico, and the disruptive effects of the emergence of two new Latin American countries, Cuba and Panama.

These factors in turn were tied up with the circumstances in which Mexico became, ideologically speaking, the leading 'progressive' country in Latin America. She did so, moreover, from a position in which she was often represented as being the most extreme expression of traditional Latin American conservatism, backwardness, militarism and dictatorship.

Certainly, the emergence of the rule of Porfirio Díaz followed a traditional Latin American pattern.[1] First came his personal distinction in the military field, in the war against the French; then a series of attempts at seizing power by violence, when constitutional methods were open to him but clearly were not seriously considered. By a military revolt in 1876 he became President, in opposition to a proposal to re-elect the incumbent. By a series of dodges he was elected to the definitive presidency from 1877 to 1880. Thereupon he retired in favour of his *compadre*, Manuel González (1880–4), and returned to the presidency in 1884. Thereafter constitutional amendment secured his re-election for the period of dictatorship which was to have so many admirers inside and outside the Americas.

But though the rule of Díaz owed its origin to simple exhaustion with the turbulence of the early years of Mexican independence, with defeat in foreign wars, and with the simple intensity of the country's internal struggles, it did also have a significant relationship to the process of economic development.

Its proximity to the United States made Mexico a natural centre for North American investment in the early stages of its world-wide distribution. A group of positivistic thinkers, as we have seen, then arose to advise how this phenomenon might best be turned to advantage. They justified the continuation of 'firm' government by the need for investment, but the extension of investment and the development of the national economy as seen from the outside world, was achieved only at the cost of accentuating that very disparity between the rich landowners and the poor Indian which had been indirectly responsible for Mexican independence itself.[2]

This occurred in two ways. On the one hand, traditional landowners, their holdings fortified by the expropriation of church property, could for the first time rely on the backing of a powerful central government in their continuing war to augment their holdings from the common lands of the Indian. On the other, a new class of landowners emerged parallel with these, but far more remote and powerful; these were the great foreign corporations, especially the colonisation companies of the last two decades of the century. Moreover, Mexico, which had had a long tradition of being plundered for mineral wealth, now became the scene of a fresh wave of speculative ventures. Until oil was discovered in 1901 none of these showed much sign of proving of permanent benefit to the Mexicans themselves. They did, however, subsequently prove the growth points for the later workers' movements which sprang up in the new ideological climate of the twentieth century.

As we have already seen, at the time the régime of Díaz was much admired. In Peru, for example, Piérola's advisers had recommended him to take the Díaz course, and to secure the future of the country by providing dictatorship in the name of economic progress. Piérola, with great wisdom, pointed out that the weakness of such a course was that it depended on the life and ability of one man. It was just this inconvenient fact that, in 1904, drove those who were dependent on the Díaz régime to attempt to prolong its existence (Díaz himself already being seventy-four) by establishing a six-year instead of a four-year term for the President, and a Vice-President as a future replacement. Signs that the régime was on the wane then rapidly multiplied, ironically, just as Mexico was triumphantly establishing itself as an oil-producing nation second only to the United States. Its strength was demonstrated on the international plane by adopting the gold standard, refunding its debt, nationalising its American-owned railways, and casting a judicious diplomatic eye on the affairs of its small Central American neighbours.

Critical pamphlets and books multiplied. A series of strikes illustrated that the traditional means of repression were failing to impress a new generation. In 1910 revolt finally broke out in the deserts and mountains of the north, and, under the inspiration of Francisco I. Madero, its leader, became a coherent force.[3] The widespread nature of the revolt made it difficult for the government to repress it, and the military régime was in any case no longer capable of doing so, as in years of speculation most of the soldiers had disappeared. Furthermore revolt in the north gave the rebels command of the frontier and the ability to import supplies privately from the United States. The morale of the government cracked. Díaz went into exile in July 1911.

It was another matter, however, to set up a durable government on the foundations he left behind. After the brief interim government of Francisco León de la Barra (1911) Madero himself was elected in open contest as he himself wished, only to find that in his adherence to constitutional processes he had lost support on all sides. His government laid the ideological foundations for future change, but had little time to do more, for Madero himself was overthrown by a complex military *coup d'état* early in 1913. In the course of this, power was seized by his Commander in Chief, Victoriano Huerta (1913–14) and the deposed President was subsequently shot in mysterious circumstances.

At this point, the new administration of President Wilson (1913–21) took office in the United States, and was confronted with a moral question of whether or not to recognise the new government, which it considered to be founded on blood.[4] Traditionally, the question of origin would not have arisen, as the power to keep order and conformity to international obligations were the only criteria used. It was Wilson's view that this ought to be changed, and his decision to use the influence of the United States to push Latin American states towards constitutional processes was to add a fresh set of obligations to the Roosevelt Corollary.

Wilson therefore refused to recognise the régime of General Huerta and by insensible steps moved from tacit opposition to him to active encouragement of his enemies, the former Maderistas and others, now grouping themselves as 'Constitutionalists' in general support of the first man to pronounce against the military government, Governor Carranza of Coahuila.

The Constitutionalists, however, were split both on military tactics and on ideological programme. They comprised roughly a diffuse group of peasants fighting for land, a more coherent group of miners and other workers, and an intellectual element which had been denied expression under the old régime. Their dissensions greatly reduced their power in face of a still strong government and the fall of Huerta came about only when, having virtually abandoned sanctions against him as being ineffective, the United States government took advantage of the so-called 'Tampico Incident' (April 1914) to take control by a force of Marines of the key port of Vera Cruz. Ostensibly this was because the

American flag had been insulted. Actually the situation of hostility without military action had got too strained for the loose American control of commanders in the field.[5]

Complete political disintegration of the country ensued. On Huerta's flight, the Constitutionalists refused to recognise a single constitutional successor, least of all the interim President Francisco S. Carvajal (1914). After a short period without central authority, a convention was called.[6] It exercised a dwindling authority under the fainéant presidencies of Eulalio Gutiérrez (1914–15), Roque González Garza (1915) and Francisco Lagos Cházaro (1915–16) but never exercised effective control over the military forces which by now were all that represented the opinions of Mexicans.

The main division that emerged was that between the agrarian interests led by Emiliano Zapata in the south, and those of the military led by Venustiano Carranza's lieutenant, Alvaro Obregón. Obregón made a successful alliance with the labour interests and sent 'red battalions' into battle. Ultimately triumphant, he continued to build up support for Carranza after the fall of the Convention, and with exhaustion widespread, Carranza's persistence gave him the presidency (1917–20). This was not, however, before he had agreed to participate in a new convention, the Querétaro convention that wrote the Mexican Constitution of 1917. Because of its advanced social features this proved a model for the rest of Latin America. These features included the detailed rights of labour, the establishment of the principle of national property of the soil and sub-soil, and the right to welfare benefits and pensions. But in itself it did not, and could not, succeed in restoring order, and without order, it was only too easy for those in authority to avoid putting the precepts of the Constitution into practice.[7]

Carranza, precluded from seeking re-election for himself, by the nature of the movement he headed, already becoming known simply as 'the Revolution', attempted to impose a weak successor whom he could control. He was overthrown and killed in the course of a military revolt led by the forces of the north.

Because this revolt originated in, and was headed by a triumvirate from the northern state of Sonora, the Presidents that followed are known as the Presidents of 'the Sonora dynasty'.[8] They were Adolfo de la Huerta (1920), Álvaro Obregón (1920–4) and Plutarco Elías Calles (1924–8). The interim presidency of de la Huerta saw the first steps towards the large scale redistribution of land which was to follow. The name of Obregón is associated primarily in most people's minds with education and with his encouragement of the indianist José Vasconcelos in his drive for universal education in Mexico, and his express support for the work of the great muralists Rivera, Orozco, Siquieros and their school.[9] In political terms, however, he is more significant as the leader of the Revolution who established his power on the political organisation of labour, the CROM (founded 1918). He was recognised by the United States only in 1923 after agreeing not to enforce the 1917 Constitution's provision on state ownership of mineral rights, but as previously the act of recognition was much more important to the United States than it was to Mexico.

De la Huerta attempted a revolt unsuccessfully in 1923, as a result of which he had to go into exile. The reversion of the presidency then fell naturally on Calles. Calles, a former school-teacher and school-inspector, was naturally concerned with the development of education. However he was also a violent anti-clerical, and his strong measures against the Church and promotion of atheism brought about the Catholic revolt known as the War of the Cristeros (1926–9). Calles meanwhile carried out a programme of financial stabilisation, including the foundation of the bank of agrarian credit, which was the necessary prerequisite for the great extra impetus which he gave to the programme of land redistribution. His radicalism, however, was severely handicapped by military necessities, and in the last two years of his term money for all projects ran short, leaving the great majority of peasants very dissatisfied.

In 1928, Calles attempted to hand power back to Obregón. But Obregón, himself not strongly anti-clerical, was assassinated by a religious fanatic before he could take office, while the very attempt to renominate him had brought about a military revolt and showed the actual instability of the 'dynasty'. Now, in the fury and fear of the Obregonistas, power vanished from the hands of Calles. In a bid for a later return to power, he took the bold step of proclaiming his adhesion to constitutional principles, and hence his retirement from office, in conjunction with the formation of an official, and hence permanent, governing political party.[10]

The years that followed were to see the development of this political party into something rather different from what anyone had intended in 1928. With its establishment the unchecked rule of the 'Sonora dynasty' was replaced by a confused time of political manoeuvring, in which the figure of Calles stood out as the chief, but by no means the only influence. It was not a transition without growing pains, but the great rebellion of the alienated generals in 1929 proved to be the last major confrontation to the old régime. It was the final achievement of the Sonora dynasty to send the soldiers back to the barracks.

To the Mexicans, the Mexican Revolution as a period of history starting in 1910 is still going on today. On all sides it is generally acknowledged to be one of the so-called 'Great' social revolutions. As a period of extensive social reform accompanied by a high level of violence, it was followed by the reshaping of land ownership, the establishment of a new system of government. In the first phase, down to 1920, millions of Mexicans died, though many of them died from privation and disease, especially in the great influenza epidemic of 1919. But there are no good grounds for supposing that these deaths were essential to social reform. Rather by dramatising the fundamental nature of the issues of violence – the desire of Mexicans to lead better lives – they impressed the importance of conserving those gains on the generations to come. In the process, they also made a deep impression on the thinking of other Latin Americans. Graphic descriptions by scores of writers, beginning with Mariano Azuela in his *Los de Abajo* ('The Underdogs') established the image of humble, downtrodden people struggling against tyranny and bossism.

The ambiguity of the reality was summed up by the character of 'Pancho' Villa, a brilliant tactician and merciless fighter who fought from uncomplicated motives of hate and shot many of his enemies himself. Yet he amassed a formidable fighting force which took eight trains (including a hospital train) to carry it into battle. With it he swung the balance for Carranza and Obregón. Disappointed by Carranza's avoidance of recognition and reluctance to carry out social reforms, he vented his rage on the United States, attacking Columbus, New Mexico, in 1916. A punitive expedition of U.S. Cavalry under General Pershing spent months roaming northern Mexico in search of him, but he easily evaded them, to meet his death at the hands of assassins in 1923, when he was a pensioner of the Obregón government.

In Central America the land question was also to be of great importance, but its resolution was to be very different.[11]

To the south of Mexico, in Guatemala, the picture in 1900 was also one of dictatorship. Guatemala in the nineteenth century had been dominated first by the figure of Rafael Carrera (1838–65), illiterate, conservative and morbidly suspicious, and subsequently by the great Liberal *caudillo* Justo Rufino Barrios (1873–85).[12] As it had been the revolt of the peasant army led by Carrera against the Liberal régime of the Central American Republic that had split the

Republic into its separate parts, so it was the ambition of the Liberals under Barrios to succeed in achieving its reunification. It was in pursuit of this aim that Barrios himself met his death in a battle against similar reunifying forces in Salvador. But in the meantime he had given Guatemala a foundation for constitutional order and indeed the first real Constitution, in the liberal principles of education, secularism and the like. Though the natural resources of Guatemala were as yet almost untapped, the future looked bright.[13]

The latter years of the century were marked by periods of constitutional administration, which came to an end in 1898 with the assassination of the younger Barrios. As a result of this, Manuel Estrada Cabrera (1898–1920) succeeded to the presidency; he was to turn into a dictatorship notorious even in Central American annals.[14] A lawyer by training, Estrada Cabrera was neurotically concerned about his own safety to the point of eating only food prepared for him by his mother, and after an unsuccessful attempt upon his life in 1907 became a virtual recluse in the Presidential Palace. Opponents were dispatched summarily or spent many years in damp and vermin-ridden cells.[15]

Estrada Cabrera, like Díaz in Mexico, still thought of himself as a Liberal. The opposition which he stirred up, however, came from within the Liberals, and centred around Manuel Lisandro Barrillas, a former President who had yielded his power constitutionally. Now, at Estrada Cabrera's instigation, Barrillas was assassinated in Mexico, also in 1907. By that time, however, the efforts he had been making had linked up with the ambitions of President Zelaya of Nicaragua to achieve Central American unification, and as will be seen later, this in turn brought into play the interest of the United States in a peaceful Caribbean settlement. The United States put pressure on the Central American countries to meet in conference to settle their differences, and in the same year, 1907, they had to sign an

agreement which bound them to submit all disputes to the
decision of a Central American Court.

The Court lasted as an effective force only down to 1919
when it fell into abeyance. Meanwhile, under the repressive
rule of its President, Guatemala had become a zone of
stability to the south of Mexico, following a policy of close
adherence to the United States, and so attracting new
investment in fruit plantations. The plantation economy
came to be dominated by the giant United Fruit Company
of the United States, which received its first concession in
1906. At the end of the first World War, therefore, Guatemala
was technically very prosperous.

The climate of the times, however, was towards the
creation of new nationalities. In this spirit the Central
American countries, including Guatemala, found that
generation of leaders stirred by fresh sentiments for unification. The ageing Estrada Cabrera was resolutely opposed to a
movement which he had not initiated and which he could
not hope to control. More than this, he was no longer up to
the job of running Guatemala as a private concern of his
own. In 1920 a spontaneous revolt in the capital, spear-
headed by a resolution of Congress to disown him, led to his
relatively peaceful fall.

The brief presidency of Carlos Herrera (1920–1) was
associated with fresh negotiations for the federation of
Central America and the signature at San José of a treaty.
But Herrera was overthrown by a military *coup* before it
could be brought into effect and the moment again passed.
Under General José María Orellana (1921–6) the traditional
Guatemalan suspicion of unification not directly under
Guatemalan auspices was again brought to the fore. The
rule of Orellana was, however, a liberal one, and while
enjoying the general wave of prosperity, Guatemalans
entered a new period of mild social reforms. When Orellana
died of a heart attack in 1926, elections returned the
reforming administration of Lázaro Chacón (1926–30).

This government did much to modernise the country, particularly by instituting public education and developing natural resources. The spirit of Liberalism which Barrios, despite his personal vagaries, had so successfully implanted, had deep roots.

Chacón too died naturally, in 1930. This time, under the stresses of the time, events followed a different course from that which they had taken in 1926. He was succeeded briefly by his First Designate (Senior Vice-President) Baudillo Palma (1930). Being antipathetic to army leaders, Palma was overthrown in a *coup d'état* executed by General Manuel Orellana, cousin of the former President, who himself held office only briefly (1930–1). The hostility of the United States administration of President Hoover (1929–33) to his seizure of power forced him to give way to an interim government under José María Reyna Andrade (1931). Andrade held fresh constitutional elections. But as in 1898, the constitutional processes only succeeded in returning a man who was determined to establish personal rule, and the name of Jorge Ubico (1931–44), rather than that of Estrada Cabrera, is the name of Guatemala's Díaz.

Under Ubico, Guatemala attained the semblance of a modern state. Travellers remarked on its neatness, cleanliness and organisation.[16] But its foundation was the system of forced labour by which every peasant gave 180 days work free in the year to the great plantations, their labour being regulated through a system of work-cards, and all that these plantations received went in the main to United Fruit (UFCO). Furthermore, in his encouragement of further capital investment, Ubico followed Díaz in passing a Mineral Law, enabling property in sub-soil deposits to be transferred to private interests. Guatemala entered the Second World War on the side of the United States, and benefited greatly from the conditions of wartime trade. It was Guatemalan chicle that provided the chewing gum for children in blacked-out Britain or liberated France.

But the exigencies of war required that as part of the bargain, United States troops should also be stationed on Guatemalan soil. And the presence of these, coupled with the dissemination in Guatemala of the liberal ideas of the Atlantic Charter, led to a new questioning spirit among a new generation of its people. In 1944 Ubico was deprived of power by a passive withdrawal of support in the capital. It did not break down even in face of military and police action, and after a few days of it, Ubico gave way. As in 1920, the end of the war for Guatemala seemed the beginning of a new and better age.[17]

Guatemala's small neighbour, El Salvador, had an interesting and rather different history in the same years, though it came to much the same conclusion.[18]

In the nineteenth century El Salvador had early become a coffee-growing country. At the same time, its political power had become vested in an oligarchy rather than an autocracy, and its recurrent violence was modest and in general limited to the time of periodic transfers of power. The others were generally the product of external military or diplomatic intervention, and, after the death of Barrios of Guatemala, in 1885, this source of conflict fell into abeyance.

Tomás Regalado (1899–1903) was the last of a succession of Presidents who attained power by force within this general framework, each subsequently holding a poll to legitimize his rule. Regalado had fought a war against Honduras which was unsuccessful, and would have been of minor importance were it not for the fact that it put an end to the hopes of post-Barrios statesmen of unifying Central America round the three 'middle' countries. It was in fact the conflicts between these three that made the whole exercise impossible. Regalado did in internal affairs succeed in ending the violent conflicts for power by the no less drastic solution of imposing his successor, Pedro José Escalón (1903–7). Escalón's position, initially shaky, was stabilised by the further course of the external conflict.

For it was Escalón who had to defend El Salvador, on the one hand from the risk of isolation with Estrada Cabrera, and on the other from the armed attack of Zelaya of Nicaragua. Zelaya had abandoned hope of peaceful unification after 1898.. He had then intervened in the succession quarrel in Honduras in 1903, before turning his attention to the support of a revolt in El Salvador. Escalón necessarily had to appeal for support to Guatemala, but received nothing except encouragement. He thereupon turned to the United States, and the situation was saved for him by the general intervention and mediation of President Roosevelt and his Secretary for State, Elihu Root.

Protected by international guarantee, the small coffee-planter oligarchy of El Salvador was able to reach agreement to transmit power peacefully. The assassination of Manuel E. Araújo (1911–13) by gunmen while sitting under a tree was considered to be the result of a personal grudge.[19] So peaceful was the situation that the presidency was held between 1913 and 1927 by members of a single family without serious dispute. This situation ended with the term of Alfonso Quiñónez Molina (1923–7). The presidency then passed by choice to an outsider, Pío Romero Bosque (1927–1931), who was prepared both to assert himself and to permit a free choice when the end of his term came. The elections of 1931 were therefore left open, with the result that no candidate received a majority.

The legislature chose Arturo Araújo as their candidate, but he was not popular in the country, and an uprising in December 1931 coupled with the withdrawal of support by the army, replaced him by his constitutional successor, Maximiliano Hernández Martínez (1931–44).

Hernández Martínez was a bizarre figure. A Theosophist, he liked to treat his people's ills with bottles of coloured water which he exposed to the sun on the roof of the Presidential Palace. Like his contemporary to the north, Ubico, he ruled as a dictator, serving as elected President,

1935-9, and by constitutional amendment in 1939 'pro-longing' his office to 1945 without further election. His treatment of opposition was as summary as his treatment of the Constitution. Faced with a revolt in 1932 fomented by Comintern agents, he retaliated with great severity, over a thousand being killed. Yet his interpretation of nationalism, by encouraging coffee growers to emerge from within the country, necessarily meant an enlargement of the ranks of the landed. This weakened to some extent the economic base of traditional dictatorship.

Hernández Martínez fell from power in the same year and in the same way as Ubico, in face of a general with-drawal of support and a general strike. But the consequences of his fall were to be rather different.

It was Costa Rica, alone among Central American States, that pursued a consistent path of constitutionalism during this same period.[20] This was the work of two men, Tomás Guardia, President from 1870 to 1876, and from 1877 to 1882, and Bernardo Soto, President from 1885 to 1890. Guardia was a dictator in fact but a reformer in spirit; a man who seized power, as a civilian, by smuggling himself into a barracks in a hay-cart, but laid the material foundation for the system of free and compulsory education which Soto later devised. It was this system which came to distinguish this country from its neighbours. Costa Rica and Guatemala were at opposite poles of development, in a sense, since the system that Carrera had imposed had actually smashed the system of education which was previously Guatemala's pride.

When the election of 1889 went against Soto's choice for President, he accepted the decision as being final. Yet this one action was by no means sufficient to establish general adherence to constitutionalism. In fact, Costa Rica entered the twentieth century under a President, Rafael Iglesias (1894–1902), who had amended the Constitution to secure his own re-election. It was still by his consent that he was succeeded by Ascensión Esquivel (1902–6). The election of

1906, however, fell short of a decisive majority and into the hands of Congress, who chose Cleto González Víquez (1906–1910) only after Esquivel had exiled three of the opposition candidates.

Under these Presidents, and under Ricardo Jiménez Oreamuno (1910–14), Costa Rica enjoyed order and economic progress.[21] The coffee and banana cultivation which had begun in the 1870s was well established but small cultivators had not been squeezed out. This was partly because many of them were not Indians but descendants of Spanish settlers who were prepared to defend their position and partly because the volcanic earth around San José proved fertile enough to be intensively farmed and still retain its value. Meanwhile the effects of public education became manifest. Organised political parties came into existence, in a state in which the old Liberal-Conservative division had lost almost all meaning.

This peaceful scene, however, suffered a momentary interruption, when Alfredo González Flores (1914–17), who had reformed taxation so as to draw more revenue from the rich, was deposed by his Minister of War, Fernando Tinoco Granados. Tinoco (1917–20) was successful in imposing himself as President, but he was less successful in making his authority effective. Even among Conservatives he lacked support. With conditions as they were and the hostility of the United States Government made plain by their refusal, under the Wilsonian rules, to recognise him, he had to resign in 1919.[22]

After the restoration of the Constitution, the pattern previously established was also restored. So much so, in fact, that Julio Acosta García (1920–4) was succeeded by the second terms of both Jiménez (1924–8) and González Víquez (1928–32), Jiménez again becoming President for the term 1932–6.

In the course of a brief revolt by an unsuccessful candidate in 1932 the United States showed its continuing support of the constitutional régime. On the other hand, despite his conservative nature, Jiménez showed that this confidence was, to some extent, justified. Not only did he take the first steps towards social security legislation in Costa Rica, but he also succeeded in arranging the return of substantial tracts of land from the United Fruit Company to the nation, for redistribution to landless farmers.

The so-called National Republican Party, which had developed to support him, had meanwhile established itself on a long-term, continuing basis. It won the elections in both 1936 and 1940, under the lead of León Cortes Castro (1936–40) and Dr Rafael Calderón Guardia (1940–4) respectively. These two administrations rapidly accelerated the development of social and welfare legislation. Conservative hostility meant that the National Republicans had to turn for added support to the left, and particularly to the Communist-inspired Popular Front organisation, Vanguardia Popular. At the election of 1944 this alliance proved to be crucial in securing the succession to Calderón, and Costa Rica found itself facing a future every bit as uncertain as that of either Guatemala or Salvador, though one for which past history suggested the omens were much more favourable in the long run.[23]

Too much stress should not be laid on the part played by United States influence in maintaining Costa Rican democracy. There as elsewhere its influence was negative rather than positive, a response to situations and not a programme for deliberate action over a period of time. But the effect of the rise of United States power on the Caribbean area as a whole certainly should not be understated, either. With the exception of the countries already mentioned, the states of that area all came under much more than influence during this period, and in some cases under actual control. This intervention did not necessarily lead to the advancement of democracy, and in fact did sometimes lead to its destruction at the point of emergence.

The reasons for this are many and complex, but they all revolve around the original cause for United States involvement. Essentially this was the concern of that country with its own strategic problems: the defence of what was perceived as its national interest against possible rivals among the European powers. Both the cause and the effect of this involvement was the emergence of two new Latin American countries at the beginning of the twentieth century: namely, Cuba and the Republic of Panama.

Cuba had long been a target for the ambitions of inhabitants of the southern states of the United States, who had seen in it a possible addition to their ranks, serving to counterbalance their interests against those of the industrial north.[24] During the Ten Years War (1868–78) between Cuban revolutionaries and Spain agitation in the United States at times reached considerable heights. Cuba was, after all, only ninety miles from the shore of Florida. But there was by then nothing the southerners could do about it. When in 1895 a fresh Cuban revolt broke out, led by the poet and patriot José Martí, feelings of Americans were naturally closely engaged in it, and by this time not only in the south.

The Spanish Government sent as their commander to Cuba General Weyler, the man who was the first to apply that 'modern' technique of counter-insurgency warfare known as the 'concentration' of the civil population in camps, employed a few years later by the British in South Africa and by the Americans in the Philippines. Then, however, it was new, and to nineteenth-century eyes, barbarous. The activation of the liberal response in the north of the United States coincided with the ambitions of a newspaper proprietor – William Randolph Hearst – to sell newspapers by creating sensational news, and the explosion of the U.S.S. *Maine* in Havana harbour in 1898 became the pretext for United States intervention. Committed to liberate Cuba by the amendment bearing the name of the distinguished liberal Democrat, Senator Teller, American forces smashed Spanish power in the Caribbean (as well as in the Philippines) in a few weeks, and on 1 January 1899 took Cuba under United States military government.[25]

This government lasted until 1902, partly for administrative reasons, but also partly because interests in the United States existed which wanted to make sure that a liberated Cuba remained officially friendly.[26] By treaty, therefore, Cuban independence was made conditional on the so-called Platt Amendment, making the United States the guardian of the new state with the right to use military force to ensure 'sound' government. Tomás Estrada Palma (1902–6) thereupon became Cuba's first President.

Estrada Palma was a distinguished hero of the war, and his administration was, on the whole, honest, as well as progressive. His desire for re-election in 1906 was not foreign in the United States context: Theodore Roosevelt himself had been re-elected in 1904. But in the Latin American view it was suspect as a desire for self-aggrandisement. Conservative opposition boiled over into revolt. Estrada Palma called in American troops, and making use of the Platt Amendment, Roosevelt's administration imposed a second military government in the island (1906–9), in the hope that this time the concept of democracy might be more generally accepted.[27] But it was the Liberals who suffered most from it, since they occupied ground too well defined to be chosen as that of settlement.

Nevertheless, their unenthusiastic acceptance of hard facts received some justification when the cautious rule of José Miguel Gómez (1909–13) was followed by the reformist administration of Mario García Menocal (1913–21). Menocal, however, achieved his re-election only with the aid of United States Marines,[28] and the ill feeling in 1920 when Alfredo Zayas was the official candidate, and was successful, called forth a fresh expression of American support, though this time only in the symbolic form of an official mission. The fact was that the United States did not need to intervene, since its agents legally controlled Cuban finances under the terms of the Platt Amendment. Cuban administrations had so little leeway in their financial policy that it was hard for them to take any action not directly concerned with Cuba's role as the world's great producer of sugar, by this time firmly tied to the rocketing United States passion for soft drinks, ice cream and candy. They therefore took no action at all. Frustration set in among Cuban intellectuals, and corruption became endemic as too many able men scrambled for resources they were not allowed to handle directly.

The re-election of Zayas (1921–5) was the signal for revolt. It was much too widespread to be controlled, and the cautious Coolidge (1923–9) did not attempt to do so. Power fell into the hands of General Gerardo Machado y Morales, effectively dictator of Cuba from 1925 to 1933. Machado's was a dictatorship more symbolic than actual, but, after the first flush of enthusiasm for change, its restrictiveness was not very popular. Worse still, from the government's point of view, it was unsuccessful. Cuba's economy had boomed on its access to the vast American market, but with the Depression the demand for a luxury item like sugar fell off sharply and Cuba suffered as severely as any country from the economic crisis.[29] Machado, despite the watchfulness of his secret police, was overthrown by a military coup in 1933. With a Democratic Administration in power in the United States, following a policy of non-interference in its neigh-bours' affairs (the 'Good Neighbour' Policy) the government of Franklin D. Roosevelt (1933–45) resigned its right of intervention in Cuba in 1934 at the precise moment at which for the first time it could have been used to advantage in a positive way, to protect the struggling rebirth of democracy.[30]

The independence of Panama resulted from a very different set of circumstances.[31] To begin with, as we have seen, it was not a colony, but part of the American state of Colombia. It had been the scene of the major fighting in the

War of 1000 Days, and it was this illustration of the disadvantages of forming a main artery of traffic for a larger country which made the Panamanians sympathetic to the idea of independence. But it was the desire of the United States to build a canal across the Isthmus that resulted in the actual occasion for its separation.[32]

To interested parties in the United States Colombia seemed to demand an excessive price for the right. There were at least three alternative possibilities for a canal route: one through the Isthmus of Tehuantepec in Mexico, one by way of the lakes near Bluefields in Nicaragua, and one in the Atrato district of Colombia proper. None, however, was anything to compare with the Panama site for shortness and ease of construction, and Panamanian interests actually killed the Nicaraguan proposal by presenting to United States senators sets of Nicaraguan postage stamps portraying a volcano that had recently been active near the proposed route. Colombia found itself in a position to profit from a monopoly position. The Colombian government turned down the United States proposals.

The revolution that broke out in Panama at this signal was successful mainly because United States ships stood off shore and prevented the landing of troop reinforcements. Once Panamanian independence had been secured, the new state was recognised by the government of President Roosevelt within five days, an act of then almost indecent haste.* No less so was the haste with which the new provisional government of Panama signed away its right to the canal, its only resource and *raison d'être*. In less than a month the United States had obtained the right to build the canal across the Isthmus, the right to defend and fortify it, and, indeed, virtual sovereign rights over a ten mile zone on each side of it. Nor was this all. In Panama itself, the constitution of 1904 granted the United States the right of intervention to maintain order.

* In 1948, however, President Truman recognised Israel in eleven minutes.

On the first occasion on which this intervention was asked for, in 1905, it was refused. But intervention subsequently did take place in connection with the 1908, 1912 and 1918 Presidential elections. These interventions aroused intense hostility among many Panamanians, conscious of the difficult position in which their government had placed them between dependence on and fear of the United States. The United States, which had paid $10 million dollars down and a rent of $250,000 per year for the canal concession, however, considered that it had made a fair bargain, in view of the dubious nature of the Panamanians' claim to the property they had traded. No time was lost in starting work on the canal, which was opened to ships on 15 August 1914, a few days after the outbreak of the First World War.[33] Almost at once the canal became a very profitable enterprise, and successive negotiations were conducted between the two sides for additional benefits to Panama, culminating first in the Treaty of 1936 which did much to satisfy symbolic demands of national pride.

Meanwhile the pattern of Panamanian politics was one of domination by a conservative oligarchy led by a few great families, whose names predominate to a startling extent in the roll of Presidents of the Republic.[34] Constitutional rule began in 1904 with the presidency of Manuel Amador Guerrero (1904–8), and his successor José Domingo de Obaldía (1908–10) who died in office. Carlos Antonio Mendoza was briefly President in 1910, holding a special election to choose a successor. This was the first of the Arosemena family, Pablo Arosemena (1910–12). Under his administration, and those of his successors Belisario Porras (1912–16), Ramón M. Valdés (1916–19), Porras again (1919–20) and Ernesto Lefevre (1920–4) the closeness of the oligarchy's control and the overriding influence of the United States resulted in a period of peace not distinguished in any particular respect.

The rule of Rodolfo Chiari (1924–8) however was marked

by the rise of trouble on two fronts. In 1925 the San Blas Indians rebelled and were suppressed by force. Meanwhile pressure for revision of the Treaty of 1903 began really to be felt. But this pressure came from the United States itself, where interests were seeking extensive commercial concessions in the Canal Zone and the government was interested in obtaining rights to airport facilities and radio communications in addition to a concession by Panama which would give them joint control with the Panamanian government of all military operations in the event of war. In 1927 the Panamanian Congress refused to ratify the draft treaty. But the refusal did not relieve Panama of its dependence, and pressures from within the country that urged an assertion of sovereignty over the Canal Zone were only with difficulty withstood. In due course private interests in the United States received almost all that their government had asked for.

The stress was such that the Conservatives went down to defeat in the 1928 elections before Florencio Harmodio Arosemena, the Liberal candidate. It was Arosemena and the Liberals, therefore, who had to take the blame for the consequences of the Depression, and who early in 1931 were overthrown by a *coup d'état* in Panama City. The coup was actually carried out at the hands of a group known as Acción Communal, a Conservative body led by Harmodio Arias (1932–6), who took over power from the military junta, headed by the interim President Ricardo J. Alfaro (1931–2).

Arias's main plank was opposition to corruption. With the return of confidence in the United States and the lifting of the Depression his administration enjoyed favourable circumstances. He was also enabled to take advantage of the change of Administration to obtain from Roosevelt a declaration that Panama would be permitted all the rights of a sovereign nation in the Canal Zone before going on to renegotiate the Treaty of 1903 in Panamanian interests. The Treaty of 1936, agreed by his successor Juan Demóstenes

Arosemena, eliminated the American right of intervention and put the Roosevelt declaration into formal words.[35]

With the general interest of the United States in the Caribbean, deriving as it did from concern to protect the approaches to the Panama Canal, it was very natural that particular attention throughout this period should have been focused on the island of Hispaniola, and on the two republics of Haiti and Santo Domingo that shared it. The course of both was deflected by the interest and intervention of their powerful neighbour, and it cannot be said that it was for the better.

In the Dominican Republic (as Santo Domingo has latterly been known) some stability had been obtained in the late nineteenth century by the dominance of the conservative oligarchy and a sequence of fairly powerful dictators. But the assassination of the last of them, Ulíses Heureaux, in 1899, left power to a series of fainéant successors, who had little ability and less support.[36] In the course of the resulting upheaval the Dominican government suspended payment of interest on the National Debt, which seemed to exist primarily to finance successful revolutions. This default incurred the keen attention of a number of European governments.

It was specifically in application to this case that in 1904 Theodore Roosevelt enunciated his second great contribution to Latin American history, the so-called 'Roosevelt corollary' to the Monroe doctrine.[37] The corollary provided that to avoid European debt-collecting expeditions in the Americas, carrying contingent possibilities for political intervention, (such as that of Venezuela in the previous year) it was in the interests of the United States to act as 'policeman' and to intervene on their behalf, as a trustee for the European nations. Accordingly, as a practical expression of this theory, in 1905 the United States persuaded the Dominicans to agree to hand over collection of the custom duties – their chief source of revenue – to the impartial services of an agent appointed by the United States, and this agreement was embodied in Treaty form in 1907.[38] By removing the prize of revolution from reach, this agreement was meant to stabilise internal politics, but though it was to last in one form or another down to 1940 it did not end internal turbulence. In fact, in one way it added to it, for it brought down the President who had signed the agreement, Carlos F. Morales (1903–5), after a term which in length did not compare very favourably even with those of his three predecessors: Juan Isidro Jiménez (1899–1902), Horacio Vásquez (1902–3) and General A. Wos y Gil (1903).

His successor, Ramón Cáceres, however, was able through ruthless use of force to hold on to his authority down to 1911, when he was assassinated. The next President, Dr Eladio Victoria (1911–12) was rapidly deposed, and the concern of the United States under Taft (1909–13) forced the leading politicians of the country seriously to consider how long they would be spared the fate of actual military occupation. They therefore chose Monsignor Adolfo Nouel, a cleric generally respected as being impartial, as Head of State. Under his arbitration order of a sort was maintained until 1913, when under the stress and strain of office, Nouel boarded a boat for Europe and wrote his letter of resignation on the way.

The politicians and soldiers showed that they had learnt little or nothing in the meanwhile. After the brief titular rule of José Bordas Valdés (1913–14) his deposition by Ramón Báez resulted in the long-threatened intervention of the United States. Since the provisional President, Dr Francisco Henríquez y Carvajal (1914) refused to grant the United States full control of finance, the American government withheld revenue until, after his death from natural causes, a fresh election had established a nominally constitutional government under Juan Isidro Jiménez (1914–16). Finally, the fall of Jiménez in 1916 at the hands of a *coup* led to invasion and the establishment of an American military government (1916–24).[39]

This régime, though alien, gave the republic the only central authority that until recently had managed to be both stable and progressive. With the external resources of a Great Power, and the experience of Colonel Gorgas in the Canal Zone to draw on, it successfully brought under control malaria and yellow fever. It established modern communications, built schools and attracted capital investment in productive enterprises. But, like all colonial administrations, it could not establish legitimacy for the rule of its chosen successors. Something more was needed, and it was natural for a military government to think in terms of a trained national guard as a disciplined force capable of maintaining order on its own.

This force served very well after the occupation was terminated by the Coolidge administration and under the administration of Horacio Vásquez from 1924 to 1930. But when Vásquez then attempted to secure his own re-election it became apparent that training had only made the traditional military *coup* many times more efficient. Vásquez was overthrown and the Trujillo régime that succeeded him, which was to last for over thirty years, was to be far more ruthless and tyrannical than anything the Dominicans had yet known.[40]

The experience of Haiti was rather similar.[41] In the early years of the Haitian Republic stability had been achieved under forms derived from the Bonapartist monarchy that had preceded it. Even after the final dissolution of the monarchy in 1859, the dictatorship of Fabre Geffrard that lasted till 1867 at least maintained order.[42] After that date the ensuing chaos permitted barely notional development while the passing government borrowed heavily from a France that for reasons of imperial grandeur was always willing to lend. The first railway, completed only in 1900, merely facilitated the path of the regular military revolts that swept down from Cap Haitien on the capital, Port-au-Prince. By then, however, the process was nearing its logical end.[43]

In 1902 it gave Haiti the presidency of an octogenarian illiterate, General Nord Alexis, who held it for six years (1902–8), and yet was lucky enough to reach the boat in which he planned to go into exile. The French Minister guarded him from a screaming mob led by the women of the market. Antonio Simón (1908–11) also escaped, his fall, however, being aided by the intervention of German ships. His successor was less fortunate. In 1912 President Leconte was blown up by gunpowder at night in the Presidential Palace.

It looked for a moment as if the age of military adventurers might have come to an end, as none came forward to fill the vacant seat held by the interim President, Tancrède Auguste, who died in office. The presidency was awarded to a civilian lawyer, Michel Oreste (1912–14). Between that time and the date of his fall Oreste made a real attempt to put right some of the evils of anarchy. Unfortunately, to do so required considerable force of character, and the accusation of despotism toppled him in a revolt that ended the hope and all semblance of stability. The brief terms of Oreste Zamor (1914), Davilmar Theodore (1914–15) and Vilbrun Guillaume Sam (1915) were shot through with increasing violence, and the rising concern in the United States was manifest. In July 1915 Sam was torn to pieces in the streets of Port-au-Prince by the exasperated mob his predecessors had generally escaped. The following day, United States Marines landed, and a military occupation began which was to last down to 1934.[44]

Haiti, however, unlike the Dominican Republic, did not undergo actual military rule. The United States merely established a protectorate, supervised the election that gave Haiti a new President, Philippe Dartiguenave (1915–22), and while retaining control over finances, allowed him to maintain civil government.[45] Dartiguenave, like Louis Borno his successor (1922–30), soon found that in fact he was proconsul for the United States, and the first act of his presidency was to sign a treaty which confirmed the protectorate. In general, however, he was able enough to disguise the fact and to moderate the effect of foreign rule. A revolt against the occupation, led by Charlemagne Perlat, took place between 1918 and 1919 but was ultimately suppressed. After that, with time the memory of the troubles of the past receded, while the influence of the United States was felt in every aspect of the national life. Even the constitution of 1918 was, it was said, written in large part by an American, the young Franklin D. Roosevelt![46]

It was, then, the Americans who carried the blame for the Depression in Haitian eyes. In 1929 riots had already broken out over a wide area against the continuation of the occupation. President Hoover thereupon dispatched a commission to the island, and it recommended elections for a new president and the withdrawal of American troops as soon as possible thereafter. The elections were held, but the troops were not withdrawn until 1934, leaving the Haitian government largely unaltered by the experience through which it had gone. In 1935, under a new Constitution, Stenio Vincent (1930–41) had his term of office extended for a further five years.[47]

The United States also intervened on the mainland, where in the early years of the century the state of Nicaragua was the principal centre of conflict.[48]

It will be remembered that under José Santos Zelaya (1895–1909), Nicaragua was the most aggressive of the Central American countries in seeking reunification, and ultimately made use of military force to secure régimes in neighbouring countries favourable to Nicaraguan leadership. Following the Conference of 1907, however, the United States government, as guarantor of the agreements, had both the interest and the legal justification for maintaining the status quo. When, therefore, Zelaya resumed his support for revolutions among his neighbours, United States determination to stop him was shown unmistakably.

Now in the nineteenth century Nicaragua had established a variation of the usual Liberal-Conservative split on a regional basis, similar to that in Colombia but more clearly defined. With Zelaya (notionally a Liberal) in power at Managua, the capital, the rival centre of León became the centre for conspiracy against him. This conspiracy spread rapidly in 1909, and, much to everyone's surprise, Zelaya did not make much of a fight but fled into exile, leaving power to his Vice-President, José Madriz (1909–10). With Zelaya gone, the forces of the Conservatives were checked. After a period of indecision, they returned to the attack, and were aided in the decisive battle at Bluefields by the intervention of United States naval forces.[49]

Conservative rule in Nicaragua thereupon became synonymous with United States intervention, for under the provisional government the United States obtained the usual control over customs revenues and a small force of Marines was landed, to uphold the government of the day.

The leader of the Conservative revolt, Juan J. Estrada, was President for only a short time (1910–11) before attempting to impose his successor. The ensuing revolt brought about the intervention of the United States and the holding of an election, returning Adolfo Díaz (1912–16). In the course of this administration, the Republicans went out of office in the United States and the Democratic Party came in. President Wilson's Secretary of State, Bryan, negotiated a treaty with the Díaz government (the Bryan-Chamorro Treaty) that would have made Nicaragua a protectorate in all but name.[50] At first the treaty was not ratified by the United States Senate, then strongly liberal, but it was in the year that Emiliano Chamorro (1916–20) became President and established virtual family rule on behalf of the Conservatives.

El Salvador submitted this treaty to the Central American Court of Justice, who declared it to be a violation of the agreements of 1907. Nicaragua ignored this decision, and thus destroyed the efficacy of the Court.[51] Thus the policy of President Wilson, designed to improve upon the Roosevelt corollary in the first instance as a guarantee of Latin American financial independence, increased – by definition – dependence on the United States. Worse still, it also destroyed the legal safeguards that the Republicans (despite their lapses) had used to safeguard the Latin Americans from one another and from themselves.

The Chamorro rule virtually came to an end when Emiliano Chamorro brought down the government of Carlos Solórzano (1925–6) by forcing the small number of Liberals (and in particular the Vice-President, Juan Bautista Sacasa) out of the government. So long as they had been permitted a minimum of participation they had not revolted. Now there was no longer any reason to hesitate, they were divided.

Chamorro himself then reassumed the presidency, but his government was not recognised by the United States, and when a Liberal insurrection against it began, the government of President Coolidge intervened and enforced an armistice. Adolfo Díaz acted as President (1926–8) until elections held under United States supervision returned the Liberal, José Mariá Moncada (1928–33). The insurrectionary Liberals, under Sandino, their military leader, resumed their guerrilla activities subsequently, and continued until Sandino himself was killed by members of the National Guard shortly after leaving a dinner given by President Juan Bautista Sacasa (1933–6).[52]

The incident was not investigated and the responsibility for it was hardly a matter for conjecture. Once more a United-States-trained security force had shown it had the power to take over the government of the country without hope of effective opposition. In 1936, that was what General Anastasio Somoza actually did.

The last of the group of countries to be specially influenced by the United States had little in common with the others but its location. This was Honduras, economically the most backward of the Central American states largely owing to the mountainous terrain that to a great extent separates it from its immediate neighbours. Unfortunately, its area of settlement around the capital is most accessible to them, while cut off from easy land access to great parts of its own territory. Its strategic position in the centre of the isthmian area nevertheless made Honduras the battleground over which the other states fought out their differences. Honduran politics at the beginning of the twentieth century were extremely turbulent; her economy entirely agricultural and essentially on a subsistence level.[53]

The chief desire of educated Hondurans was to escape from their predicament. They believed that they had done so when in 1906 they reached agreement with Nicaragua on a boundary settlement in the Mosquitia area, and the Conference of 1907 agreed that their territory was to be guaranteed neutrality. Both hopes were to be dashed. Nicaragua denounced the settlement in 1912. And Honduras had to undergo United States military intervention in 1911 and 1922 before stability was achieved.

Fortunately, however, Honduras did not control a vital approach to the Panama Canal. Unlike Nicaragua, therefore, there was no military government, and the United States had little or no inclination to involve itself there at other times.

After the death of Barrios, Honduras developed towards constitutionalism under the impetus lent to it by those of his followers in Honduras who had given it the liberal constitution of 1880.[54] The Conservatives returned to power in 1891, whereupon the Liberals allied themselves with Zelaya, and Policarpo Bonilla emerged as their supreme chief. It was his nominee, General Terencio Sierra (1899–1903), who was President at the turn of the century. When he tried to prolong his term of office, he was deposed and replaced by Manue Bonilla (1903–7).

Manuel Bonilla was not sympathetic to the new, autocratic Zelaya, and was overthrown with the latter's aid by Miguel R. Dávila (1907–11). After the fall of Zelaya, Bonilla returned to challenge Dávila in a two year civil war ultimately ended by United States mediation and an armistice to hold and abide by the results of a fresh election. This election returned Manuel Bonilla as President for a fresh term (1911–13).[55] He died in office and was succeeded by his Vice-President, Dr Francisco Bertrand, whose popularity secured his election to office in due course and his survival until challenged in turn by a fellow-Liberal, Rafael López Gutiérrez (1920–3).

So far the strength of the Liberals had depended largely on their monopoly of organisation. Now it was the turn of the Conservatives. Gutiérrez, faced with their victory in the elections of 1924, tried to prevent their candidate, Tiburcio Carías Andino, from assuming office. The Conservatives then turned for aid to the government of President Coolidge. It severed relations with Gutiérrez and landed troops. Gutiérrez was killed in battle.[56] The victory of the Conservatives ended the civil war, and by United States mediation they now had to stand back while still under the provisional administration of Vicente Tosta (1924–5) fresh elections were held. In this election Carías Andino stood down, but the candidate of the National Party (as the conservative organisation was known) topped the poll.

In the event, the administration of Miguel Paz Barahona (1925–9) was reasonably progressive, and constitutional stability was maintained by Carías's refusal to revolt when the Liberal candidate, Dr Vicente Mejía Colindres (1929–1933), won the election of 1928. Nevertheless, taking the period as a whole, little was achieved, and Honduras remained very much the 'odd man out' in Central America and backward economically. Even the incursion of the United Fruit Company in search of the elusive banana did not disturb the equanimity of its citizens to any marked extent, and if it made them no richer, at least it made them no poorer.

The course of United States intervention, therefore, had widely differing effects. But with the possible exception of Haiti, it deeply affected the course of history of all the Caribbean countries to a great extent. Now the whole of Latin America – and the United States – was to realise that there were greater forces in the world even than that of the United States government; forces, in fact, which were as powerful to the United States as they were to the other countries of the hemisphere. And the Great Depression, which we have already observed in various of its aspects on more than one occasion, marks the great divide in twentieth-century Latin America.

1. Wilfrid Hardy Calcott, *Liberalism in Mexico, 1857–1929* (Stanford, Stanford University Press, 1931) is the best guide in English to the last days of the *Porfiriato*; see also the indispensable Daniel Cosío Villegas, *Historia Moderna de México*, 8 vols (Mexico, Editorial Hermes, 1955–).

2. Carleton Beals, *Porfirio Díaz, dictator of Mexico* (Philadelphia & London, Lippincott, 1932).

3. Charles Curtis Cumberland, *The Mexican Revolution, Genesis under Madero* (Austin, University of Texas Press, 1952); Stanley Robert Ross, *Francsico I. Madero, Apostle of Mexican Democracy* (New York, Columbia University Press, 1955).

4. Peter Calvert, *The Mexican Revolution, 1910–1914; the diplomacy of Anglo-American conflict* (Cambridge, Cambridge University Press, 1968).

5. Robert E. Quirk, *An Affair of Honor: Woodrow Wilson and the Occupation of Vera Cruz* (New York, McGraw-Hill, 1964).

6. Robert E. Quirk, *The Mexican Revolution, 1914–1915; The Convention of Aguascalientes* (Bloomington, Indiana University Press, 1960).

7. Frank Tannenbaum, *Peace by Revolution: an interpretation of Mexico* (New York, Columbia University Press, 1933).

8. John W. F. Dulles, *Yesterday in Mexico, A Chronicle of the Revolution, 1919–1936* (Austin, University of Texas Press, 1961).

9. José Vasconcelos, *A Mexican Ulysses, an autobiography* trs. and ed. W. Rex Crawford (Bloomington, Indiana University Press, 1963) pp. 151–187.

10. Peter Calvert, 'The Mexican Political System, a case study in political development', *Journal of Development Studies*, iv, 4 (October 1968), 464.

11. Parker is the best and most recent guide; Dana Gardner Munro, *The Five Republics of Central America. Their political and economic development and their relations with the United States* (New York, Oxford University Press, 1918) and the same author's *Intervention and Dollar Diplomacy in the Caribbean 1900–1921* (Princeton, Princeton University Press, 1964) together give the fullest picture of Central American history in these years available in any language.

12. Paul Burgess, *Justo Rufino Barrios* (Philadelphia, Dorrance, 1926).

13. A view of Guatemala at the turn of the century is given by Anne Cary and Alfred Percival Maudslay, *A Glimpse at Guatemala and some notes on the ancient monuments of Central America* (London, J. Murray, 1899).

14. Cf. W. F. Sands, *Our Jungle Diplomacy* (Chapel Hill, University of North Carolina Press, 1944). This account follows Chester Lloyd Jones, *Guatemala, past and present* (Minneapolis, University of Minnesota Press, 1940; New York, Russell & Russell, 1966).

15. Hugh Wilson, *The Education of a Diplomat* (London, Longmans, 1938) pp. 48–50.

16. Vera Kelsey and Lily de Jongh Osborne, *Four Keys to Guatemala*, 2nd ed. (New York, Funk & Wagnalls, 1945).

17. Ronald M. Schneider, *Communism in Guatemala 1944–1954* (New York, Praeger, 1959).

18. This account follows Parker, pp. 150–2. See also Lily de Jongh Osborne, *Four Keys to El Salvador* (New York, Funk & Wagnalls, 1956).

19. Sir Thomas Beaumont Hohler, *Diplomatic Petrel* (London, John Murray, 1942), p. 181.

20. Chester Lloyd Jones, *Costa Rica and civilisation in the Caribbean* (Madison, Wis., University of Wisconsin Press, 1935) is the only definitive study. See also Parker, pp. 263–77.

21. Stacy May *et al.*, *Costa Rica, a study in economic development* (New York, Twentieth Century Fund, 1952).

22. Munro, *Intervention & Dollar Diplomacy*, pp. 426–48.

23. Cf. John D. Martz, *Central America, the crisis and the challenge* (Chapel Hill, University of North Carolina Press, 1959) pp. 212 ff., where Calderón is dismissed very lightly.

24. Basil Rauch, *American Interest in Cuba, 1848–1855* (New York, Columbia University Press, 1948).

25. David Healy, *The United States in Cuba, 1898–1902, Generals, Politicians and the Search for Policy* (Madison, University of Wisconsin Press, 1963); Richard Butler Gray, *José Martí, Cuban Patriot* (Gainesville, University of Florida Press, 1962) gives depth to the central aspect of Cuban independence.

26. Russell H. Fitzgibbon, *Cuba and the United States, 1900–1935* (New York, Russell & Russell, 1964) pp. 30–66. See also Hermann Hagedorn, *Leonard Wood, a biography* (New York, Harper Brothers, 1938).

27. Allan Reed Millet, *The Politics of Intervention; the military occupation of Cuba, 1906–1909* (Columbus, Ohio State University Press, 1968).

28. Leo J. Mayer, 'The United States and the Cuban Revolution of 1917', *H.A.H.R.* x, 2 (May 1930) 138.

29. R. L. Buell *et al.*, *Problems of the new Cuba* (New York, Foreign Policy Association, 1935).

30. E. David Cronon, 'Interpreting the New Good Neighbor Policy, Cuban Crisis of 1933', *H.A.H.R.* xxxix, 4 (November 1959) 538.

31. M. W. Williams, *Anglo-American Isthmian Diplomacy, 1815–1915* (Washington, American Historical Association, 1915).

32. Munro, *Intervention and Dollar Diplomacy*; see also Philippe Bunau-Varilla, *Panama: the creation, destruction and resurrection* (London, Constable, 1913).

33. Miles P. DuVal, *And the Mountains Will Move: the story of the building of the Panama Canal* (Stanford, Stanford University Press, 1947).

34. Panama lacks a good internal history, cf. L. O. Ealy, *The Republic of Panama in World Affairs, 1903–1950* (Philadelphia, University of Pennsylvania Press, 1951).

35. Cordell Hull, *The Memoirs of Cordell Hull* (London, Hodder & Stoughton, 1948) i, pp. 344–5.

36. Bemis, pp. 151–9.

37. Sumner Welles, *Naboth's Vineyard: the Dominican Republic, 1844–1924* (New York, Payson & Clarke, 1928).

38. J. F. Rippy, 'The Initiation of the Customs Receivership in the Dominican Republic', *H.A.H.R.* xvii, 4 (November 1937) 419.

39. Carl Kelsey, 'The American Intervention in Haiti and the Dominican Republic,' *Annals of the American Academy of Political and Social Science*, c (March 1922) 109.

40. C. A. Thomson, 'Dictatorship in the Dominican Republic', *Foreign Policy Reports*, xii, 3 (15 April 1936).

41. J. G. Leyburn, *The Haitian People* (New Haven, Yale University Press, 1941), is the principal history.

42. J. E. Bauer, 'The Presidency of Nicolas Geffrard of Haiti', *The Americas*, x (April 1954) 425.

43. A not overtly hostile account of the condition of Haiti at this time is H. Hesketh Prichard, *Where Black rules White: A Journey Across and About Hayti* (London, Thomas Nelson, 1910).

44. This account follows Munro, *Intervention and Dollar Diplomacy*, pp. 326–87.

45. A. C. Millspaugh, *Haiti under American Control, 1915–30* (Boston, World Peace Foundation, 1931).

46. Arthur M. Schlesinger, Jr., *The Crisis of the Old Order, 1919–1933* (London, Heinemann, 1957) pp. 357, 377, says that this claim was grossly exaggerated.

47. Herbert Hoover, *The Memoirs of Herbert Hoover; The Cabinet and the Presidency, 1930–1933* (London, Hollis & Carter, 1952) p. 333; Hull, pp. 345–6.

48. Account follows Parker, pp. 225–7; see also W. H. Koebel, *Central America: Guatemala, Nicaragua, Costa Rica, Honduras, Panama and Salvador* (London, Fisher Unwin, 1917) for the state of Central America in the early years of the century.

49. Munro, *Intervention and Dollar Diplomacy*, pp. 160–216.

50. T. A. Bailey, 'Interest in a Nicaragua Canal, 1903–1931', *H.A.H.R.* xvi, 1 (February 1936) 2; see also I. J. Cox, *Nicaragua and the United States, 1909–1927* (Boston, World Peace Foundation, 1927).

51. M. O. Hudson, 'The Central American Court of Justice', *American Journal of International Law*, xxvi (1932) 759.

52. Parker, p. 227; see also Joseph O. Baylen, 'Sandino: Patriot or Bandit?', *H.A.H.R.* xxxi, 3 (August 1951) 445.

53. Account follows Parker, pp. 187–8.

54. William S. Stokes, *Honduras, an area study in government* (Madison, University of Wisconsin Press, 1950).

55. Munro, *Intervention and Dollar Diplomacy*, pp. 225–35.

56. Theodore P. Wright, Jr., 'Honduras, A Case Study of United States Support of Free Elections in Central America', *H.A.H.R.* xl, 2 (May 1960) 212.

4 Soldiers and States

So far the impact of the Great Depression on Latin America has been considered primarily as affecting directly the economic well-being of countries in the hemisphere whose economies, as primary producers, were closely linked to the world market. But the Depression itself was world-wide and hence associated with phenomena far more widespread and significant in the political field. The consequent effects were to divert the course of Latin American history.

Among these were the inward-turning of the United States itself, and the consequent withdrawal from the outside world after the change of administration in 1933. The Depression was also associated with the fall of the Spanish monarchy in 1931, and paradoxically lent significance to the successful stabilisation, both political and economic, of Portugal after Dr Salazar became Prime Minister in 1932. The latter went together in the public mind with the physical achievements of Italian fascism under Benito Mussolini (1922-43), himself, not wholly aptly, named after the great hero of Mexican liberalism! There were, after all, by this time very many Latin Americans of Italian origin living in Argentina, Brazil and Chile, while the rise of German Nazism struck a response from members of the widely dispersed German trading colonies as well as from German settlers in all those countries, in Paraguay and Bolivia, and, curiously enough, in Guatemala.

In any case, the traditional tendency of the Latin American military to have recourse to violence provided fertile ground for the growth of radical ideologies both of the Left and of the Right. In 1930 the governments of the Dominican Republic, Bolivia, Peru, Argentina, Brazil and

Guatemala were toppled by forcible intervention. The following year, 1931, those of Panama, Chile, Ecuador and El Salvador followed, while in 1932 Chile suffered forcible changes of government no less than four times. Finally in 1933 Uruguay and Cuba, previously stable, underwent

Table 5

Assassination, Coup d'État and Revolution, 1901–68

No	Country	Dates
1	Uruguay	1933
3	Colombia	1909, 1953, 1957
3	Costa Rica	1917, 1919, 1948
5	Honduras	1911, 1919, 1924, 1956, 1963
6	Brazil	1930, 1946, 1954, 1955(2), 1964
6	Venezuela	1909, 1945, 1948, 1950^b, 1952, 1958
8	Cuba	1906, 1933(2), 1934, 1936, 1952, 1959(2)
8	El Salvador	1913^b, 1931, 1944(2), 1948, 1949, 1960, 1961
8	Mexico	1911, 1913, 1914(2), 1915(2), 1916, 1920
8	Nicaragua	1909, 1910, 1911, 1926(2), 1936, 1947, 1956^b
9	Argentina	1930, 1943(2), 1944, 1945, 1955(2), 1962, 1966
9	Chile	1924, 1925(2), 1927, 1931, 1932(4)
9	Guatemala	1920, 1921, 1930, 1944(2), 1954(2), 1957^b, 1963
9	Panama	1903^a, 1931, 1941, 1949(3), 1951, 1955^b, 1968
9	Peru	1914, 1919, 1930, 1933^b, 1936, 1948, 1962, 1963, 1968
11	Bolivia	1920, 1930, 1934, 1936, 1937, 1939, 1943, 1946, 1951, 1952, 1964
12	Ecuador	1906, 1931(2), 1935(2), 1937, 1944, 1947(2), 1961, 1963, 1966
15	Dominican Republic	1902, 1903(2), 1905, 1911, 1912, 1913, 1914, 1916, 1930, 1961^b, 1962, 1963, 1965(2)
15	Paraguay	1902, 1904, 1908, 1911(2), 1912(2), 1921, 1936, 1937, 1940, 1948, 1949(2), 1954
16	Haiti	1902(2), 1908, 1911, 1912^b, 1914(2), 1915(2), 1946, 1950, 1956, 1957(4)

^{a} Secession. ^{b} Assassination.

violent alteration (though in the Uruguayan case admittedly a small one) while the President of Peru was shot (see Table 5, p. 96).

It is interesting to notice how those states that escaped this pattern of intervention did so for very different reasons. In Colombia and Mexico, the political process was sufficiently developed to allow peaceful transfer of power when a government lost support. In Costa Rica too the constitutional order withstood the strain without in this case involving a change. Honduras, Nicaragua, and Haiti, which avoided changes otherwise only too probable, were stabilised by the presence of United States forces. The Venezuelan dictatorship, which needed no outside resources, stood firm. Bolivia and Paraguay went to war.

Before turning to the course of this war, the Chaco War (1932–5), which is the greatest international conflict to break the peace of Latin America in this century, we must first take a closer look at the backgrounds of the two countries principally concerned. They had a great many things in common. They were both land-locked countries, dependent on others for their trade route with the outside world. Bolivia, however, was one of the world's only two major producers of tin, the metal indispensable to the most versatile and universal system of food preservation. This made it alarmingly dependent on the production of a substance with a particularly wide fluctuation of price, but tin, coupled with the output of the silver mines of Potosí, was sufficient in itself to give it economic potential far in excess of that of Paraguay, a largely agricultural nation. Otherwise, both states had in the nineteenth century passed through appalling wars, in which they had lost men, territory and prestige beyond their capacity to replace in generations. Both accordingly came to turn their interest inwards towards one another and so the scene was laid for their conflict.

First of all, however, let us take the case of Bolivia.[1]

Bolivia was not only the stronger, but in the late nineteenth century the more frustrated of the two. As the result of the War of the Pacific she had lost the littoral provinces she had previously possessed. Pending peaceful settlement between her government and that of Chile she had no satisfactory means of transit to the coast, since the route to Peru by way of Lake Titicaca – the highest lake in the world – was hardly a viable alternative. At the same time, Bolivian statesmen had an exasperating dependence on Chilean good will for the contingent possibility of a settlement.[2]

In common with the other Andean countries, Bolivia shared the division between coast, upland and mountain, and the intense regional differences, focused in this case on the traditional conflict of interest between the legal capital Sucre and the administrative capital La Paz. Although after the War of the Pacific Bolivia enjoyed relative political stability under a series of Conservative governments, the stability was born of exhaustion, not agreement, and was easily disturbed by a revival of traditional disputes. Thus when José Pando (1899–1904) came to power by military coup, it was because his predecessor had attempted to transfer the administrative functions to Sucre. He well illustrated the phenomenon which we have already observed in the case of Colombia, namely obsession with a single goal in international affairs to the exclusion of all other desirable possibilities.

Pando, the President successful in obtaining the negotiations with Chile which led to the Treaty of 1904 and agreement on the access question, was the same man who signed away the Acré region to Brazil for rubber plantation, in consideration for a cash indemnity of $10 million and a concession to build a railway into Brazil.[3] It was Pando's successor, however, Ismael Montes (1904–9), who actually signed the treaty with Chile. Chile conceded very little, for she only admitted Bolivia's right to the Atacama Desert, most of which was in the hands of Peru. The guarantees

which the treaty included for the construction and operation
of the Arica–La Paz Railway were much more to the
advantage of Bolivia than to Chile, but certainly Chile only
stood to benefit from development of the entrepôt trade.
The railway was built between 1904 and 1912, just as tin
began to come into general use for its modern purpose.

Montes also carried out an enlightened policy of religious
toleration and took important steps towards the development
of public education. In the term of his successor, Eleodoro
Villazón (1909–13), and in the second term of Montes
(1913–17), Bolivia underwent a continuous spell of progress
in which her prosperity based on new access to the world
was fanned by the new need for food preservation in war-torn
Europe. The confidence of governments of this period was
well illustrated by their attempts, especially in 1913, to
delimit the boundary with Paraguay in the region of the
Chaco, along a line, as things then stood, very acceptable to
both parties.

But Bolivia was to discover that not all the products of the
War were to her advantage. The term of José Gutiérrez
Guerra (1917–20) was one of disillusion. The wartime boom
came to an end. Worse, Bolivia approached the newly
formed League of Nations from which idealists hoped for so
much in an attempt to reverse the Treaty of 1904 and
restore her claim to the territory of Arica. Her statesmen
were disillusioned to discover, as did so many others, that
possession of a good case before the League was not the same
thing as being able to make it good. Gutiérrez Guerra was
then overthrown by a military *coup d'état*. This incident, plus
the need for self-assertion and the possibility of new economic
resources, turned the attention of the Bolivian government
once more towards the Chaco.

The Gran Chaco is a great area of upland plain, stretching
across several countries from Brazil in the North to Argentina
in the South. The area with which the Bolivians were
concerned was the Chaco Boreal, a flat area of scrubby

semi-desert which turns to swamp during the rainy season. It stretches westwards from the foothills of the Bolivian section of the Andes as far as the Paraguay river, so that its edge lies just across the Pilcomayo river from Asunción, the Paraguayan capital. There were no obvious geographical features in this region which might serve to delimit the boundary and no very obvious interest before the term of Bautista Saavedra (1920–5) which might impel the Bolivians to go to war for it. On the other hand, the possession of at least part of the Chaco was of very great strategic importance to Paraguay. A Bolivian frontier on the Paraguay River, the extreme Bolivian claim, was not to be thought of. What was mainly a matter of glory for Bolivia was a matter of national survival to Paraguay.

But under Bautista Saavedra, Bolivia itself had undergone a considerable economic boom, with the growth of new investment in mining. Bolivia had been even more fortunate to locate oil especially around Camiri in the south, sufficient for her needs and more. Geological surveys now suggested that further oil reserves might be discovered under the Chaco Boreal, and this cast a very different light on the situation. Oil was not just the objective of the war, but the means by which it could be waged.

The situation of the new Bolivian President was extremely unstable. José Cabino Villanueva (1925) was the subject of intense hostility outside ruling circles because of the fraud connected with his election, and he was forced to flee the country. Hernando Siles (1926–30) was therefore open to constraints from all sides, and military adventurism on the frontier was inopportunely coupled with an aggressive, forward policy from his Foreign Minister. It may only have been intended to improve a bargaining position, but for whatever reason the Bolivian claim was extended to the maximum possible, beyond both the line of 1913 and the de facto limit of Paraguayan military defence. Both sides then built forts and sent out patrols in the region of the Chaco and in 1928 the first armed clash occurred.

Fortunately for Paraguay, Bolivian interest was temporarily diverted by the possibility of a fresh settlement with Chile of the Tacna–Arica question. This hope was dashed by the 1929 Treaty between Chile and Peru. External mediation by American nations, notably Argentina, allowed the Chaco dispute to linger on without solution.

The fall of President Siles in 1930 as the result of a military *coup* further delayed the issue. His régime was unpopular because of the economic depression and the fall of the price of tin on the world market. In the turbulence that followed, it was some time before a stable administration was formed. The interim government of General Carlos Blanco Galindo (1930–1) eventually held an election, however, and Daniel Salamanca (1931–4) was returned, only to find that the delay had forced on Bolivia a radical revision of tactics.

The history of Bolivia in these years was much more stable, however, than that of Paraguay.[4] Paraguay had also entered the twentieth century under a Conservative régime, that of the so-called Colorados. But the problem for every government was the dominant position of the Army in a country in which the Army was traditionally the chief end of the state. On the other hand, the abnormally small male population, a generation after the War of the Triple Alliance, made the problem of maintaining the Army particularly acute. As it could not hope in those years to fight successfully against any foreign enemy, it was natural that much of the Army's interest should be focused on intervention in domestic politics to secure its own ends. It was in fact the chief regulator of political change.

When President Emilio Aceval (1898–1902) was overthrown by his Vice-President, Héctor Carballo (1902) it was as the immediate result of an armed battle on the floor of Congress, arbitrated by the Army. The fact that the fight had occurred in Congress at all, though, showed that there were surviving traditions in Paraguay other than military ones. The Liberalism which had assumed the burden of reconstruction after 1870, in a country shorn of over one-third of its territory by Brazil and Argentina, had not entirely disappeared. Though the Conservatives retained office, the making of a full scale civil war was already apparent. President Juan A. Escurra (1902–4) was the last of the line, and was overthrown by the Liberals in a three month campaign, marked by a number of heroic and dramatic episodes around the railway from Asunción to the Argentine frontier. Fighting was terminated by negotiation and the Pilcomayo Agreement of 1904.[5]

The interim President Juan B. Gaona (1904–5) was then replaced by the Liberal nominee, Professor Cecilio Báez (1905–6), who held an election, at which the leader and General of the Liberals, Benigno Ferreira (1906–8) became definitively President, and sought to carry out the liberal programme.

Now, a leading item in this programme was, not surprisingly, the destruction of military power in politics. Ferreira's Minister of War, Colonel Albino Jara, was entrusted with this task in his capacity as leader of the radical group. Feeling that his chief, once in power, was not keen to put the reform into effect, Jara seized power from him after a pitched battle in Asunción. There the military barracks were shelled from a gunboat on the river, until the garrison of Concepción revolted and aided the radicals to victory.

Jara himself remained Minister of War under the interim President, Emiliano González Navero (1908–10), and it was he who carried through the dissolution of the old Army and the creation of a new one based on universal military service. In 1910 a fresh election was held, and Manuel Gondra (1910–11) elected to constitutional office. Gondra, a lawyer, was a moderate, and when he tried to rid himself of his dominating Minister, he was overthrown by him. Jara

(1911) then took the presidency for himself, but his dictatorial style made many enemies and he fell in months, being arrested in a bloodless *coup* by the moderates. A third set of elections under liberal auspices were then held.[6]

The radicals planned a last desperate assault on the capital. Their plans were betrayed by a telegraphist and the government sent a train loaded with dynamite down the track towards the village of Sapukai where their forces were assembling. It exploded in the station with tremendous force and blew to pieces the expedition, the village and the hopes of further radical reform. Jara himself was killed in battle near Paraguari.

Yet freed from their internal divisions the Liberals were able at last to justify some of the hopes placed in them. Eduardo Schaerer (1912–16), in serving a full term of office, developed trade through Argentina with the outside world. His successor Manuel Franco (1916–19) died in office; his Vice-President, José Montero (1919–20), succeeded without incident. Unluckily, this run of good fortune then came to an end, for the re-election of Gondra (1920) only confirmed that he was too academic a personality to stay in office. But his fall brought to the fore the Ayala brothers who were to dominate Paraguayan politics for a decade.[7]

Eusebio Ayala (1921–3) was therefore succeeded by his brother Eligio (1923–4); the interim government of Luis Riart (1924) being employed as a device to allow the re-election of Eligio Ayala (1924–8). Ayala's administration was one of social reform and development, and he transmitted power without incident to his chosen successor José Guggiari (1928–31). It was Guggiari who had the job of preparing for the Chaco War. For it was quite apparent to the Paraguayans that war was the only possible outcome that could guarantee their national survival. They proceeded to make desperate efforts to build up the strength of their army while exhausting every diplomatic outlet that appeared to be available to them, and they were fortunate enough after 1930 to enjoy the tacit support of the Argentine military governments and the services of the new Argentine foreign minister, Saavedra Lamas.

It was Paraguay that brought the Chaco question before the League. Their attempt to invoke the League's aid, however, was frustrated by the dispute within the American states and the fact that the United States, not being a member, preferred to build up some Pan American alternative. But United States intervention meant hostility within the camp. The Pan American Conference was unable to make a satisfactory agreement and the major Latin American powers were neither willing nor able to enforce one. Skirmishes continued in the disputed area, while a generally accepted alternative became the return to the *status quo ante*.

News soon reached Paraguay that the Bolivians too were increasing their military strength. In a desperate throw to forestall an invasion, the Paraguayans initiated hostilities in mid-1932 by attacking a Bolivian advance guard on the near side of the Chaco. Action, they hoped, would bring into effect the customary general ban on exports of arms to either party, and this, they believed, would leave them with the advantage. Regrettably for the Paraguayan hopes, the Chileans were prepared to let the Bolivians have arms, though the instability of Chilean administrations in mid-1932 suggested that this was probably not a result of deliberate planning. This did not matter much militarily, as the Paraguayans had greatly underestimated their power and the Bolivians proved unable to resist.

But politically it was a miscalculation as it placed the Paraguayans in the unenviable position of being branded as an 'aggressor' by the League of Nations. The League's obsession with questions of who fired the first shot in the end led to the ban on arms being lifted in favour of Bolivia. By then, however, the Paraguayans had been able to drive the Bolivians entirely out of the Chaco region, so that the actual position the latter found themselves in was not only worse than when they had started, but worse than any position of demarcation proposed since 1879! The Bolivian president, Salamanca, was overthrown by military revolt in December 1934 and his successor, Vice-President José Luis Tejada Sorzano (1934–6) was overthrown when he proposed to make peace.

In their victory, the Paraguayans were helped above all by the physical conditions of the Chaco.[8] The difficulty of communications across the swamp and desert meant that the Bolivians were fighting at the end of an over-long line of supply. The same factor, when the Paraguayans' victory had put them in the same position, forced them to stop short of the Bolivian heartland in 1935. A truce was then hastily concluded by the Bolivian government, and the Paraguayans were prepared to make a reasonably generous peace, until military *coup d'état* achieved the unlikely end of overthrowing the victorious government of Eusebio Ayala (1931–6).[9] It was replaced by a military régime under General Rafael Franco (1936–7) while at the same time the government of Tejada Sorzano in Bolivia was overthrown by a revolt led by Germán Busch and replaced by a socialist/fascist régime under José David Toro (1936–7).[10]

It soon became clear that the régime of Franco was tending the same way. Both countries, therefore, had been given dictatorial régimes bound towards the reconstruction of every aspect of the national life. Both attempted by the development of rigid controls over the people to develop the economy and military infrastructure, especially through the nationalisation of key industries. But in neither case did they last long. In 1937 the régime of Toro was terminated by Busch (1937–9) who modified some aspects of his pro-gramme, while Franco was overthrown by a bloodless liberal *coup* and replaced by the constitutional régimes of Félix Paiva (1937–9) and subsequently Marshal José Félix Estigarribia (1939–40). Political changes removed Saavedra Lamas from office in Argentina and into dignified retirement with a Nobel Peace Prize (for doing more than any other single man to prolong the Chaco War). Peace was at last signed under pressure from the United States in 1938. The concessions made by each side were disguised under the forms of a so-called 'arbitral award' agreed between them in advance.[11]

The results of the war were profound. It played an important role in damaging the reputation of the League, the secession from it of Paraguay in 1935 being rapidly followed by a wave of secessions by other Latin American states with axes to grind. Paraguay was greatly strengthened, and, indeed, regained territory almost equal to that which she had lost in the War of the Triple Alliance, but only at the cost of adding to the pride of the military and reinstating their habit of intervention in politics. The fact of military success, however, did enable the Liberals for a time to restore civilian government.

Bolivia was greatly weakened, and humiliation was greatly exacerbated in its corrosive effect by the pressure of the division between Bolivia's military rulers and the workers who provided the economic resources of the country. Disgust with oligarchy had even developed an intellectual movement for the liberation of the Indian, exemplified by Alcides Argüedas's *Raza de Bronce*. This division was reflected in a social cleavage in the Army. Poor conscript soldiers, struck down by the diseases of the lowlands, blamed the incompetence of the officers for their failure. At the same time the example of radicalism gave them grounds for believing that their lot could be changed, if only they knew how.[12] The ultra-conservative rule of Gérman Busch was terminated by his suicide in 1939. That of his successors, Carlos Quintanilla (1939–40) and Enrique Peñaranda del Castillo (1940–3), however, continued military rule, that lasted altogether almost six years and imposed totalitarian control on national life. Peñaranda was pro-Ally and so enjoyed for a time the benefit of the new wartime boom. When he was overthrown in 1943 Bolivia was ripe for radical change.

The war, then, played an important part in bringing out the latent conflict between the Hispanic and Indian elements of society in the Andean region. It was a development which, by the nature of Latin American cultural similarity, had great importance for the rest of the continent. Like the Mexican José Vasconcelos in his book *La raza cósmica*, Argüedas and other writers attached positive virtue to the Indian, while other writers (such as the Ecuadorean, Jorge Icaza, author of *Huasipungo*) stirred humanitarian feelings on the Indian's behalf by describing his appalling condition of starvation and degradation in the face of the rich landowner.

One other result of the war, ironically, was to stand for many years: the creation of the myth of that inter-American co-operation of which the war was itself the negation.

The Chaco War, however, was only the most dramatic test of the complex of inter-related strains and pressures that made up the uneasy balance in Latin America between internationalism and nationalism. The rise of the United States between 1898 and 1915 as a power in Latin America undoubtedly was the major factor in forming this interaction for it brought about both revulsion and admiration. There was little competition for the role of the United States Government, for Brazil was not much involved under the Old Republic in the politics of the hemisphere at large. She was following the ancient policy of the Empire in advancing (in the language of the pseudo-science of 'geopolitics' then fashionable in strategic circles) towards the 'heartland' of the South American continent, considered by Brazilian strategists as lying in the Charcas region of Bolivia.[13] After an interlude in the era of Getúlio Vargas, this policy was resumed in the 1950s, the creation of Brasilia being seen only as one of the more conspicuous ways in which it could be implemented.

Argentina, on the other hand, though powerful, was

ideologically tied to Europe. After 1910 she had a rival with more striking relevance to the problems of the Andine region and Central America. This was, of course, Mexico, which had, after all, been the first Spanish American power admitted to the international community and one of the few successful in creating a distinctive, non-European personality. Apart from the ideological contribution, though, Latin American countries generally showed their reconciliation of nationalism and internationalism in practical ways.

Firstly, there was the contribution to international law. The Monroe doctrine, which had become the keystone of United States policy in the hemisphere, was interpreted by the Latin Americans as well as by North Americans. If they tended in general to see the doctrine as the expression of a tendency towards 'imperialism' (the word was coined in 1902) they can scarcely be blamed for that, for that was the side of it they saw. Here it was the example of Argentina that paved the way. Under the leadership of her eminent jurists, as has been seen, a programmed response to pretensions of intervention was developed. If the Drago doctrine of non-interference was easily challenged by sheer force, the legal subtleties of the Calvo clause were not, for in the absence of a developed organ of international law the clause was not successfully challenged in any court until the 1920s.[14] By then it was so much accepted doctrine that the creditor countries found it impossible to fight on all fronts.

In particular the United States was notably open to obstruction by legal means. Republican administrations, basing their policy on the rule of law, were indeed more reluctant than Democratic administrations to attack the Calvo clause, whose implications tended to harm their businessmen supporters far more.

Secondly, there was the contribution to diplomacy. Latin American countries, however, were no less active in developing a multilateral approach to foreign policy than a bilateral one. The greater movement towards hemispheric solidarity arose from North American interests, but the significance of Pan Americanism was the fact that it included all countries of the hemisphere. Its rise came at a time when (with the customary exception of Central America) the ideal of reunification had been generally abandoned among the Spanish American countries. Yet that was where it had begun, in the abortive Conference of 1826 summoned by Bolívar for the purpose of unifying the hemisphere against Spain.

The concept had lived on, if not the desire. And yet it was a North American, James G. Blaine, who was the next to invoke it, and so include the North. In 1889 the first Conference met at Washington, D.C., and its most important achievement was to establish a permanent bureau there. This was the ancestor of the Pan American Union, reconstructed in 1947 within the United Nations as the Organisation of American States (OAS).[15]

It was not until the turn of the century that the first meeting was followed by another, and the Second Conference of American States took place in Mexico in 1901–2, making Pan Americanism very much a twentieth-century phenomenon. It established the general principle that meetings ought to take place every five years. The Third and Fourth Conferences, therefore, took place at Rio de Janeiro (1906) and Buenos Aires (1910). They were successful in a host of minor but useful activities concerned with the promotion of trade and intellectual contact in the hemisphere and this side of their activities has continued to be of great importance to the present day.

In the course of the disturbances in the Caribbean and the United States intervention associated with this and with the early stages of the Mexican Revolution, Pan Americanism had a mixed success in promoting peace. The United States clearly had no interest in using it to obstruct its own policies, but was, as with the so-called ABC (Argentina, Brazil, Chile) conference at Niagara Falls in 1914, very interested indeed in it as a method of promoting them.[16] Decisions continued to be made on a bilateral basis. It was not until after the war and the establishment of the League, when the Fifth Conference met at Santiago de Chile (1923) that a formal development of multilateralism seemed a possibility to the Latin Americans, and they saw its advantages.

In this second period, therefore, they began to combine to press their wants on the United States. At the Fifth Conference negotiations were opened for the Pan American Treaty for the Pacific Settlement of Disputes (the Gondra Treaty, so named after the Paraguayan statesman, its sponsor). This was the document subsequently invoked by all as grounds for seeking an 'American' settlement in the Chaco. The Sixth Conference at Havana (1928) followed a visit by President Coolidge to Latin American states and was to be followed by a similar visit by President-elect Hoover.[17] At the conference the Pan American Union was established on a treaty basis, and subordinate conferences were established to deal with other matters of common concern.

However, it was also at this conference that it became clear that Latin American delegates were more concerned with establishing the principle of non-interference by the United States than they were with regulating affairs amongst themselves. The division between them made the intentions of the conference largely symbolic. By the Seventh Conference at Montevideo (1933) the atmosphere had changed. The new Administration in the United States, having given a name to the 'Good Neighbour' Policy, was anxious to show its sincerity in implementing it.[18] Delegates who had seen the financial power of the Colossus of the North brought low in a few brief weeks in 1929 were much less afraid of it than they had been four years previously. As a result the United States' delegates had had to sit for many hours through harangues on their government's wickedness in the past – harangues which, perhaps, they were rather too ready to accede to. Nevertheless the favourable impression which they created did go far towards establishing a new rapprochement.

In the five years that elapsed before the conference at Lima (1938) common interests drew closer together. A special meeting in 1936 at Buenos Aires accepted the principle of consultation in case the peace of the continent should be threatened. A convention was drawn up providing for a common policy of neutrality in the event of conflicts between American states. And at the Lima conference, all states adopted the Declaration of Lima reaffirming the sovereignty of the various states, and their determination to defend themselves against 'all foreign intervention or activities that may threaten them'.

When in the following year the United States in the consciousness of its military power acted unilaterally in proclaiming the separateness of the Western Hemisphere from the outbreak of the European conflict, there was wide agreement in Latin America that the 'Hemispheric Safety Belt' was a good thing. Even the acquisition by the United States from Britain of a chain of naval bases to complete her circle round the Panama Canal in the Caribbean area did not cause much alarm.[19]

Throughout, it is important to note, the differences between American States were often significant in creating the results notionally said to be the product of co-operation. For instance, after 1936, the polarisation between friends of Nationalists and Republicans in Spain led to a great deal of ill feeling, in turn strengthening the position of the neutral United States as a pacific mediator. The 1930s, therefore, saw the end of the period of open negotiation between fully independent states; the following decade was to bring the first stirrings of the desire of Latin American states to exact material benefits from the United States, on which the United States in turn could reasonably demand a return. Yet we must not forget that, if Latin Americans were in general disillusioned with the League, their presence and membership of that body was extremely influential, especially in aiding it to secure what definite advantages it achieved.

The polarisation just alluded to was reflected in the internal behaviour of the Latin American states themselves, in that they pursued solutions to the problem of economic reconstruction in ways that emphasised differences rather than similarities between them. Four countries achieved varying degrees of success in providing these solutions within the tradition at their disposal, namely Mexico, Brazil, Chile and Colombia.

In the case of Mexico the crisis was met in part by the appearance of an institutionalised structure of interest management associated with orderly regulation of the succession to the presidency. The structure, the Party of the National Revolution (PNR), was also the agency by which the inbuilt conflict between the three groups of peasants, workers and middle class (subsequently known as the 'Popular' Sector) was eventually reconciled. Power remained where it always had been, with the politicians.[20]

Under the presidency of Emilio Portes Gil (1928–30) the government defeated the last of the great military challenges (1929), established the PNR as an official institution by levying a precept on the salaries of all government officers, stepped up agrarian reform and began the codification of the rights granted by the 1917 Constitution. The shift towards peasant interests, in part dictated by the collapse with Calles of labour domination, was reinforced by the strength they gave to the government faced with rebellion. In return, Portes Gil quietly ended the Cristero revolt by agreement.[21]

Pascual Ortiz Rubio (1930–2) – chosen as a compromise between the two great groups, and personally colourless – proved unable to command the strength of the presidency; under him Calles re-emerged as 'Supreme Chief' of the Revolution, at least to his intimates. Political manœuvring became intense, for labour groups backed the attempt of the Calles faction to ease the agrarian leaders out of power. Their domination of the government in a time of economic crisis, however, only discredited them, and in late 1932 Calles eased Ortiz Rubio out of office.[22] In Congress, a new provisional President was chosen, a general with associations with Sonora. Abelardo Rodríguez (1932–4), in the brief space allotted to him, did not attempt to assert himself very much, but his personality and his support suggest that the presidency itself had once more clearly become the focus of power. He proved strong enough, at least, to 'hold the ring' while the diverging interests composed a common programme in the Six Year Plan 1933–9.

The new President, Lázaro Cárdenas (1934–40) was a devoted Callista, but a man of known probity and great character, prepared to use the power of the presidency to the full. An agrarian leader by instinct, he won support by his extensive tours of the country, meeting the people of the villages. Outflanking all other groups by radicalism and the personal touch, he forced Calles himself into exile in 1935–6. Land distribution was again stepped up, this time fivefold. The Six-Year Plan was dramatised and so made effective. National pride was restored by the nationalisation of foreign-owned oil properties in 1938. Above all, the popularity of the President harnessed the machinery of the official party to the office rather than the man, and made the new institutional system really part of Mexican life.[23]

The retirement of Cárdenas in 1940, therefore, was the final point at which the principle of no re-election, sought since 1910, became fact. The presidency of Manuel Ávila Camacho (1940–6) emphasised this by reducing the military to a purely unofficial role within the government. The President himself, moreover, was a practising Catholic. Mexican participation in the Second World War marked a more decisive break with the past and gave the people a new feeling of self-confidence, and the great boom in Mexico that began in these years has continued with only minor interruptions down to the present.[24]

The response of Brazil to the Depression was very different. For Brazil, the years between 1930 and 1945 were the years of the great *caudillo* of Rio Grande do Sul, Getúlio Vargas.[25]

Vargas had, as we have seen, come to power by a peaceful (though massive) revolution. The forces behind him were those concerned with rebuilding the state on a new plan, to end the recurring cycle of boom and slump so unhappily characteristic of their country at that time. At first the strong constitutional tradition ensured that he lacked the powers necessary to enforce distasteful measures notably in the great state of São Paulo. The resistance of the Paulistas was therefore particularly effective, but when in 1932 it developed into an armed outbreak, Vargas used the suppression of it to institute a new Constitution, embark on a programme of vigorous reform, and institute a planned programme of industrialisation under state auspices. A barter arrangement with Germany, avoiding the restraints of world trade, brought in valuable revenue. Vargas's own political base, however, was anomalous in being fascist in hue rather than fact: the Brazilian Labour Party (PTB), created on the foundation of his power, survived him to become a leading power in the post-Vargas era. What did most to extend his support was his enfranchisement of Brazilian women. However a revolt in Pernambuco in 1935 was used as the excuse to arm the government with greater emergency powers than were reasonably necessary, and the government did not choose to relinquish them.

Shortly after this, Vargas should have been due for re-election. The struggles over the succession went on, and by 1937 Vargas had moved nearer the Mussolini style; his new Constitution of that year continued his term while equipping him with full dictatorial powers and the trappings of the corporative state. The Vargas version was known as the 'Estado Novo'.

The Vargas years gave Brazil the most important aid to economic development: a heavy steel and engineering industry, which subsequently developed capacity to produce most basic commercial adjuncts from motor cars to shipping. The harnessing of the energy reserves available in hydro-electric schemes and the formation of a state petroleum corporation (Petrobras) similar to that in Mexico were necessary corollaries. Of course, Vargas was fortunate in the resources that his country held, but his attitude to the Second World War proved that his dictatorial tendencies had something more than a personal justification. Brazil moved closer to the United States from 1939 onwards, and in 1942 came into the war following Axis attacks on Brazilian shipping. The only power on the South American continent to join the Allies, it was a founder member of the United Nations. A contingent of troops was sent to aid the Allied effort in the Pacific campaign.

Vargas's fall came when the defeat of the Axis made his style of government old-fashioned, if not reactionary. In 1945 military support was withdrawn from him, and he was replaced by the interim rule of Chief Justice Linhares. Elections then established a more conventional régime, though under a member of Vargas's own party.

Chile's road out of the slump was the road of exhaustion. The intense politico-military conflicts of 1932 ended in a characteristically conservative compromise, forced by an army command that saw in the rise of the 'socialist republic' of Carlos Dávila, Arturo Puga and Marmaduque Grove (1932) a threat of dissolution to the state itself.[26] The compromise, improbably enough, was the recall of Arturo Alessandri to power. He was confronted by unemployment, inflation and a soaring national debt. Cynical about democracy, his remedy was repression, and within the uninspired limits of his policy he was successful, in that he stayed in power to 1938 and the end of his term. Disorientated by repression, the Left had nevertheless gained in power and support, and made an alliance with the forces of the Chilean Nazis. As late as 1937, Alessandri showed even some measure of real popularity, when in the congressional elections of that year his right coalition achieved overwhelming victory.

But a fascist revolt that occurred shortly afterwards so alarmed moderates that they threw their support in the 1938 presidential elections to the newly formed, communist-inspired 'Popular Front', and its working-class candidate Pedro Aguirre Cerda (1938–41).[27] Since the Nazis were also backing the Front, its victory was inevitable. But Cerda was not himself a strong leader, and no leader, however strong, could have held the Front together through the ideological storms of the era from the Molotov–Ribbentrop Pact to the German attack on Russia. Chile remained neutral in the War. The Cerda Administration, moreover, sustained an appalling blow in the shape of the great earthquake of 1940 which imposed a huge burden of reconstruction and rebuilding on every sector of the community. In 1941, racked by illness, Cerda retired to die.

In a special election the remnants of the Front were swept aside by the conservative coalition backing Juan Antonio Ríos Morales (1942–6). The new government maintained the policy of neutrality, though Chile severed relations with the Axis in 1943. The country profited enormously from the wartime boom in copper and nitrates, which finally ended the legacy of the Depression. With more confidence, the Ríos government declared war on Japan in 1945 and secured membership in the United Nations. There it instituted a quarrel with the United Kingdom over the Palmer Peninsula of Antarctica, to which it advanced the tendentious claim that it lay within the area of the world granted to Spain by Alexander VI. Ríos died naturally in 1946, having been a more successful president than anyone would have predicted. He left to his successor the problem of fragmented politics and the strongest left-wing organisation in Latin

America – a difficult legacy to handle in the years of the Cold War.[28]

Lastly, in Colombia the peaceful transition to liberal government in 1930 led to a measured and orderly economic recovery.[29] But in retrospect it lost most of its value by the fact that it also deepened traditional political rivalries at a time at which the old order was being challenged by new men with radical ideas. Under Enrique Olaya Herrera (1930–4) the Liberals took reasonable steps towards social security, and established legislation guaranteeing minimum rights to labour. Coupled with public works and aid to coffee planters to replant, these measures maintained economic stability while averting the worst of the effects of the slump.

Unfortunately, however, the Olaya Administration became embroiled in a dispute with Peru over the upper Amazon territory of Leticia. Though it carried it to an eminently satisfactory conclusion from the Colombian point of view (since the Colombians had no direct naval or military presence in the disputed area) the Conservatives were influenced by it into accepting the leadership of the intransigent Laureano Gómez.[30] Gómez made the serious blunder – not the last in his twenty-year career – of boycotting the election of 1934, so that Alfonso López (1934–8) was returned with an all-Liberal Congress. The new government produced a new constitutional code of civil rights including power to intervene extensively in economic matters, and embarked on a forward policy in social legislation. This included an income tax, a system of secular education and toleration for all religious groups. The bill for this, in conservative opposition and Catholic resistance, was not presented in the term of Santos (1938–42) nor in the second term of López himself (1942–5). In this period Colombia entered the war against Japan and adhered to the United Nations. But Colombia did not benefit much from the war, proportionately, and deep unrest began to become evident. The Liberal Party split, hiving off a radical wing under the charismatic leadership of Jorge Eliécer Gaitán, who formed a necessary complement to Laureano Gómez. López resigned in 1945, handing over leadership to the moderate Alberto Lleras Camargo (1945–6), but the split ensured the return of the Conservative candidate in the elections that followed. Time was to show that the very success of the Liberals, in carrying out the measures which they had fought for for so long, had rebounded, bringing to the fore the most extreme and least adaptable elements among the Conservatives at a time at which their most active supporters were demanding a further instalment of reform.[31] The result was the release of violence which shook Colombia for some twenty years to come.

Nevertheless, Colombians could congratulate themselves on the success with which they had avoided the turbulence that had afflicted other countries in the thirties, or the dictatorships of the forties. They had escaped from the Depression by their own efforts.[32] This consideration is particularly notable when we turn to the position of the area of the Río de la Plata. Both Argentina and Uruguay (though in very different ways) had resort to temporary dictatorship to solve the emergency, but perhaps without the success that Vargas attained.

The military *coup* of 1930 in Argentina, which brought to power General José Félix Uriburu (1930–2) seemed at first to have resulted in the establishment of a government concerned only with the holding of power.[33] No original ideas were forthcoming and the persecution of the Radicals was no substitute for action. With the rigged succession of General Agustín P. Justo (1932–8) the conservative coalition behind the military government became more noticeable. In despair, many Radicals had voted for him in the hope of action of some kind. In return, Justo continued the repressive measures, controlled elections by fraud, and extremism grew and flourished on the left and on the right.

It was greatly aided by the adoption at Ottawa in late

1932 of the system of Imperial Preference for the British Empire. Argentine Conservatives found that their British counterparts could be quite as tough as they were, for when they sought alleviation of the catastrophic effect of this tariff on their exports of meat to Britain, they received only a guarantee to buy the same amount for three years on terms that heavily increased their dependence on Britain. The Roca–Runciman Agreement was regarded as a national humiliation. But being in the hands of the government the Radicals were unable to offer an effective alternative course.[34]

Under the Justo administration a widespread reaction to world circumstances was the absorption of fascist attitudes, though they did not become coherent. Under the presidency of the businessman and civilian Roberto M. Ortiz (1938–42) they were seen to be sufficiently deep-rooted as to involve intense dissension among the army. Ortiz himself was personally honest and the elections of 1940 were held in a free atmosphere and marked by the return of a radical majority in the Chamber of Deputies. Ortiz himself shortly afterwards ceased to be able to perform his job as President, which devolved on the Vice-President, Ramón S. Castillo, who became President in fact on Ortiz's resignation in 1942.[35]

Ortiz met the outbreak of war and the economic crisis that followed by cutting government expenditure. The major export market for Argentine meat was cut off by German submarine warfare. After he had ceased to direct affairs, a great land-sale scandal darkened his reputation, and the Vice-President easily returned to the policy of electoral fraud and repression. Once in power in his own right, however, Castillo's known partiality for the Allied cause brought about his overthrow at the hands of the Army.

Conflict within the army junta brought about the fall of General Arturo Rawson (1943) after only three days; his successor, General Pedro P. Ramírez (1943–4) was then in turn deposed with Allied support by the younger group of officers known as the GOU. The administration of General Edelmiro Farrell (1944–6) became a holding operation for the traditional military régime, and was principally distinguished by the rise to power from the Labour ministry of the figure of Colonel Juan D. Perón.

This rise was not accomplished without incident. At one stage Perón was exiled to an island in the Río de la Plata, before a popular demonstration for his recall alarmed the government into conceding it. Then the American Ambassador, Spruille Braden, incautiously published his disapproval of the Perón programme. Swept along by a wave of anti-Americanism, Perón's campaign brought him the presidency by an overwhelming majority. The age of Perón had arrived.

Though technically Uruguay also became a dictatorship of a sort, it was only for a brief period and under a ruler essentially constitutional. President Gabriel Terra (1931–8) used relatively gentle methods in handling his traditionally turbulent country. His basic remedy for the Depression itself was the familiar one of instituting public works. As in, say, the United States, the developed condition of the country made such activity seem pointless enough, and a certain measure of discontent boiled over into demonstrations and was met by conservative police methods. In 1933 Terra went further, dissolving Congress and calling a Constitutional Convention. The use of force in this way so distressed ex-President Brum that he committed suicide.[36]

The assumption of dictatorial powers to reshape the Constitution the following year, however, marked the high water of unconstitutional action. The new Constitution actually deepened the impact of the elder Batlle upon the political tradition of Uruguay. It decentralised government, involved opposition participation further, and increased the responsibility of the government for the social welfare of the citizens.

Under Alfredo Baldomir (1938–43) the government continued its newly orderly course. It became a firm supporter of the Allies, instituting national military conscription and embarking on a counter-intelligence operation to remove fascist agents who had made use of the tolerant régime of Montevideo as a centre for subversive activities in the hemisphere. Only formal complaints were lodged when the *Graf Spee* was sunk in territorial waters by its German crew after pursuit by three British cruisers; it was, ironically, the President of remote Panama who chose to speak up about belligerent acts in American waters.

In 1942, Baldomir dissolved Congress and called fresh elections, feeling that the Congress, dominated by pro-Axis elements, was deliberately obstructing the conduct of government. Nevertheless, later in the year free elections were held at the proper time to choose the new President, and Juan José Amézaga (1943–7) carried on Baldomir's tradition of rule with relatively little incident. Amézaga's successor, Tomás Berreta (1947), died after only five months of office. His death brought the nephew of José Batlle y Ordóñez, Luis Batlle Berres (1947–51), to the presidency. His influence was to have a decisive effect upon its future, though not the one which he had intended.

Uruguay, therefore, survived both the Depression and the war with the minimum of emergency legislation, soon afterwards revoked. In its case the post-war Radicals were represented by Luis Batlle and his faction (*lema*) of the Colorado Party, the so-called Lema 15. It was Batlle's misfortune that he was successfully opposed from the one quarter from which a challenge could succeed – from the rival faction of his own party headed by Batlle's son. This collision shaped post-war Uruguay.[37]

Depression, therefore, was accompanied by widely differing effects in Latin America. In Bolivia and Paraguay there was war. In Mexico, Brazil, Chile and Colombia there was peace. In two countries – Argentina and Uruguay – there was dictatorship for emergency. But in a large remainder, dictatorship for emergency became permanent dictatorship under one exceptional personality. It has already been seen how Ubico ruled Guatemala, and Hernández Martínez guided El Salvador. Even more impressive, and long-lasting, were the dictatorships of Tiburcio Carías Andino in Honduras (1933–48), Anastasio Somoza in Nicaragua (1936–56), Rafael Leonidas Trujillo Molina in the Dominican Republic (1930–61), and Fulgencio Batista y Zaldívar in Cuba (1933–59), the dates in each case being those of their overlordship rather than those of their intermittent presidencies.[38] With the exception of Costa Rica, the remaining countries in these years had administrations that could only be described as 'unstable'.

The Depression years, in short, were associated with a marked divergence in social, economic and political styles. The relationship between them was immensely complex. The withdrawal of the United States presence from the Caribbean made permanent dictatorship possible there, where to the south the resurgence of dictatorship in Europe stimulated instability. With the approach of the Second World War internal upheaval brought international co-operation, but international co-operation stopped short of removing hostile and distasteful régimes. The cessation of intervention on behalf of investors accompanied the emergence of a post-war generation of statesmen intensely hostile to the United States and all its acts, for good or ill. The continent of the 1940s and 1950s was to be the scene for the resolution of these and other paradoxes.

1. For Bolivian history generally see Harold Osborne, *Bolivia, a land divided*, 3rd ed. (London, Oxford University Press for Royal Institute of International Affairs, 1963) and for the position in the early years of the century, Paul Walle, *Bolivia, its people and its resources . . .* (London, Fisher Unwin, 1914). Enrique Finot, *Nueva Historia de Bolivia. Ensayo de Interpretación Sociológica* (Buenos Aires, Imprenta López, 1946), covers the period down to 1930 in pp. 337–77.

2. W. J. Dennis, *Tacna and Arica. An account of the Chile Peruvian boundary dispute and of its arbitration by the United States* (New Haven, Yale University Press, 1931) traces the whole history of the dispute.

3. F. W. Ganzert, 'The Boundary Controversy in the Upper Amazon between Brazil, Bolivia and Peru', *H.A.H.R.* xiv, 4 (November 1934) 427.

4. For the history of the Chaco conflict Bryce Wood, *The United States and Latin American Wars, 1932–1942* (New York, Columbia University Press, 1966) is indispensable and this account is based on its interpretation.

5. George Pendle, *Paraguay, a riverside nation* (London, Oxford University Press for Royal Institute of International Affairs, 1956), needs supplementing by Warren, esp. pp. 264–7 for the early years of the century and the Liberal Revolution of 1904. See also, however, Efraim Cardozo, *Paraguay Independiente* (Barcelona, Salvat Editores, 1949).

6. *The Times*, 7 July 1911.

7. Cardozo, p. 294.

8. The course of the war is described by P. M. Ynsfran, ed., *The Epic of the Chaco: Marshal Estigarribia's memoirs of the Chaco War, 1932–1935* (Austin, University of Texas Press, 1950).

9. Harris Gaylord Warren, 'Political Aspects of the Paraguayan Revolution, 1936–1940', *H.A.H.R.* xxx, 1 (February 1950) 2.

10. Herbert S. Klein, 'David Toro and the Establishment of "Military Socialism" in Bolivia', *H.A.H.R.* xlv, 1 (February 1965) 25.

11. Wood, pp. 150–66.

12. Herbert S. Klein, 'American oil companies in Latin America: the Bolivian experience', *Inter-American Economic Affairs*, xviii, 2 (Autumn 1964) 47.

13. Lewis A. Tambs, 'Geopolitical factors in Latin America', in Norman A. Bailey, ed., *Latin America, Politics, Economics, and Hemispheric Security* (New York, Frederick A. Praeger for the Center for Strategic Studies, 1965) p. 31.

14. D. R. Shea, *The Calvo Clause. A problem of inter-American and international law and diplomacy* (Minneapolis, University of Minnesota Press, 1955).

15. Arthur P. Whitaker, *The Western Hemisphere Idea: its rise and decline* (Ithaca, Cornell University Press, 1954); Gordon Connell-Smith, *The Inter-American System* (London, Oxford University Press for Royal Institute of International Affairs, 1966).

16. Arthur S. Link, *Woodrow Wilson and the Progressive Era, 1910–1917* (London, Hamish Hamilton, 1954).

17. Alexander DeConde, *Herbert Hoover's Latin American Policy* (Stanford, Stanford University Press, 1951).

18. Bryce Wood, *The Making of the Good Neighbor Policy* (New York, Columbia University Press, 1961).

19. Lawrence Duggan, *The Americas: the search for hemisphere security* (New York, Holt, 1949).

20. Cf. Howard F. Cline, *The United States and Mexico* (Cambridge, Mass., Harvard University Press, 1953).

21. See Emilio Portes Gil, *Quince Años de Política Mexicana* (Mexico, Ediciones Botas, 1941).

22. Frank Tannenbaum, *Peace by Revolution*, the classic statement of this view of the Revolution.

23. C. F. William Cameron Townsend, *Lázaro Cárdenas, Mexican democrat* (Ann Arbor, George Wahr, 1952) and Nathaniel and Sylvia Weyl, *The Re-Conquest of Mexico: the years of Lázaro Cárdenas* (New York, Oxford University Press, 1939).

24. Howard F. Cline, *Mexico, Revolution to Evolution 1940–1960* (London, Oxford University Press for Royal Institute of International Affairs, 1962).

25. For the recent period see especially Thomas E. Skidmore, *Politics in Brazil, 1930–1964; an Experiment in Democracy* (New York, Oxford University Press, 1967). For a contemporary account of Vargas see Kurt Loewenstein, *Brazil under Vargas* (New York, Macmillan, 1942); Jordan M. Young, *The Brazilian Revolution of 1930 and the Aftermath* (New Brunswick, N.J., Rutgers University Press, 1967).

26. Jack Ray Thomas, 'The socialist republic of Chile', *J.I.A.S.* vi, 2 (April 1964) 203. Chile had seven Presidents in this year, namely: Juan Estéban Montero Rodríguez, Arturo Puga, Marmaduque Grove, Carlos Dávila Espinosa, Bartolomé Blanche Espinosa, Abraham Oyandel and Arturo Alessandri.

27. J. R. Stevenson, *The Chilean Popular Front* (Philadelphia, University of Pennsylvania Press, 1942).

28. On recent Chilean politics see Federico Gil, *The Political System of Chile* (Boston, Houghton Mifflin, 1966).

29. Fluharty, pp. 43–83.

30. Wood, *The United States and Latin American Wars*, pp. 169–251 covers.

31. For recent politics see John D. Martz, *Colombia, A Contemporary Political Survey* (Chapel Hill, University of North Carolina Press, 1962).

32. Benham and Holley, p. 118.

33. Alfred Hasbrouck, 'The Argentine Revolution of 1930', *H.A.H.R.* xviii, 3 (August 1938) 285. See also José Luis Romero, *A History of Argentine political thought* introduced and trans. Thomas F. McGann (Stanford, Stanford University Press, 1963), for events of period.

34. V. L. Phelps, *The International Economic Position of Argentina* (Philadelphia, University of Pennsylvania Press, 1938).

35. Ruth and Leonard Greenup, *Revolution before Breakfast: Argentina 1941–1946* (Chapel Hill, University of North Carolina Press, 1947).

36. Philip B. Taylor, Jr., 'The Uruguayan Coup d'État of 1933', *H.A.H.R.* xxxii, 3 (August 1952) 301.

37. Taylor, *Government and Politics of Uruguay*, cited above.

38. Interesting descriptions of these and other personalities of the late thirties are preserved in John Gunther, *Inside Latin America* (New York and London, Harper Bros, 1940).

5 Peace and Social Justice

As will already be apparent, the strains of the Second World War for Latin American countries were numerous. Almost all of them were affected to some degree by United States and Allied pressure for their support in the global conflict. Some were affected also by the opposing pressures from the Axis in the search for an outflanking alliance in the Western Hemisphere. To a few, it was a matter of urgent concern who was going to win.

The translation in the immediate post-war period, say from 1945 to 1949, to the world of the Cold War implied some crucial rethinking of trends and alliances.

This was, generally, a period of relatively left-wing régimes, differing both in their adventurousness and in their success. Of them, many romantic stories have been told, both in the Caribbean area and in the Andes. In this chapter it will be necessary first to separate truth from legend. The main consideration is the effect of countervailing pressures in the region in which the stress resulting from them appeared most intense, namely the Caribbean. But before approaching these it is important to know what happened in Bolivia between 1943 and the present.[1]

It will be remembered that when in 1943 the dictatorship of Peñaranda was overthrown circumstances had prepared the way for a radical administration. The first and most radical development was that the overthrow of the President was achieved by an organised political party based upon the organised support of the tin miners. Tin was booming under wartime conditions and the tin miners had not been receiving the reward they believed they deserved. The government of Guilberto Villaroel (1943–6) therefore would have had much in its favour if it had played its cards right.

Ideological considerations, however, required that it secure control of the mines, many of which were under foreign and especially United States ownership, by following a widespread programme of nationalisation. After the first enthusiasm and national pride had died down, the government still had to run the mines. At the end of the war, predictably, the price of tin collapsed. Intense rioting in La Paz in 1946 came to a macabre climax when a mob broke into the Presidential Palace, shot the President, threw his body out of the window and then hanged it on a lamp-post.

Despite the discouraging precedent of General Bilbao Rioja, who had been beaten up by the Army in 1940 when he advocated open elections, the new interim president, Nestor Guillén (1946–7) attempted to do so. His successor, Tomas Monje Gutiérrez, was more careful. Perhaps because of this, in the results the conservative trend was very noticeable. The administrations of Enrique Herzog (1947–9) and Mamerto Urralagoita (1949–51) were not successful in reconciling the demands of the Conservatives on whom they depended for support with those of the tin miners on whom the country depended for money. The elections of 1952 brought about a renewed burst of enthusiasm for the programme of radical reform. Víctor Paz Estenssoro, the MNR candidate, was returned for the term 1952–6. The army then intervened to try to nullify the elections and was defeated only after three days of hard fighting by MNR supporters in the capital. Their success gave the new government a crucial advantage, that of being able to reconstitute the armed forces in a radical mould.

Paz Estenssoro carried out the long-awaited nationalisation of the tin mines which had been cut short in 1946. The grudging acquiescence of the United States government of President Eisenhower in what they had hitherto regarded as an act of usurpation is generally attributed to the fact that La Paz was not popular with Republican supporters on account of its altitude and the new administration was capably represented there by career diplomatists.[2]

The new Bolivian president, however, had more to offer than good luck. He was effectively in control of his party and made of it a useful instrument of government, enabling the government to monitor the effects of its actions with some precision. This continued to be the case in the term of his successor, Hernán Siles (1956–60), and Bolivia continued on its radical course. It began to fail after 1960, the year Paz entered on his second term. The penetration of the tin miners' union, under its socialist leader Juan Lechín, had been so rapid in the year since the appearance of Castro in Cuba that their demands began to exceed that which the government could allow and still survive. They had, in fact, formed themselves into a virtually autonomous socialist republic of the mining fields, and clashes over all sorts of conditions carried heavily political overtones. The newly constituted armed forces began to display something of the same restiveness as had characterised the old.

Finally, when Paz himself sought a third term in 1964, they stepped in.[3] Since that time Bolivia has been effectively under the rule of the former commander of the Air Force, René Barrientos, who was elected to constitutional office in 1966. Barrientos put into effect the programme of counter-insurgency developed in the United States by the orders of the Kennedy Administration from 1963 onwards. Bolivian troops marched into the tin mines in 1965 and after days of bloody fighting suppressed the paramilitary workers' shock troops.[4] About the same time, former activists of the Cuban Revolution of 1959, under the revolutionary leader Ernesto ('Ché') Guevara, set up the nucleus of a guerrilla force in the south, but the nucleus was hunted down and destroyed by United States-trained special forces late in 1967.[5] It had been disowned by the regular Communist Party in Bolivia some time before. But with it died Guevara, who seemed likely to become a legend for a new generation.

If this was all that Barrientos had achieved it would not have been much. But as the first president in Bolivian history to speak Quechua in public, he did maintain the revolutionary impetus within the constitutional framework. The groundwork was laid for economic diversification with the aid of funds from the Alliance for Progress. Economic equality, social security and welfare legislation were incorporated in the government's programme, while a by-product of the military emergency was the completion of badly needed trunk roads.[6]

The rule of the MNR in Bolivia has been called the period of the 'Bolivian Revolution'. If a 'Revolution' is taken to be a broad rearrangement of the social order accompanied or directed by violence, then this is certainly too much to claim for it. The violence was, to a large extent, incidental, and the social change was not very drastic. The term is probably even less applicable to the corresponding period in Guatemalan history, which, however, was to become a more popular slogan in the Cold War and so was to have rather wider repercussions.

When widespread riots brought down Ubico in 1944, the commander of the Army, General Federico Ponce (1944), tried to continue the system but was overthrown in a similar fashion. The Guatemalan urban *élite* turned to a very unlikely candidate, a member of the literati and a novelist, who in exile as a Professor of the University of Tucumán, Argentina, had gone so far as to abandon Guatemalan nationality.

Juan José Arévalo (1945–50) described himself as a 'spiritual socialist'. A prophet of Indo-America, along the lines of similar thinkers in Mexico and Peru, he offered the descendants of the Maya a vision of a broader destiny for the continent. His own term of office offered mild social reform, but mild as it was it caused a considerable stir in the

Caribbean at that time. Like Paz in Bolivia, he was lucky enough to have had the opportunity to reconstitute the Army, and a struggle for succession between his two leading generals enabled him to last out his five-year term.[7]

Finally in 1949 General Arana, the leading contender, was machine-gunned from ambush, a car belonging to the wife of his rival, General Jacobo Arbenz, being identified at the scene of the incident. Arbenz (1950-4), always 'left' in his sympathies, moved further in that direction, embarking in 1952 on an extensive programme of land reform. In particular, he challenged the large tracts held fallow by the United Fruit Company, which the Company claimed were indispensable to the proper rotation of banana cultivation. Acrimony became intense. In 1954 an attack was launched across the Honduran frontier by a force of Guatemalan exiles, under the leadership of Carlos Castillo Armas, a devout Catholic and an unsuccessful conservative candidate for the presidency in 1950.[8]

Castillo Armas, though aided by three small aircraft lent to him by the United States Central Intelligence Agency (CIA), did not succeed in advancing more than 25 miles, before Arbenz decided to arm the workers of the capital with Czech weapons and send them to the front. The army scented danger, refused to distribute the arms, and deposed Arbenz. A conference between Castillo Armas and the general of Arbenz's forces resulted in the succession of the former to a presidency (1954-7) which he never put to the test of election.[9]

Though Castillo Armas did not destroy the reforms of the Arévalo period, he did not contribute anything new to social welfare in Guatemala, while his disregard for constitutional forms (going beyond Estrada Cabrera, after all) did not suggest that he could offer much in the way of democracy. In 1957 he was assassinated, probably as the result of a personal grudge, while going in to dinner in the Presidential Palace. A period of turbulence ensued.

The first set of elections to be held were set aside by military intervention when their inconclusive result led to disturbances. Provisional President Luis González López (1957) was deposed and replaced by Guillermo Flores Aveñado (1957–8), his constitutional successor. At a second election the victor was the old style military leader, Miguel Ydígoras Fuentes (1958–63). Ydígoras himself had contested the 1950 election, afterwards being arrested in the course of an unsuccessful revolt, he made a spectacular escape from prison which brought him no little popularity.

His régime, especially after 1959, was marked by a constant series of communist plots, but his government, though 'firm' was reasonably restrained.[10] It suppressed both army and air force revolts. It dealt with the bizarre case of the tins of Cuban pineapple which on examination were found to contain one hand grenade each. Finally it succumbed not to pressure from the left but from military *coup*. The change reflected the Army's fear that its wish to return to normal and allow the re-entry of ex-President Arévalo was the sign of communist infiltration.[11] Between 1963 and 1966 the country was ruled by a military régime under Ydígoras's Minister of Defence, General Enrique Peralta Azurdia.

The Peralta government was largely occupied in counter-insurgency. Its arrival was the sign for a dramatic increase in the number of guerrillas operating in the country, and both urban and rural violence became widespread. Despite this, it stabilised the economy and held fresh elections in 1966. The candidate of the moderate Left was shot shortly after his nomination for the presidency, and in a triumphant campaign his brother, Julio César Méndez Montenegro (1966–), carried the day.[12] The combination of insurgency and military suspicion has not allowed the Méndez government to go too far in its programme of social reform. Nevertheless, the government has survived, despite intense propaganda from the Left, the kidnapping of the Archbishop of Guatemala and the assassination of the United States Ambassador.

The Arbenz episode in Guatemala was the occasion for two object-lessons. One was that it was possible for an extremely left-wing régime to assume power within the hemisphere and maintain itself, for some time at least, even in face of the tacit or merely vocal opposition of the United States. The other was that the United States administration of President Eisenhower (1953–61), unlike its predecessor, was prepared to lend its physical aid to remove it. A less cautious administration might well use force itself if necessary to put an end to a similar situation. But the association of CIA agents with the Castillo Armas forces, which was made the excuse for the failure of Arbenz himself to weigh up the balance of the political situation correctly, was overestimated on both the left and the right. Had the United States been significantly engaged in Guatemala the next development in the Caribbean area would have been almost inexplicable.

This time the centre of conflict was located in Cuba. It will be remembered that in 1933 President Machado of Cuba had been forced out of office by a military revolt led by Sergeant Batista. His interim successor, Carlos Manuel de Céspedes, held office for less than a month, before Batista again intervened and replaced him by another candidate. Batista himself had in the meanwhile been promoted to Commander of the Army.[13]

The new President was a radical and the choice of the Congress. Ramón Grau San Martín was a Professor of the University of Havana, and had built his support on his students. The uncontrollable chaos of his government, his lack of pliability and his zeal for reform led, after the United States had refused to recognise his government, to his replacement in 1934 by Carlos Mendieta (1934–5).[14]

The United States was important to Cuba because Cuban recovery from the slump depended on the negotiation of a new sugar agreement. It was this element in the negotiations which led to the abrogation of the Platt Amendment (see above, p. 77) which made the brief régime of Mendieta particularly important, as the negotiations were especially successful on this point. Shortly afterwards, Mendieta resigned and was succeeded by the interim José A. Barnet y Vinegeras (1935–6). A special election a month later returned Miguel Mariano Gómez (1936), but he proved unable to work with Batista, and was forced to resign in favour of his Vice-President, Federico Laredo Bru (1936–40), who had no such difficulties.

Directed by Batista, Cuba was moving towards the corporative state. Opposition was ruthlessly suppressed. In 1937 the then customary Plan was adopted, this one for three years. It involved state control of the sugar and mining industries, the reorganisation of agricultural schools and the redistribution of land to small landowners. Then in 1940 a new Constitution was drafted under which Batista became President himself for the first time. This 1940 Constitution was distinctive in that it embodied a semi-parliamentary system with a prime minister acting as head of government.[15] Its adoption marked the end of the repressive phase and the beginning of a period of democratic forms.

In his first term, therefore, Batista ruled as a constitutional President. His presidency, and those of his successors Grau San Martín (1944–8) and Carlos Prío Socarrás (1948–52) were marked by free competition between the political parties, of which the main ones were the so-called *Ortodoxos* and *Auténticos*, each claiming descent from the former Liberal Party. With the inception of the Cold War the government was beset with strikes and took severe counter-measures against labour movements rather than trying to satisfy their needs. Forcible intervention reached even into the Army in a search for subversive elements. These were years of prosperity for a country that according to most indices of individual wealth was one of the most affluent in Latin America It was, however, an affluence based insufficiently on primary industry and the wealth of Havana came from corruption, the tourist industry and the illegal operations of the great gambling syndicates.

In 1952, Batista seized power once more in a military *coup* that was a classic of its kind for precision and planning. It began at precisely 2.43 a.m. and was all over by breakfast.[16] This second term, renewed to 1959, was one of repressive government and conspicuous expenditure, in which the government became closely identified with the strong-arm methods of the world of syndicated crime. Constitutional guarantees lapsed, one of the few organised movements allowed by the dictator to survive as an entity being the Communist Party. As long as communist deputies sat in Congress Batista could always point to them as evidence both of his attachment to democracy and of his need for foreign aid![17]

It must not be thought that this repression was either universal or undiscriminating. When in 1953 a group of young men attempted to carry out a *coup* at the Moncada barracks, they were gaoled for only a year before being released under amnesty. One of them, Fidel Castro, who made an impassioned speech at his trial claiming: 'History will absolve me!', went into exile in the United States and prepared to try again. In 1956 he landed on the coast of the Oriente province with a group of followers from the hired motor boat *Granma*. Having announced his intention to create a popular uprising by radio beforehand, his troops were massacred by Batista's soldiers. Only twelve escaped to the mountains of the Sierra Maestra range, where for two years little was heard of them.[18]

Then the enterprising American journalist Herbert L. Matthews secured an interview with Castro. The outside world was informed that, unknown to them, a dedicated band of simple agrarian reformers were toiling there to overthrow the tyranny of Batista. Meanwhile, the traditional Cuban opposition to re-electionist government was growing fast. The collapse of the government in face of the withdrawal of civil and military support left power to the dramatic figure of Castro, who from his mountain stronghold promised anything and nothing. A small local victory over a detachment of troops in November 1958 precipitated the withdrawal and confirmed, it seemed to many, his claim to power.[19]

Castro himself had little idea what to do with his victory. He became Prime Minister and the government of Manuel Urrutia Lleo (1959), his choice as interim President, embarked on a programme of democratic reform. The taxes that had been lost through corruption were recovered, labour laws enforced, and savage reprisals taken against the police of the Batista régime. Castro's personal daring and hostility to the United States – where he was received with a caution his extravagant demands for aid ($30,000,000,000) made reasonable enough – inclined him to accept the backing of the Soviet Union, as suggested by his friends and associates. Castro thereupon took the government on his own shoulders, forcing Urrutia to resign by denouncing him on television to the crowd of the capital, and following a clandestine course towards the ultimate declaration in 1961 that he adhered to Marxism-Leninism.[20]

This course meant that an integrated workers' party was formed based mainly on the old pro-Batista Communists, while the defence of the new state was entrusted to a well-organised militia, which was used as the pretext and the agent of universal political indoctrination. Elections were not held and the new President, Osvaldo Dorticos Torrado (1959–) was a cypher. Real pride in the early achievements of the régime, however, was shown in the volunteer effort that went into the 'Year of Literacy' in 1961 (Table 6).

The promised programme of redistribution of land was transformed into a programme of collectivisation, rather to

the alarm of Cuba's new Soviet advisers, who were con-
servatively unwilling to admit that anything could be done
better in Cuba than in their own country. It was not the
only way in which Cuban haste, carelessness and personalism

Table 6

Literacy, c. 1950

Country	Per cent. popn. over 16 literate	Year
Argentina	86·4	1947
Bolivia	32·1	1950
Brazil	49·4	1950
Chile	80·1	1952
Colombia	62.0	1951
Costa Rica	79·4	1950
Cuba	77·5	1950
Dominican Republic	59·9	1956
Ecuador	55·7	1950
El Salvador	39·4	1950
Guatemala	29·4	1950
Haiti	10·5	1950
Honduras	44·0[1]	1960
Mexico	50·0[2]	1950
Nicaragua	38·4	1950
Panama	65·7	1950
Paraguay	65·8	1950
Peru	47·5	1950
Uruguay	80·9	1950
Venezuela	52·2	1950

[1] 'Never attended school'.
[2] Adjusted from population aged 6 and over.
SOURCE: Bruce M. Russett *et al.*, *World Handbook of Political and Social Indicators* (New Haven, Yale University Press, 1964).

alarmed them. Yet the gratuitous gift of a communist state
90 miles from Miami could not be foregone, and in August
1960 Mr Khruschev, the Soviet Chairman of the Council of
Ministers and First Secretary of the CPSU, announced that

the Soviet Union would defend Cuba with intercontinental missiles, if necessary.

State intervention was extended into every aspect of the national life. Printers were encouraged to take over newspapers, sugar planters their plantations. Fishermen were urged to form co-operatives. Meanwhile the dislocation of agriculture reached such a point that by 1962 there was a shortage of black beans, staple foodstuff of the poor and something that had never been known to be in short supply before. Now, with wheat, potato and other foodstuffs in short supply already, the basic filler was no longer sufficient.[21]

Hunger suggested the possibility of revolt, even by a people who had gained dignity and self-respect from the ideal of communal ownership. Such a possibility, anyway, was suggested to the newly elected government of President Kennedy (1961–3) of the United States. Though reluctantly and against his instinct, the new President backed an attempt by Cuban exiles to carry out an invasion, yet because of the need to preserve appearances, denied them the overt support of the United States Air Force which they needed to ensure success. The ground fighting itself was conspicuously unsuccessful, since, because of the inclination of their military advisers to favour military attitudes among the members of the expeditionary force, it came to be made up mostly of Batistianos who commanded no sympathy among Cubans in general.[22]

In the excitement this fiasco occasioned for Communism in general and the Cuban version ('as Cuban as the pine trees', Castro said) in particular, the Cuban government overreached itself. It was already encouraging a general guerrilla revolt on the American continent in terms that alienated such likely sympathisers as Betancourt of Venezuela. But it was playing great-power politics without the resources; most critically, it lacked oil for its own needs, having broken with the United States on the issue of compelling the oil refineries to refine oil bought cheaply in the Soviet Union. The acceptance of oil from that source brought reciprocal obligations, and the Soviet Union took advantage of this by offering Cuba medium-range ballistic missiles (MRBMs) to outflank United States defence systems based on the Polar confrontation with the USSR.

These weapons had an offensive capability against not only the United States but also Mexico and the other Caribbean states. Confronted by evidence of their presence, the other countries of the hemisphere combined with the United States in demanding their removal, and by acceding to this demand the Soviet Government made clear the subordinate role of the Cuban government in world politics.[23]

The Castro régime found solace in the growing division of opinion between the Soviet Union and China, from which country they received a certain amount of platonic encouragement. Effort was redoubled to make the Andes 'the Sierra Maestra of South America', and it was in pursuit of this aim that 'Ché' Guevara left for Bolivia in 1965. At the same time, the Tricontinental Congress held in Havana called for insurgency from all undeveloped nations against the United States and her allies. As far as Latin America was concerned, at least, the moment was favourable. The early sixties saw guerrilla movements in Guatemala, Colombia, Peru, Bolivia, Venezuela and Brazil. In Colombia, indeed, tiny 'communist republics' had existed in remote places for some time. For most of these, as in Bolivia, the essential weakness of their power and strategy was too great for success. In 1968 it seemed that only the discovery of oil could save Castro's régime from moral, political and economic collapse.[24] It had brought neither economic prosperity to Cuba nor revolution to Latin America, and of all its promises of 1958 only that of improving education had really been achieved.

If there was one place in which Castro might have hoped for success, it was in the neighbouring island state of the Dominican Republic. Since 1930, after all, it had been under the dictatorship of Generalissimo Rafael Leonidas Trujillo Molina.[25] Trujillo ran his country like a limited liability company, the liability being limited to others. He and his family formed the board of directors not only of the state, but of a host of private corporations which used the power of the state legally to provide themselves with corporate and personal wealth.

Trujillo was personally vain. The model of the Freudian explanation of dictatorship, he showed his desire to be loved by erecting vast statues to himself as 'Benefactor of the Fatherland', not only in the capital (renamed Ciudad Trujillo) but in every town and village. He served as President himself from 1930 to 1938, after which the official headship of State was held by Jacinto Peynado (1938–40) and then by Manuel de Jesús Troncoso de la Concha (1940–2), before being resumed by Trujillo (1942–51) in his own name. In 1951 he transferred the title to his brother, Héctor Trujillo (1951–60).

The régime, supported as it was by a vigorous secret police, was able to crush opposition and to maintain an appearance of great tranquillity. Inevitably this brought investment from American business interests seeking a tax haven, and their political influence was exercised in its favour through conservative politicians. This had bizarre consequences: for example there was no income tax, since the revenue from on-the-spot traffic fines met the official needs of the state. Big business, however, included racketeering, and in the changed political climate in the United States after the death of Dulles (1959) and the return of liberal Democrats to the United States Congress, the Trujillos came under pressure to present a more democratic image. Rising criticism from Latin Americans had to be met.

In 1960 Héctor Trujillo resigned the presidency, and a moderate liberal, Joaquín Balaguer (1960–2) was installed in his place. All the signs were, however, that the Trujillos were retaining power. Then the strength of the family was broken at one stroke by the assassination in 1961 of Rafael Trujillo himself, machine-gunned from ambush on a lonely road. The other countries of the hemisphere, in the Organisation of American States, imposed sanctions on the Balaguer administration until such time as it could prove itself democratic. To make its support of this policy abundantly clear, the Kennedy Administration sent a fleet of ships to Dominican waters in 1962. The Trujillos left the Republic in a private yacht, taking with them the body of their dead relative in a refrigerator that in happier times had sheltered only refreshments.[26]

Shortly after their departure, however, Balaguer himself was overthrown by a military *coup*. His designated successor Rafael Bonnelly (1962) was arrested. The military held fresh elections, won by the candidate of the Left, Professor Juan Bosch (1962–3). He in turn was overthrown by force by the right, who did not dare to attempt further elections at once. Their interim government continued in office until the temporary unity of the Army broke up in 1965.

This resulted in a savage battle in the centre of Santo Domingo between the forces of the Left (pro-Bosch) under General Francisco Caamano Deno and those of the Right under Brigadier General Eliás Wessin y Wessin. A stalemate seemed to be developing, when the battle was cut short by the first landing by United States military forces in Latin America since the 1920s.[27] The Left were extremely reluctant to accept stalemate and the formation of a coalition under Dr Héctor García Godoy, as they argued with some justice that they had had marginally the upper hand, that their candidate was the lawful President, and that intervention and compromise could only result in the choice of someone else. This in fact proved to be true. The President chosen by the new elections in 1966 was once more Balaguer, and while time had shown there could be no real doubt of the sincerity of his intentions there was much doubt about what he would be able to achieve.

For supporters of the revolutionary Left the situation of the Dominican Republic was seen as the clear proof they had always expected of the imperialist intentions of the United States. Since the position of the United States was in fact by any standard anomalous this is an appropriate point at which to consider why.[28]

It will be remembered that in 1939 the United States government, faced by the outbreak of war in Europe, had taken the initiative in proclaiming the neutrality of the Americas. Very many Latin Americans were doubtful about this move, which some considered might even act as a provocation. Nevertheless at the Second Meeting of Consultation of the Foreign Ministers of the American states at Havana in 1940 the United States was remarkably successful in obtaining agreement, both for a permanent Inter-American Peace Committee to keep watch and for a number of resolutions including Resolution VIII opposing 'subversion' in the hemisphere. The coming of war in 1941 stilled many of the objections to both. Transformation of the Peace Committee into a Committee on Political Defense in 1943 marked a further stage on the road to institutionalisation of inter-American relations.

For the duration of the war, however, the United States was primarily interested in the creation of the larger world body of the United Nations. It was only after the Dumbarton Oaks Conference in 1945 that a Special Conference of the American states was called to discuss common problems. At this Conference, held at Chapultepec Castle in Mexico, it became clear that Latin Americans had their own views on the new world organisation, and, furthermore, that they were in direct conflict with the United States as a Great Power. Their demands were of more than passing interest in view of later developments: they included two permanent seats on the Security Council, stronger powers for the General Assembly, an effective International Court and greater provision for co-operation. Without United States support they had no chance of getting them, though in 1948 they did obtain the Economic Commission for Latin America (ECLA).

The Act of Chapultepec, however, did formalise the organisation of inter-American co-operation. In future, there were to be regular quadrennial conferences with annual meetings of the Foreign Ministers in the off years. A large number of resolutions indicated that the object of the states remained one of peace and non-intervention. Ironically, in view of later events, it was Guatemala that proposed Resolution XXXVIII, calling on the American states to defend democracy and oppose anti-democratic régimes.

With the development of the Cold War this was increasingly interpreted in the United States as opposition to militant communist attack and subversion. By the Rio Pact (1947) the United States government established a formal military defensive alliance with other Western Hemisphere countries. When, therefore, the first regular post-war Conference met at Bogotá in 1948 the atmosphere was not propitious for quiet discussion of economic and social problems. Scarcely had the Conference met when the assassination of Gaitán, the Liberal leader, touched off the three days of rioting known as the *Bogotazo*, which raged through the conference centre itself and then receded leaving badly shaken delegates to respond as best they could. North Americans blamed communist agitators; Latin Americans the prevalent poverty and misery of the continent.

As a result, the Ninth Inter-American Conference produced little of lasting value. Latin American delegates advocated non-intervention and spoke out against further pacts. The United States delegation, led by Secretary of State Marshall, did not accept the need for a Marshall Plan for Latin America, pointing out that European recovery was of vital necessity for the recovery of Latin American economies too. At the same time the Point Four programme, by increasing United States private investment, particularly

in the extractive industries of Latin America, was actually
going to create greater suspicion of United States economic
motives. The Conference did however formally create the
Organisation of American States (OAS) as a regional
organisation under the United Nations provisions for such
bodies.[29]

With the outbreak of the Korean War United States
official interest in Latin America waned, not to revive till
1958. Latin American interest in the United States did not,
the more so since the war meant a recession and the return
of the Republicans in 1952 seemed to presage support for the
generally dictatorial régimes of the time. The Tenth Inter-
American Conference took place at Caracas in 1954 in a
state of general gloom.

To begin with, Costa Rica refused to attend in protest
against the régime of Pérez Jiménez, under whose auspices
it was being held. Then it became clear that the United
States delegation under Secretary of State Dulles was only
interested in obtaining an anti-communist resolution aimed
at the Arbenz régime in Guatemala. This the other delegates
refused to accept. A substitute, in very vague terms, was
passed without the support of Mexico and Argentina, and
with severe reservations by Uruguay. Dulles then left without
staying to hear what the Latin Americans felt about
economic problems. Shortly afterwards the Guatemalan
government fell. While other Latin American states rid
themselves of their dictators it seemed to have become one of
the most authoritarian states in the hemisphere.

The world climate of opinion was changing. New states
were admitted to the United Nations after 1955 and the
views of their leaders were nearer to those of the Latin
Americans than to any of the Great Powers. The United
States itself seemed to be seeking a rapprochement with the
Soviet Union. But the Soviet Union, from October 1957
onwards, was newly magnified into a global power with the
ability to strike with nuclear rockets at many points on the

earth's surface. It was as much in derision as in hatred that
students in Lima and Caracas attacked Vice-President Nixon
of the United States on his Latin American 'goodwill' tour
in 1958. Nixon returned from his experience a wiser man,
prepared even to consider President Kubitschek's proposal
for an 'Operation Pan-America' to raise economic conditions.[30] But by that time it was impossible for the government of the United States to appear to act gracefully in face
of the mounting demands upon it.

After the death of Dulles in 1959 Eisenhower conducted
his own foreign policy, and tried to do so in a humane spirit.
The establishment of the Castro government in Cuba,
however, dominated his Latin American policy, since the
military threat that it presented was in fact so urgent that
economic counter-measures took second place. In 1960
meetings of the Foreign Ministers of the hemisphere voted
sanctions against Trujillo in the Dominican Republic, but
refused to express more than mild disapproval of a Castro
who had had the boldness to take the initiative and ask
the United States for so much money.[31] By itself Cuba
seemed too small a state to present a serious threat, and
sympathy for the Fidelistas was widespread among the
literati and students. Best of all, in Latin American eyes, the
Monroe doctrine was 'buried'.

It was the Eisenhower Administration that obtained the
first instalment of economic aid to Latin America from a
reluctant Congress – some $600,000,000.[32] This the new
Kennedy Administration proposed to expand into a so-
called 'Alliance for Progress'. Before this could get under
way, however, the Administration had committed its serious
blunder in backing the exile invasion of Cuba that failed so
dismally at the Bay of Pigs. Significantly, the continuing
readiness to use force in defence of perceived national interests
which this action signified was met with very much muted
criticism when it took the form of intervening in the Dominican
Republic to drive out the Trujillos later the same year.

To restore its position the Kennedy Administration then turned to securing a vote of condemnation of Cuba from the OAS. Failing to obtain any sign of a majority on initial soundings, their delegates then elected to press for the formal sanction of expelling Cuba from the organisation. Here for the first time since the 1930s there were signs that the United States government had realised the advantage it had in its skill in competitive politics in an open forum, provided only that it had as its delegates able politicians. With a deft combination of indirect pressure and inducement the necessary majority was secured and the resolution passed.[33] Not until the missile crisis of October 1962, however, were many Latin Americans convinced that their countries' votes had been cast the right way, and then only temporarily.

In spite of the appearance of unanimity it engendered, the position of the United States against Cuba had by late 1963 actually been weakened. In the larger context of world politics, the bargain with which the crisis had been concluded precluded the United States from mounting an actual invasion of the island. But after the assassination of Kennedy the government of Johnson (1963-9) was able to continue the policy of combined negotiation and power politics with notable effectiveness, its hand strengthened by the wave of military *coups* from 1962 onwards culminating in the fall of the Goulart régime in Brazil.[34] After the Ninth Meeting of Consultation of Foreign Ministers in Washington in January 1964 only Mexico continued to have diplomatic relations with Cuba, and the embargo established in 1962 was greatly strengthened.

This new strength even survived the unilateral intervention in the Dominican Republic in 1965. This was a clear breach of the Charter of the OAS but was justified on the plea of the presence of known communist agents. With more than ten thousand American troops in the island the United States government secured a bare two-thirds majority for its action, of which the vote of the disputed government of the

Dominican Republic itself was one![35] Even this, however, would have been unthinkable a decade previously. The Alliance for Progress had by this time contributed greatly to creating the political climate in which this could happen, though its economic benefits were still dubious. That it was still uncertain was shown by the great and continuing reluctance to hold the scheduled Conference due in 1958 in Quito.

Economically the establishment of the Alliance for Progress at Punta del Este, Uruguay, in August 1961 was the turning point its authors intended it to be. It made reality of the financial provisions of 1960 and the foundation of the Inter-American Development Bank in that year by establishing the principle of reciprocal obligations. The United States would provide $20,000,000,000 over ten years. In return the republics of the hemisphere must carry out necessary social and economic reforms. After that there was no other way for those governments to turn, for the only alternative to the United States seemed to be Cuba. The successful establishment of the Central American Common Market (CACM) in 1960 and the Latin American Free Trade Area (LAFTA) in 1961 were steps of perhaps more immediate significance, and certainly more interesting in that they represented an independent initiative less subject to political considerations from the world at large.[36]

CACM and LAFTA both derived from the experience of the United Nations Economic Commission for Latin America (ECLA). Many U.N. agencies have worked in Latin America, and UNESCO in particular has done much to promote education in the poorer regions. ECLA, however, was something special: a regional agency created for their own needs by the Latin Americans themselves. As such, its first task was to make the first accurate survey of the material and human resources of the region. Subsequently the dissemination and application of this information was based on the same document, the 1949 report of the distinguished Latin American economist, Raúl Prebisch, who subsequently acted as Secretary-General to the Commission.

CACM had, as has been seen, a historical basis for its existence in the traditional current of local opinion in favour of the reunification of Central America. But it has a serious objection: that for this very reason the Central American economies were similar and not complementary. The founders' hope for planned diversification in Central America, with different countries specialising in different products, has worked to some extent. Intra-regional trade expanded sixfold between 1961 and 1967. But the regional organisation has yet to persuade its members effectively to lower their customs barriers and unify their tariffs and currency, and until this is done diversification may even tend to promote political disunity rather than political unity.

LAFTA, on the other hand, which is composed of all the South American states plus Mexico, is stronger both absolutely and proportionately, on a level at which there is scarcely any point in comparison. But the problem of communication is formidable, and though diversification already exists, great care has had to be taken that unification does not kill technologically advanced industries. Furthermore, it has to contend with the general lack of economic development of the poorer members and the alarming inability of development anywhere satisfactorily to keep pace with the rapid rise of population. Despite these difficulties, intra-regional trade doubled in its first six years and its formation stimulated the emergence of useful sub-regional development organisations, in the Andes and the River Plate Basin (1968).

Given this climate of opinion, at the Third Special Inter-American Conference at Buenos Aires in 1967, the American presidents attending, and the Prime Minister of Trinidad and Tobago, issued a Declaration resolving to press on with the unification of Latin America in a Latin American Common Market within fifteen years. In this grouping, the

United States (which already dominates the economies of Central America) would take part, and it would have to sacrifice its traditional economic exclusiveness for it.

By this declaration the American presidents have affirmed that, despite the example of Cuba, the future development of Latin America depends on co-operation, not conflict, with the United States. There is therefore no prospect of inter-American co-operation providing in the foreseeable future an effective financial counterpoise to United States capital, such as existed down to 1920 in European invest-ment. In part this reflects the decline of European capital, which the Soviet Union is neither able nor willing to replace. Though in the last decade West German interest in Latin American trade and investment has in most places risen to second place among foreign countries, it still lags far behind.

After all, the respective standing of Latin America and Europe has changed. Europe is no longer regarded as the repository of all wisdom. France's culture is still honoured, but no longer by the old aristocracy. Britain's currency has declined until it is now less stable than that of Venezuela. Latin American states generally can now supply much of their own capital needs. One Europe-based authority alone remains: that of the Church.

The primary role of the Church in Latin America in recent decades has been what it always has been – the cure of men's souls. The overwhelming majority of Latin Americans have been, and remain, at least nominal Catholics. Secularisation, lay education – even the policy of militant atheism pursued by the government of Mexico under Calles – none of these has altered the allegiance of the peasant majority, even to the extent that it has succeeded in making them literate. At the same time, the *nouveaux riches* and new men in government have adopted the customs of formal observance of the class they displaced.

This does not always mean that the Church is as powerful as its number of adherents would suggest. The proportion is around ninety per cent in most places except Cuba. In Bolivia and Uruguay – to take two very dissimilar examples – the Church has little political power. However, its complex and far-reaching structure where it is strong (as in Paraguay and Colombia) has made it a necessary component of the political process. The Latin American hierarchy, as has been seen, has been native-born since colonial times. It continued to be conservative well into the present century, stressing the doctrine of obedience to lawfully constituted authority, and authority was held to be lawfully constituted if it received formal assent from the National Assembly after it had been set up. In the economic sphere, Leo XIII's encyclical on labour and social problems, *Rerum novarum*, was discounted in favour of traditional *laissez faire*. Particularly after 1945, reform generally was frequently equated with Communism.

At this stage, Latin America did not share in the rise of Christian Democracy in Europe. The traditional elements were too strong to admit it, while the schism between the hierarchy and the junior priesthood and laity widened. Then came Castro's rise to power in Cuba. Already some of the younger clergy had followed the example of the 'worker priests' of France and Italy and had been reproved. Now others allied themselves with insurgency, especially in the case of the 'Peasant Leagues' of Francisco Juliao in north-east Brazil, though such events reflected sometimes the attitude of individual diocesans, such as the Archbishop of Recife. At the same time the failure of traditional dictatorship had already led to a severing of the traditional alliance. For example, Colombian bishops dissociated themselves publicly from Rojas Pinilla, while a fiery sermon from Father Severo Velásquez touched off the rioting which brought about the dictator's fall.

At the Vatican Council the Latin American bishops generally found themselves divided on social issues much as their colleagues in other countries. On one such issue they were notably radical. Many spoke strongly in favour of revising the stance of Pius XI against the use of reliable means of birth-control. The equivocal consequences of closer links between Latin Americans and the Church at large was highlighted by the visit of Paul VI to Bogotá in 1968. The Pope – the first to visit Latin America while in office – was received with unaffected enthusiasm by vast crowds of upwards of half a million at a time. The crowds at one and the same time symbolised the intensity of Catholic devotion, and the pressing problem of a rapidly growing population crowding into the capital region, which the Pope's recent encyclical *Humanae vitae* could hardly be expected to alleviate.

Even the Church, therefore, has been affected by the social and economic pressures of the day. Central America, of all parts of the continent, was the area most open to such pressures, not just for strategic reasons. The fate of Cuba and the Dominican Republic under their dictators was harsh. But vicariously at least some of their inhabitants received some material return from them. In Haiti, Honduras, Nicaragua and Panama itself this was less certain. Yet in none of them was any move from the Left successful, either in the form of the traditional gradualism of Soviet diplomacy or of Fidelista guerrilla attacks.

Most backward of all was the condition of Haiti. The withdrawal of United States troops in 1934 left the military force of the Garde d'Haiti the sole regulator of the state's politics. It was perhaps preferable to the spontaneous armies of pre-intervention days, but not much.

The President elected under the occupation, Stenio Vincent (1930–41), retired after two terms of relatively successful government. Thereupon the traditional pattern reappeared of attempted *continuismo* tempered by armed revolt. Thus Elie Lescot (1941–6) was deposed and replaced by Dumersais Estimé (1946–50) and Estimé in turn by Paul E. Magloire (1950–6), when each attempted to secure re-election. For a year no one candidate proved able to achieve power, six different Presidents or juntas holding office in as many months. Exhaustion brought agreement to an election, its winner being a physician named François Duvalier, said to be a dominant figure in the cult of Voodoo which the early slaves had brought with them from Africa.

With this aid, and that of his palace guard and a private force of thugs nicknamed the 'Ton-tons Macoutes', Duvalier (1957–) established a control over the poverty-stricken republic such as had not been known since Geffrard. No further elections were held. Congress appointed Duvalier President for life, and to all critics he returned the smiling answer that the Haitian people loved him so much that they would not dream of rebelling against him. In consequence, Haiti received little or no official aid from the United States, and its position as the poorest state in the Caribbean remained unchallenged.[37]

Honduras, the poorest of the mainland states, had a very different history. The strong rule of Tiburcio Carías Andino (1933–48) was not unchallenged, but such was his imposing personality that he retained his dominance over the National Party into his eighth decade. His own rule was maintained by unabashed *continuismo*: a self-conferred six-year term in 1936 and a ten-year term in 1939.[38] The country received the kind of intense centralisation that had previously been the characteristic of Guatemala, and coherence brought economic growth, investment, and the decline of the subsistence economy. The appearance of the United Fruit Company was now followed by vast expansion to the north, Honduras becoming the only Central American state literally a 'Banana republic'.

When Carías Andino wisely decided to retire, he conferred the presidency on a chosen successor, Juan Manuel Gálvez (1948–54). Gálvez, though a Conservative, made a considerable attempt to restore constitutional government, and permitted free choice at the elections of 1954, giving the

Liberals a majority.[39] The majority was so narrow, however, that in the ensuing dispute, Vice-President Julio Lozano Díaz seized the executive office by force, holding it thereafter for two years (1954–6) before being deposed and rereplaced by an interim junta.

The presidency of Ramón Villeda Morales (1957–63) then proved that both energy and honest intentions were able to achieve success. It was terminated by another of the incidental hazards of Central American politics, a *coup* carried out before the elections to ensure that power did not pass into the hands of a more radical successor.[40] The military junta that conducted the *coup* held the power in its own hands for three years before 'legitimizing' itself with a Constitutional Convention. At fresh elections General Osvaldo López Arellano was elected President (1966–   ) to serve a six-year term.

This *coup*, and the military régime itself, had virtually no significance as far as the people of the country were concerned. The same could not be said for the corresponding phenomena in Nicaragua.

For many years, Nicaragua has been in practice the private estate of the Somoza dynasty. General Anastasio 'Tacho' Somoza, the elder, dominated the country from 1936 until he was shot at a reception in León in 1956,* thus anticipating the fate of his contemporary Trujillo. Like him too, he was a capitalist, but he was a more able, more gregarious and more restrained ruler. His power, as we had seen, rested on that National Guard in which United States observers (not without accuracy) had placed their hopes for stability. If nothing else, he established the first real unity the country had known, and if it was the unity of a private estate, it gained something of the prosperity of an estate well run. On his death it passed to his son, Luis

* President Somoza's tenure of the presidency was interrupted between 1947 and 1950 by the terms of Leonardo Argüello (1947), Bènjamín Lacaya Sacasa (1947) and Víctor Román y Reyes (1947–50).

Somoza Debayle (1956–63), who withdrew when he felt the new liberal climate made it expedient.

Under strong United States pressure from Presidents Kennedy and Johnson the Somozas made progress towards broader participation in government. Secret ballot was instituted in 1963, for example, for the election of René Schick Gutiérrez (1963–6). Furthermore, the Somozas being nominally 'Liberals', there was a strong conservative opposition to *continuismo*, led by the Chamorro family. Against this the Somozas retained the National Guard and the tacit support of foreign interests. When the United States was involved elsewhere in the mid-sixties and its attention appeared momentarily to have wandered, Anastasio 'Tachito' Somoza, the younger, assumed the presidency peacefully (1967–).[41]

Panama, at first sight, seems to be an entirely different problem. Not only was it spared a long period of dictatorship; its history is so far from being monotonous that it is confused almost beyond belief.[42]

Harmodio Arias (1932–6) was succeeded by the pro-Fascist Juan Arosemena (1936–9), who died in office. The elections that followed resulted in the defeat of the liberal coalition that had held power for so long, by Arnulfo Arias, son of Harmodio. Arnulfo Arias ran on a platform of opposition to United States influence. In the circumstances this was both a popular and a dangerous line to take. When with the spread of the war to the Western Hemisphere in 1941 it became clear what the implications were, Arnulfo was deposed by military *coup*.

For the war and immediate postwar period, therefore, Panama was tied closely to the success of the Allied cause, and the fall of Ricardo Adolfo de la Guardia (1941–4) came because of his personal desire to stay in office, rather than for broader reasons of policy. The course of government was not again diverted until the bizarre events of 1949, when following the death in office of Domingo Díaz Arosemena

(1948–9) Daniel Chanis (1949) became President. Shortly afterwards, he resigned 'for reasons of ill health'. Regretting his resignation a few days later, he led a march on the Presidential Palace to recover it from his successor, Rodolfo Chiari.

The Supreme Court on appeal held Dr Chanis to be the lawful President, but at this point new interests stepped in. Since Panama had dissolved its army, this took the form of intervention by the police, who in a *coup d'état* installed ex-President Arnulfo Arias for a new term.

Arias served from 1949 to 1952, during which time a rapprochement took place between Panama and the United States. In the post-war years Panama was becoming ever more prominent as a country of registration for ships of other nations, flying a so-called 'flag of convenience'. Her tanker fleet became one of the largest in the world; not an unmixed blessing as it raised the question of how much longer tankers would be able to pass through the existing canal and its system of locks. The older generation of Panamanians were beginning to appreciate the advantages of their unique position and to accept it in some degree.

In 1952 Arias tried to prolong his term by restoring the old (1941) Constitution, and was arrested and impeached before the National Assembly under the guidance of the commander of the police, José Antonio Remón. The acting presidency devolved on Alcíbades Arosemena, and at the new elections Remón assumed the presidency in his own name. A man of some ability, Remón gave Panama three years of strong government before his car was ambushed leaving the racecourse at the capital in 1955. His Vice-President, José Ramón Guizado, who momentarily assumed the presidency after the assassination, proved to have been implicated in it, and was impeached by the National Assembly. The Second Vice-President, Ricardo Arias Espinosa, was thereupon sworn in in Guizado's place.[43]

It was Arias Espinosa (1955–6) whose administration negotiated a fresh treaty with the United States replacing the agreement of 1936. It increased the annuity paid by the United States government for its rights over the canal, and provided Panama with a greater share in the revenues of the Canal Zone. His successor, Ernesto de la Guardia (1956–60), became the first President for many years to survive a regular term of office. Yet his term was marked by great bitterness at the smallness of the United States concessions and riots became endemic, involving at one stage a full-scale invasion of the Canal Zone by angry students and others. Wiser for the events elsewhere in the hemisphere, the Eisenhower Administration made the symbolic concession of the right to fly the Panamanian flag in the Zone, and the violence subsided.

Under Roberto Chiari (1960–4) the issue continued, however, and was solved only by the rational decision formally to transfer sovereignty over the Zone to Panama, leaving the status of the canal unaltered.[44] Since 1964 Marco Aurelio Robles has served a term which by comparison with those of his predecessors had been uneventful until the time for elections came round again. Much bitterness remains at the client state of the country, especially among students and members of the literati. But with Panama an associate member of the CACM its economy has picked up and a new sense of nationhood seems to be growing.

It would be very misleading to stop at this point and leave the impression that the twentieth-century history of the Caribbean areas has been one of unrelieved violence and degradation. Certainly there are many who from safe distances take a broad social-democratic view of the problems of Latin America and recommend violent revolution as the panacea for them. There is no proof, of course, that violence as such brings economic betterment; in fact, there is good evidence that it prevents it. The major violent upheavals of Latin America have not been conspicuously successful in providing economic well-being. Yet on the other hand, certainly, dictatorial rule has not been successful in providing political acceptance and small incidents of violence go far in making dictatorship work. In fact, those régimes in the Caribbean area which have provided a measure of democracy have tended to be those which have made progress also.

Most striking of these is the picture presented by modern Mexico.[45] The election of 1946 was noteworthy in Mexican history because of the return of a civilian, Miguel Alemán Valdés (1946–52) – proof of the retirement of the military to the position of informal lobbying characteristic of advanced political systems.

The Alemán presidency began under conditions of great economic difficulty. The industrial achievement of its last four years was the more spectacular for this. The huge industrial complexes in the neighbourhood of Monterrey and in the environs of the capital were expanded. Public works projects were stepped up, concentrating on the infrastructure necessary to continued growth. Glory was, however, not neglected: the 'University City' was built for the University of Mexico, today a showpiece for visitors because of its superb murals and grand scale. The statue of its patron was largely smashed and daubed with paint by students in a riot in 1966. For Alemán has since become a symbol of the Right, while corruption among members of his administration went beyond accepted limits.

The presidency of Adolfo Ruiz Cortines (1952–8) took as its theme a 'March to the Sea'. It was aimed at bringing into use the fish protein which was being neglected, in developing communications and, in particular, linking the Yucatán Peninsula with the rest of the nation – with a great consequent increase in tourism. Rail links were also established with Guatemala and work advanced on the Pan American highway intended to link Alaska with Cape Horn.[46]

The task of coping with Castro and competition from those on the Left who considered that the Mexican Revolution had lost sight of its goals fell to Adolfo López Mateos (1958–64). López Mateos, who came to his post from the Secretaryship of Labour, proved popular as President for his defence of labour interests and extension of social security provisions. More dramatically, he carried through the nationalisation (by purchase) of the electricity industry, and proclaimed a new policy for the Frontier region. In the main, however, his name is likely to be associated with the last resurgence of the policy of land redistribution, for which his record stood only short of that of Cárdenas himself. With the population standing at 36 million at the end of his term, it was observable that despite this, the failure of the *ejidos* (co-operative farms) of the official ideology to equal the rate of production of private land was bringing about a long-term trend in favour of increased central control and dominance of the bureaucracy within the revolutionary family.

Mexico, the only nation by 1964 still to retain diplomatic links with Cuba, was on any account difficult to attack from the Left. Cuban agents were nevertheless continually being arrested in the country, and propaganda from them strengthened the hand of more conservative elements. In 1964 the new President, Gustavo Díaz Ordaz, generally regarded as coming from the Right of the revolutionary party, still won a unanimity of support from all but Cárdenas himself which had been denied his predecessors. Like his two predecessors, he exemplified the trend to the technocrat of proved ability.[47]

Outside the circle of the revolutionary family, however, there was growing cynicism at the complacency of those in power. Incidents of unrest in the states from time to time were put down by local officials with strong-arm methods, culminating in the heavy-handed repression of student unrest in the capital itself, on the occasion of the XIX Olympic Games in October 1968. The Olympics, the first to be held in Latin America, were to have been the occasion for the

world to see that Mexico had really become the modern
state its economic indicators suggested. The parallel with the
Centenary celebrations of 1910 – held as the first cracks
appeared in the Díaz edifice – was too close to be comfort-
able, but was almost certainly misleading.

To the south, in El Salvador, the picture of social change
has been much less dramatic, but still on the whole encouraging.[48] The fall of Hernández Martínez in 1944 was
followed by the military government of Salvador Castañeda
Castro (1944–8), and, following his deposition, by that of a
military junta (1948–50). Constitutional government was
restored in 1950, however, at a time when it was not
particularly fashionable elsewhere. The presidencies of
Oscar Osorio (1950–6) and José María Lemus (1956–60)
were administrations of moderate reformers, and El Salvador
played a leading role in the negotiations for the setting up
of CACM.

Unfortunately, towards the end of his term Lemus
showed signs of attempting personal rule and *continuismo*,
and was therefore overthrown by a coalition of opponents
of the continuing influence of the military on the political
process. Much had been achieved in social security and
welfare legislation. The question of land distribution, under-
lying the aristocratic-military domination of the government, had not even been raised. Now in the ensuing unrest
and turbulence this and other problems came under serious
consideration for the first time. In 1962, after two years of
nominal rule by shifting juntas moderated by student
demonstrations, elections returned the sole candidate of the
new reforming coalition, Colonel Julio Adalberto Rivera
Carballo (1962–7). He was succeeded peacefully by Fidel
Sanchez Hernández (1967–).

As already indicated, much more important than internal
change for El Salvador has been the growth of CACM, linking her small economy with that of the other Central
American states. Stabilisation of currency and establishment

of new trading patterns were fundamental to the development in the long-term of a welfare state. Politically and
contrary to pessimistic forecasts, this development seems on
the whole to have accelerated the trend towards democratic,
rather than just constitutional government.

Politically, the most interesting and progressive country
of Central America has continued to be Costa Rica.[49] This
is the more surprising since in 1948 it looked as if the process
of constitutional development had come to an end there,
leading to a revolt of exiles under the former Spanish
Republican officer José Figueres. The fall of Teodoro
Picado (1944–8) was, however, clearly not a military revolt
in the old style, nor was Figueres a Tinoco. Picado had been
backing former President Calderón for the presidency.
Following the coup, however, his opponent Otilio Ulate,
who had been declared elected and then disqualified, was
reinstated in office.

It was a curiously convenient time for constitutional
debate since Costa Rica had just disbanded its army as
superfluous and, indeed, potentially dangerous. Acting
under the Rio Pact of 1947 the new government was able to
invoke the aid of the OAS to maintain its territorial integrity
in face of conservative opposition from its neighbours.
Ulate was officially inaugurated in 1949 following formal
investigation and agreement. Costa Rica thus became the
first state to rely wholly on international agreement to
maintain her national interests. It was not, perhaps, a
position that many other states would be well advised to try
to emulate, but it proved a very remarkable success.

Almost inevitably, the successor to Ulate (1949–53) was
Figueres himself (1953–8). When Figueres was challenged
by an invasion of Costa Rican exiles from Nicaragua in 1955
(similar to the attack on the Arbenz régime the previous
year) his government again invoked the OAS, and received
military aid, though the Costa Rican militia proved easily
capable of defending themselves and the country against the

insurgents. Under Mario Echandí Jiménez (1958–62) and
Francisco José Orlich (1962–6) the Figueres programme of
social democracy continued. Today Costa Rica is a prosperous state, with one of the highest authentic literacy rates in
Latin America. Its president, Dr José Joaquin Trejos
Fernández (1966–) was elected in a free, secret and direct
ballot, contested by several parties, and one to which international observers were invited.[50]

There is, of course, no direct correlation between high
literacy and political stability, as Table 5 indicates. Costa
Rica had more: an early tradition of broad citizen participation based on universal education, something that Cuba (for
example) conspicuously lacked.

In recent years by fits and starts the long term trend
towards broader participation has continued, as part of the
general development of the Caribbean basin. But in
political terms it is still the contrasts that catch the eye.
They generate not only conflict, but the forces that make
for co-operation. Internal instability has brought the
strongest movements for international organisation. The
particular problem of the proximity of a Great Power has
forced a deeper consideration of the relative advantages and
disadvantages of an international order dominated by
'policemen' against one of equals. Characteristically, it is
through the states bordering on the area that many of these
ideas have been filtered to the great continent to the south.

1. Robert J. Alexander, *The Bolivian National Revolution* (New
Brunswick, N. J., Rutgers University Press, 1958) is considerably outdated
but as yet there is no satisfactory substitute.
2. Richard W. Patch, 'Bolivia: U.S. Assistance in a Revolution
Setting', in Richard N. Adams, ed., *Social Change in Latin America Today*
(New York, Harper & Row for Council on Foreign Relations, 1960)
p. 108.

3. Edwin Lieuwen, *Generals versus Presidents, Neomilitarism in Latin America* (London, Pall Mall, 1964).

4. For a view of this process by a celebrated Marxist advocate of revolution in Latin America see Régis Debray, *Revolution in the Revolution?* (London, Monthly Review Press, 1967).

5. Daniel James, ed., *The Complete Bolivian Diaries of Ché Guevara and other captured documents* (London, Allen & Unwin, 1968).

6. *The Times*, 10 and 18 October 1967.

7. Ronald M. Schneider, *Communism in Guatemala, 1944-1954* (New York, Praeger, 1959) pp. 11-34; Martz, *Central America*, pp. 28 ff.; Samuel Guy Inman, *A New Day in Guatemala, a study of the present social revolution* (Wilton, Conn., Worldover Press, 1951).

8. Schneider, pp. 35-43; see also Kalman H. Silvert, *A Study in Government: Guatemala* (New Orleans, Middle American Research Institute, Tulane University, Publication No. 21, 1954).

9. Schneider, pp. 301-17; David Wise and Thomas B. Ross, *The invisible government* (London, Cape, 1965) pp. 165 ff.

10. Mario Rosenthal, *Guatemala, the Story of an Emergent Latin American Democracy* (New York, Twayne, 1962).

11. Lieuwen, pp. 37-45; cf. Miguel Ydígoras Fuentes, *My War with Communism*, 'as told to' Mario Rosenthal (Englewood Cliffs, N.J., Prentice-Hall, 1963), p. 167.

12. Kenneth F. Johnson, *The Guatemalan Presidential Election of March 6, 1966; an analysis* (Washington, Institute for the Comparative Study of Political Systems, n.d.).

13. Edmund A. Chester, *A Sergeant Named Batista* (New York, Holt, 1954) is a contemporary biography. See also Batista's apologia *Culsa Betrayed* (New York, Vantage Press, 1962).

14. This account follows the interpretation of Boris Goldenberg, *The Cuban Revolution and Latin America* (London, Allen & Unwin, 1965).

15. William S. Stokes, 'The Cuban Parliamentary System in Action, 1940-47', *Journal of Politics*, xi (1949) 335.

16. William S. Stokes, *Latin American Politics* (New York, Thomas Y. Crowell, 1959) pp. 314-15.

17. Goldenberg, pp. 105-8.

18. For an account of the war in the Sierra Maestra by a participant see Ernesto 'Ché' Guevara, *Reminiscences of the Cuban Revolutionary War*, trans. Victoria Ortiz (London, Allen & Unwin, and Monthly Review Press, 1968).

19. There are many works on Castro and his controversial role in world affairs. See *inter alia* Russell H. Fitzgibbon, 'The Revolution Next Door: Cuba', *Annals of the American Academy of Political and Social Science*, cccxxxiv (March 1961) 113; Leo Huberman and Paul Sweezy, *Cuba: Anatomy of a Revolution* (New York, Monthly Review Press, 1960); Theodore Draper, *Castro's Revolution, Myths and Realities* (New York, Frederick A. Praeger, 1962) and Goldenberg, *cit sup*.

20. Rufo López-Fresquet, *My 14 months with Castro* (Cleveland and New York, The World Publishing Co., 1966) pp. 65-126.

21. Goldenberg, pp. 255-7.

22. Theodore C. Sorenson, *Kennedy* (London, Hodder & Stoughton, 1965), pp. 294-309; Arthur M. Schlesinger, Jr., *A Thousand Days: John F. Kennedy in the White House* (London, André Deutsch, 1965), pp. 194-270.

23. Henry M. Pachter, *Collision Course; The Cuban Missile Crisis and Coexistence* (London, Pall Mall, 1963); Sorenson, pp. 667-718.

24. Sir Herbert Marchant, 'Cuba hamstrung by economic troubles', *The Times*, 6 February 1968. For the most balanced account of present day Cuban politics see C. A. M. Hennessy, 'Cuba, the politics of frustrated nationalism', in Martin C. Needler, ed., *Political Systems of Latin America* (Princeton, Van Nostrand, 1964) p. 183.

25. A. Terry Rumbo, 'Dominican Republic', in Needler, *Political Systems of Latin America*, pp. 172-4. See also Germán E. Ornes, *Trujillo: Little Caesar of the Caribbean* (New York, Nelson & Sons, 1958).

26. De Lesseps S. Morrison, *Latin American Mission, An Adventure in Hemisphere Diplomacy*, ed. and intro. Gerold Frank, pp. 112-43 (New York, Simon & Schuster, 1965).

27. Morrison, pp. 150-2. See also Juan Bosch, *The Unfinished Experiment, Democracy in the Dominican Republic* (London, Pall Mall, 1966).

28. This account follows Connell-Smith, pp. 146-88.

29. O. Carlos Stoetzer, *The Organization of American States, An Introduction* (New York, Praeger, 1965).

30. Richard Milhous Nixon, *Six Crises* (London, W. H. Allen, 1962) pp. 183-234.

31. Goldenberg, pp. 182-3.

32. Dwight D. Eisenhower, *The White House Years, Waging Peace, 1956-1961* (Garden City, N.Y., Doubleday, 1965) pp. 515-20, 537-9.

33. Morrison, pp. 177-96.

34. For details, see Lieuwen, *Generals versus Presidents*.

35. Connell-Smith, p. 339.

36. David Huelin, 'Economic Integration in Latin America: Progress and Problems', *International Affairs*, xl, 3 (July 1964) 430; C. M. Castillo, *Growth and Integration in Central America* (London, Pall Mall, 1967); Miguel S. Wionczec, *Latin American Integration: Experiences and Prospects* (New York, Praeger, 1966).

37. Rayford W. Logan and Martin C. Needler, 'Haiti', in Needler, *Political Systems of Latin America*, p. 149.

38. Martz, *Central America*, pp. 112-63; Parker, pp. 188-96.

39. See also William S. Stokes, *Honduras: An Area Study in Government* (Madison, University of Wisconsin Press, 1950).

40. Lieuwen, *Generals versus Presidents*, pp. 63-8.

41. James L. Busey, 'Foundations of Political Contrast: Costa Rica and Nicaragua', *Western Political Quarterly*, xi, 3 (September 1958) p. 627 Martz, *Central America*, pp. 164-209; Parker, pp. 227-34.

42. John Biesance and Luke M. Smith, 'Panamanian Politics', *Journal of Politics*, xiv (August 1952) p. 386.

43. Larry LaRae Pippin, *The Remón Era, an analysis of a decade of events in Panama, 1947-1957* (Stanford, Stanford University Institute of Hispanic American and Luso-Brazilian Studies, 1964).

44. Jules Dubois, *Danger over Panama* (New York, The Bobbs-Merrill Co., 1964); Martz, *Central America*, pp. 264-319. See also American University, Washington, D.C., Special Operations Research Office, *Special warfare area handbook for Panama* (Washington, United States Government Printing Office, 1962).

45. Cline, *Mexico 1940-1960*, pp. 31-4, covers this period. See also Frank R. Brandenburg, *The Making of Modern Mexico* (Englewood Cliffs, N.J., Prentice-Hall, 1964).

46. William P. Tucker, *The Mexican Government Today* (Minneapolis, University of Minnesota Press, 1957); cf. Robert E. Scott, *Mexican Government in Transition* (Urbana, University of Illinois Press, 1959).

47. Calvert, 'The Mexican Political System', cited above.

48. Parker, pp. 263-77; Martz, *Central America*, pp. 210-63.

49. Busey, cited above; see also James L. Busey, *Notes on Costa Rican democracy* (Boulder, University of Colorado Press, 1962).

50. Paul G. Stephenson, ed., *Costa Rica Election Factbook, February 6, 1966* (Washington, Institute for the Comparative Study of Political Systems, 1966).

6 South America Today

THE great surprise of modern South America has been the drastic reinvigoration of historic Venezuela. For South Americans generally, it carries more hope than the experiences of Costa Rica and Mexico.

After its long spell under dictatorship, Venezuela had the good fortune in 1935 to fall into the hands of a relatively civilised military leader, Eleázar López Contreras (1935–1941). López Contreras worked hard to promote the transition from constitutional to democratic government, leaving the choice of his successor to Congress. He set up the National Bank, organised public works and rural schools and divided the great estates in a programme of land redistribution that produced favourable economic results. In this he was aided by the power of strong government and the absence of financial restraints.

His successor, Isaías Medina Angarita (1941–5) benefited from the wartime boom, but proved inflexible during the recession of 1945–6, when the market for oil fell off. He was deposed by a popular revolt in the capital, under Rómulo Betancourt, founder of the movement known as Acción Democrática (AD). Betancourt (1945–8) as interim President, carried out a programme of nationalisation of major industries and assumed substantial regulatory powers. His party won the 1948 election with Rómulo Gallegos, distinguished novelist and *pensador*, author of *Doña Bárbara* – a telling critique of his country's problems in the guise of fiction – and former Minister of Education under López Contreras.[1]

Unfortunately this election, and the permanence of left-wing rule which it implied, revived suspicion among conservative elements in the military. They overthrew Gallegos in 1948 and replaced him by a junta under Carlos Delgado Chalbaud (1948–50). Fanned by the Cold War atmosphere, extremism grew, not only on the Left, but on the Right, and the strains within the Army were reflected in the duration of interim rule. Then in 1950 Delgado Chalbaud was kidnapped, his body subsequently being found in a suburb of Caracas in circumstances that cast considerable suspicion on his colleagues. The provisional presidency of Germán Suárez Flamerich (1950–2) proved only a transitional phase, covering the rise of a new generation and in particular the figure of Col. Marcos Pérez Jiménez.

Pérez Jiménez (1952–8) came to power by national election, but the intimidation that accompanied it was a foretaste of dictatorship in the new style. His secret police used the most sophisticated means of terror known in Latin America down to that time, and accounts of refined tortures showed that they too were fully comparable with the latest European practices. But he had two traits of the old-style dictator which made his régime especially vulnerable. Megalomaniac building plans turned Caracas into a showplace of modern barracks and super-highways. But the highways ended in shanty towns that soon became known as the worst in the hemisphere. And the dictator himself flaunted his personal gains in the style of *nouveaux riches*. Excluded from real power by the growth of the police state, army officers were successful in establishing a secret conspiracy and deposed Pérez Jiménez with the agreement and encouragement of the AD leaders in exile.[2]

The military junta of Admiral Wolfgang Larrazábal (1958–9) held to their promise and held open elections. Betancourt was elected to a full term as President (1959–63) and became the first President in Venezuela's history to complete it. To do so he had to survive dissension and unrest on all sides. Foolishly, however, forces of Cuban sympathisers tried to overthrow him in favour of a conventional communist government. By so doing they strengthened his position immeasurably, and at the same time lost a possible ally.

It was Pérez Jiménez who had coined the phrase that most aptly described the policy by which Venezuela maintained its economic base for progress. 'Sembrar el petróleo' ('sowing the oil') meant reinvestment of the product of an extractive industry in enterprises of more lasting economic and social value. This policy Betancourt continued. Raúl Leoni (1964–1969) took over power peacefully and continued the Betancourt policies. The Leoni administration successfully contained the local version of the guerrilla movements of the day, and concerned at the proclaimed possibility of a junction between guerrillas and forces of discontent in the shanty towns, has developed workers' housing on the grand scale.

In an ironic comment on AD's constitutional success, its nominee was defeated without violence at the 1968 elections by the candidate of the opposition Christian Democrats, Dr Rafael Caldera.

Despite its very different background, Colombia too passed through a period of dictatorship in the 1950s. Its circumstances were bizarre and its consequences very nearly fatal for the continued domination of the traditional aristocracy. In a sense this arose from the very attainment of the conservative succession in 1946 which brought a man of unusual calm and restraint to the presidency.[3]

Mariano Ospina Pérez (1946–50), had he had less of either, could not have survived the events of 1948. The Conservatives were in a minority, their election having resulted from the division in the Liberals. From this division it seemed by then that the radical wing under Gaitán was gaining most, and Gaitán himself might well become his party's nominee in 1950, with consequences that could not be forecast. At this point he was assassinated. As the news spread the capital city erupted in a fury of violence and destruction, indiscriminate and not channelled in the direction of the United States though to some extent open to the interpretation put upon it by the Americans of being communist-inspired.[4]

The *Bogotazo* ('the blow of Bogotá') was perhaps a nine days' wonder in itself, as far as other countries were concerned acting mainly to strengthen those calling for repressive government. In Colombia itself the effect was catastrophic. The President himself refused to resign, but the Conservatives swung towards their hotheaded reactionary leader, Laureano Gómez, who duly became their candidate. Leaderless, the radical Liberals had lost heart. Gómez easily triumphed at the elections of 1950.

Gómez (1950–3) was stubborn without having the ability of his predecessor, and his extreme position was untenable as it allowed no room for compromise. In three years he alienated virtually every element of potential support. Even the Army felt impelled to depart from its old tradition of abstention from politics lest the system break down altogether. Ironically, it was its apolitical nature that brought it into politics. Gómez resigned; the Liberals refused quixotically to assume the obligation of opposition, and the commander of the Army, the incapable Gustavo Rojas Pinilla (1953–7) felt it incumbent upon himself to assume power in place of the politicians.[5]

So sharp a departure was this from custom that Colombians could hardly realise what had happened. Soon, however, they found that with the support of the Army this unintelligent man with his three hundred multicoloured uniforms was very hard to dislodge. The Conservatives had first to detach themselves from the sulky Gómez before they could come to terms with the Liberals. Only after Rojas Pinilla's fall was the breach healed and a united front formed at the Pact of Sitges (1957).

The fall of Rojas Pinilla was actually achieved when he tried to arrest the opposition candidate for the presidency and was given an ultimatum by his leading generals. The military junta proceded to return power to the civilians. Under the Pact of Sitges the sixteen-year experiment began of alternating governmental offices between the two parties in strict proportion. This experiment in *rotativism* has now lasted successfully through the terms of Dr Alberto Lleras Camargo (1958–62) for the Liberals, Guillermo León Valencia (1962–6) for the Conservatives, and Dr Carlos Lleras Restrepo (1966–) for the Liberals again. The elections to Congress have been 'fixed' to give equal holding of seats by control of the nomination process. Yet despite the agreement between the parties these have also been the years of *La Violencia*, a form of endemic banditry arising from poverty, despair, desire for revenge, and revolt against authority and officialdom. Continuous fighting, intense at times, has ranged between the supporters of each party and even between villages in the upland districts. Buses and lorries have been periodically ambushed, and many casual passers-by shot. Reaching a peak in the early 1960s *La Violencia* is now in decline, but its convenience for contemporary practitioners of guerrilla warfare could hardly be exaggerated.[6]

Nevertheless some measure of social reform has been achieved. After the inert presidency of Valencia – a disappointment after his bold opposition to Rojas Pinilla – there were many who believed that the left-wing position of Lleras Restrepo would bring fresh intervention from the army. So far this has not happened. However disillusion with the Liberal–Conservative rule is such that in 1966 only some 27 per cent of the electorate bothered to vote and there was a strong groundswell of support for the desperate alternative, the return of Rojas Pinilla. Interestingly enough, despite the premium on left-wing leadership in Colombia – as in Mexico, El Salvador, Costa Rica, Venezuela – its governments have been far more influential as critical allies of the United States than any old-style dictatorship. It was, furthermore, the absence of United States intervention that has made such a position politically possible.

This is particularly important since diplomacy after 1945 has been based on the new forms of political organisation discussed earlier in this chapter. If the United States has gained from realising its potential as a country whose leaders are trained in competitive politics in an open forum, Latin American states stand to do likewise. As they do so, United States diplomatists and politicians may come to realise a little better the limitations of the rigid stance of the 'Monroe doctrine' as popularly interpreted. So far from protecting the United States from foreign involvement, by its extension to Hawaii and to the Asian mainland it has actually endangered the United States' vital interests in the Caribbean.

The open forum has also tended to increase the significance of the South American countries to the United States. Even by modern standards they are large and powerful states with rapidly rising populations (Table 7). As allies and friends, however, it has been in their interest that the United States has found it necessary to make a return to them by acknowledging and even enhancing their stature. This has been particularly important to the bigger South American states, who in the world forum of the United Nations have acted as 'opinion leaders' to the large Latin American bloc.

The growth of Latin American involvement in world politics is set out in summary form in Table 8. It shows clearly how the smaller states, so active as allies in two wars, retain their importance as a numerical majority for voting purposes. But it is the larger states that have taken part in international peacekeeping and taken on a significant part of the costs that go with it. Independence of the United States, however, and the development of separate juridical personalities, does not mean that the larger states wholly lack cohesion, if only on matters outside Latin America. United Latin American support was an important factor in carrying the Spanish resolution in the

United Nations for the annexation of Gibraltar. Many Latin American boundary claims (such as that of Guatemala for British Honduras or that advanced in 1968 by Venezuela for part of Guyana) have even less justification in modern terms of a world of peoples rather than legal formulae.

Table 7

Population and Ethnic Composition, c. 1960

Country	Date	Population	Eur	Mes	Ind	Neg	Other
Argentina	1960	20,009,000	98	2	—	—	—
Bolivia	1965[e]	3,598,000	5	25	70	—	—
Brazil	1965[e]	82,200,000	61	21[3]	2	15	1
Chile	1964	8,515,023	37	60	3	—	—
Colombia	1964	17,482,000	30	40	5	7	18[1]
Costa Rica	1965	1,413,531	48	47	2	3	—
Cuba	1953[c]	5,829,029	73	—	—	26[3]	1[4]
Dominican Republic	1965[e]	3,221,000	5	14	—	81	—
Ecuador	1962[c]	4,777,194	10	41	39	10[3]	—
El Salvador	1965	2,878,000	8	80	10	—	—
Guatemala	1964[c]	4,278,341	1	45	53	—	—
Haiti	1965[e]	4,600,000	—	—	—	90	10[1]
Honduras	1965	2,130,000	1	90	9	—	—
Mexico	1965[e]	40,000,000	10	60	30	—	—
Nicaragua	1964[c]	1,559,526	tr	77	4	9	10
Panama	1965[2]	1,243,860	12	72	1	14	—
Paraguay	1962	1,820,000	—	99	tr	—	—
Peru	1965	11,800,000	13	37	49	1	—
Uruguay	1963	2,556,020	90	10	—	—	—
Venezuela	1961[c]	7,555,799	12	68	10	10	—

[c] = census.   [e] = estimate.
[1] Mulatto.   [2] Ethnic data on 1940 census.
[3] incl. mulatto.   [4] Chinese.
SOURCES: *The South American Handbook* (1967); *Whitaker's Almanack*.

Paradoxically, in terms of communication the great South American states are nearer to North America today than ever before.

The countries of South America which hitherto were

largely independent of United States influence have therefore had to take stock of their position in recent years. The
growth of that influence has varied greatly from country to
country. Certainly in none of them does it wholly dominate
national attitudes as it does in some Caribbean states. Yet
in part this is due to the way in which the pressures in the
Caribbean described in the last chapter have acted to call
into being countering forces in South America and in the
outside world.

The chief of these forces has been that for the mobilisation
of sectors of the population not hitherto part of the political
process: the leaders of working-class organisations, the
workers themselves where sufficiently concentrated, certain
peasant groups, and in places the lower orders of the clergy.
This mobilisation has been primitive, in that it often lacks
developed organisation and clearly articulated goals. It
shares the characteristics of personalism with traditional
politics, and though where it amounts to a mass movement
called forth by a single leader it has been dignified with
the title 'populist', it is not by any means clear where the
old politics end and the new begin.

Such mass movements are easily sealed off from access
to the formal political process by ruthless governmental
action. In the Caribbean region this has been the normal
pattern of response. In South America, however, the more
open and sophisticated culture, the numbers involved and
the influence of European and North American ideas other
than those of businessmen, meant that populistic methods
were accepted as a path to power and populist leaders
entered government. The leading example is the case of
Argentina.

Since 1943 Argentine political life has been dominated
by the figure of Juan D. Perón – first as ruler and then as
spectre. It has already been shown how as a young colonel
he channelled the frustrations of those Argentine leaders
who had expected the Axis to win. Hostility to the emer-

Table 8

Latin America in War and Peace

Country	Great War	Acceded to League	Seceded from League	World War	UN membership	Korea	Other
Argentina	—	1920[1]	1921–33	27 Mar 45	11 May 45[2]	Aid	Congo
Bolivia	13 Apr 17[8]	1920	—	7 Apr 43	27 Apr 43	Aid	—
Brazil	27 Oct 17	1920	1928	22 Aug 42	8 Feb 43	Aid	{ Suez / Congo
Chile	—	1920	1938	14 Feb 45	12 Feb 45	Tps	*
Colombia	—	1920	—	28 Nov 43	22 Dec 43	Aid	Suez
Costa Rica	23 Mar 18	1920	1925	9 Dec 41	1 Jan 42[3]	Tps	—
Cuba	7 Apr 17	1920	—	9 Dec 41	1 Jan 42[3]	—	—
Dominican Republic	Occ. by USA	1924	—	9 Feb 45[5]	7 Feb 45	Aid	—
Ecuador	8 Dec 17[8]	1934	—	8 Dec 41	1 Jan 42[3]	Aid	*
El Salvador	—	1924	1937	8 Dec 41	1 Jan 42[3]	—	—
Guatemala	23 Apr 18	1920	1936	8 Dec 41	1 Jan 42[3]	—	—
Haiti	12 Jul 18	1920	—	8 Dec 41	1 Jan 42[3]	—	—
Honduras	19 Jul 18	1920	1936	8 Dec 41	1 Jan 42[3]	Aid	—
Mexico	—	1931	—	1 Jun 42	5 Jun 42[4]	Aid	—
Nicaragua	8 May 18	1920	1936	8 Dec 41	1 Jan 42[3]	Aid	—
Panama	7 Apr 17	1920	—	9 Dec 41	1 Jan 42[3]	Aid	—
Paraguay	—	1920	1937	9 Feb 45	12 Feb 45	Aid	—
Peru	6 Oct 17[8]	1920	—	12 Feb 45	11 Feb 45	Aid	*
Uruguay	7 Oct 17[8]	1920	—	22 Feb 45	23 Feb 45	Aid	*
Venezuela	—	1920	1938	16 Feb 45	16 Feb 45	Aid	6

8 = severed diplomatic relations only.
* Offer of troops for UNEF not taken up.
1 Withdrew from Assembly 1921 after rejection of resolution; resumed full membership 1933.
2 Invited to join after UN Conference on International Organisation, 30 April 1945.
3 Signed Declaration.
4 Troops actively participated outside hemisphere.
5 Declared war on Japan only.

gence of the United States as a world power fitted in perfectly with the new form of protest which he represented, and which owed so much of its style to Fascism. Neither of these things in itself, of course, would have enabled him to put his imprint on a whole generation.

Perón (1946–55) based his power on the support of the dispossessed of Argentine society, the *descamisados* or poor industrial workers (lit. 'shirtless ones'). With the control of the Press and the aid of the techniques of mass manipulation refined at Nuremberg and Berlin, he whipped up fluid discontent into a stable though chauvinistic nationalism. His marriage to the film star Eva Duarte made his position unassailable, for she was as politically skilful as she was beautiful. Her death in 1952 initiated his downfall. There were, however, other factors.

In a grand gesture, Perón bought out the British-owned railways when they were on the point of bankruptcy. He embarked on a programme of visits in pursuit of national glory, and tried to solidify his claim to hegemony, amongst other things, by reviving a claim to the British-owned Falkland Islands. After Eva's death, his self-glorification and pressure for state centralisation swelled to the point of open conflict with the Church, hitherto tolerant. In 1955 the Air Force revolted, joined forces with elements of the Army, and dismissed him from power.[7]

Since that time the Army leaders have been consistent in their determination not to let Peronism return, lest its implications divide them again. General Eduardo Lonardi, Perón's immediate successor, was dismissed when he proposed to allow the Peronistas to vote.[8] His successor, General Pedro Eugenio Aramburu (1955–8), was unable to amend the Constitution on this score owing to the size of the Peronista block. In a dictatorial flourish, he finally resorted to proclaiming the return of the old Constitution and the Sáenz Peña Law of 1912! Under it, the country was fortunate enough to secure a moderate liberal as President,

Arturo Frondizi (1958–62). He was able to channel energies back into economic development and so take advantage of the boom of the late 1950s. So successful was he that the forces of Peronismo began to divide, between those who wanted Peronismo *con* (with) Perón, and those who would be content with Peronismo *sin* (without) Perón. A fatuous attempt by the former President to create a national rising by visiting Brazil in 1963 merely accelerated the trend towards the latter, and, indeed, away from Peronismo altogether.[9]

But Frondizi moved too quickly in trying to get this movement under control by allowing Peronistas to vote in 1962. The Army, which had learnt little since 1955, promptly overthrew him. Since no one was prepared to take on such a thankless task, the presidency, held for a brief period by José María Guido (1962–3) devolved on a poor country doctor, Arturo Illía (1963–6), whose complete honesty and hard work made him remarkably successful. When it looked as if the situation might really be improving at long last the army leaders, who had scarcely bothered to conceal their contempt for his régime, stepped in again and this time took over power themselves on a programme of national 'renovation'.

Since 1966, under the leadership of General Juan Carlos Onganía, now still serving as Provisional President, it has become clear that nationalism has brought its own nemesis. Renovation has become a crusade to purge Argentina of outside corruption, such as long hair and kissing between couples in public. Argentina is still rich and powerful. Her heavy industry can sustain shipbuilding and her government can afford to buy nuclear reactors. Little or no progress has been made in meeting the real needs of the discontented.[10] If Britain, Argentina's best customer for meat, for whatever reason turns to alternative sources of supply, the future of Argentina's self-imposed role of hemispheric leadership would be doubtful indeed.

As in previous decades, the history of Paraguay since 1939 has shown interesting parallels with that of Argentina. As an inland nation dependent on its larger neighbour for its links with the outside world, it was, however, not subject to the same stresses of wartime production. The principal cause of turbulence under Higinio Moriñigo (1940–8) came from the internal growth of industrialisation in Asunción. In 1946 the existence of the Liberal Party was recognised, even though the military régime had dissolved all other forms of organised opposition.

In 1947 rebellion against the repressive rule of Moriñigo broke out under the leadership of General Rafael Franco. In a savage internal war the rebels were defeated, and the hopes of the Liberals for a return to power dashed. Yet they were partially successful that in the following year Moriñigo himself did not seek re-election. His chosen nominee was elected, but was deposed on the penultimate day of the year by military *coup*.

In a curious reversal of practice elsewhere the armed struggle between factions that followed was resolved by the compromise of an election. Starting as an interim choice, Federico Chávez (1949–54), who based his power on an alliance with Perón, thus remained for almost five years. Then he was forced to resign by General Alfredo Stroessner (1954–), descendant of one of Paraguay's many German immigrant families.

Stroessner's rule is old-fashioned in its paternalistic style, but since the Nixon tour in 1958 has been subjected to liberalizing pressures from the United States and elsewhere. Early in the 1960s opponents of the régime bid for recognition and were permitted to register as a legal political party. This recognition has since been extended to all other constitutional groups and contested elections held since 1963 confirmed in office the dominant Colorados. Liberal opponents in exile in Buenos Aires were expelled in 1966 and many of them have chosen to return home.[11]

Paraguay has not been able to advance industrialisation to any great extent. It remains an enclave of traditional ways little known to the outside world, though in the last few years a growing number of people have heard about and come to appreciate the extraordinary richness of its musical heritage.

As we have seen, the third state of the Platine region has remained, for reasons of convenience to both sides in the Cold War and thereafter, an oasis of calm. This, however, was to a great extent the product of the Uruguayans themselves, rather than of their leaders. Luis Batlle Berres (1947–51) was certainly the representative in his day of the humane, reformist tradition. His presence, however, led to the crystallisation of opposition around the rival figure of the elder Batlle's son, stressing the leading factor of the tradition above all. This was, of course, opposition to *personalismo* of every kind. Andrés Martínez Trueba (1951–2) achieved his victory on this theme, and at once having made a deal with the leaders of the Blancos, introduced constitutional reform for the collegiate system that had been José Batlle's ultimate ambition.[12]

The functions of the presidency were entirely vested in the Executive Council of nine members. One of the majority served for a year at a time as nominal head of state. The experiment initially justified the confidence that democrats had placed in it. In 1958 the Blancos won the elections for the first time in ninety-three years, and it seemed that this was further confirmation. Their traditionalist Conservatism was muted, and the change of policy virtually imperceptible in the pervasive atmosphere of consensus and good management. Uruguay continued to maintain the most advanced social services in the world – including unemployment and industrial injuries' insurance, family allowances, old-age and social security benefits – and to do so on an economic basis which was still largely agricultural rather than industrial. Violence had become something associated with football, not politics.

Meanwhile, however, an inflationary trend set in which struck at the middle-class confidence and trade union-centred bargaining process which were the substructure of the system. It was already noticeable in international affairs, as at the 1962 Meeting of Consultation at Punta del Este, that the Uruguayan government had great difficulty deciding on a positive rather than a negative approach to any given situation. It was an institutional problem. But in internal matters it threatened to endanger the structure of the state itself. As rising prices made a mockery of wages and pensions, the politicians seemed to be doing nothing.[13] In 1966 a further constitutional amendment ended the experiment with conciliar government for the sake of rapid decision-making. It was an unhappy coincidence that the first post-conciliar President, General Oscar Gestido (1967) died after only a few months in office. His successor, President Carlos Pacheco Areco (1967–) has made it very clear that in its present crisis Uruguay needs the help of every one of its citizens, who are rightly proud of what their country has achieved.[14]

It is still too early to say how the return to presidential rule will benefit Uruguay. Decisions of themselves (as others elsewhere have learnt) are not enough to ensure the attainment of the socio-economic millennium. Uruguayan optimism, however, gives grounds for hope.

Turning to the Andean states we find more strenuous conditions for social reform, and no less interesting responses.

Chile, since 1946, has been passing through a period of firm institutions and evanescent political parties.[15] Of all the states of Latin America, it offers the clearest evidence of the curious attraction doctrines of systematisation (such as Marxism) hold for members of Latin American ruling *élites*. With its advanced industrial substructure, working-class movements, and political organisation, the communist movement was in 1946 more deeply based there than anywhere else. With the experience of the Popular Front period

– and actual participation in government – behind it, it was natural that the González Videla Administration (1946–52) should have contained several Communists, who were thus as well placed in Chile as, say, in France or Czechoslovakia.

What was curious was their blind lack of common sense. Their major aim was to take over labour from within the government – much as Perón had done in Argentina a few years previously. But simultaneously they used their positions to foment strikes to put pressure on their governmental colleagues. In 1948 the President summarily expelled them from his Cabinet and outlawed the Communist Party. By this time, with the drawing of Cold War lines, their chance had passed.

Nevertheless Gabriel González Videla did not himself provide the leadership which many considered necessary. As a result, the electorate turned back in 1952 to the improbably charismatic figure of Carlos Ibáñez, now to serve a term as a democratically elected President (1952–8). It was the first Chilean presidential election in which women had the vote. Ibáñez justified confidence in that he had no further dictatorial ambitions. But economic conditions after the Korean War worsened steadily and the ageing President seemed quite unable to take the decisions for which he had been elected. Only one further solution seemed possible, though widely unacceptable: a government of the extreme Left under Salvador Allende. This was averted by coalition between the Centre and Right that secured the return of Jorge Alessandri Rodríguez (1958–64) but with a minority vote for Allende that seemed to augur well for his election in 1964.

Alessandri's term had hardly begun before Chile was struck by the great earthquake of 1960, which spread destruction from Arica to Puerto Montt. The magnitude of the disaster stultified the Administration. It was not lacking in ideas but, lacking support in the divided and fragmented Congress, was unable to have them enacted. Despite the apparent impossibility of any alternative to Allende in 1964, one was already emerging in the form of the new Christian Democratic Party, ideologically on the left as far as progressivism was concerned, and with a personable leader in Senator Eduardo Frei. In 1964, the polarisation of support resulted in a clear majority for Frei.

The Frei Administration (1964–) was so successful in generating support that it went on to achieve the remarkable feat of obtaining a majority overall in the Chamber of Deputies in 1965. This created an expectation of dramatic change which was not fulfilled and perhaps never could have been. Disillusion with economic stagnation brought renewed unrest. Nevertheless, under its new régime Chile appeared to outside observers to be maturing as a Latin American democracy, still capable of responding to the need for economic stabilisation and industrial growth.[16]

Hope also seems appropriate for the future of Peru. The history of Peru since 1930 has very largely been the tale of why Haya de la Torre did not achieve political power.[17] His first chance came with the fall of Leguía, when his exile movement was formed in Peru in the early days of the rule of Sánchez Cerro (1930–3). Sánchez Cerro used sharp repression against the new movement, and his assassination in 1933 was said to have been the product of a plot hatched by elements of Haya's radical nationalist group, the Apristas. It gave his successor, Oscar Raimundo Benavides (1933–9) an excuse for further repression, to which in any case his conservative instincts made him prone. When Haya tried to challenge the autocracy in 1936 his name was simply removed from the ballot. The Benavides régime achieved little of lasting value and Benavides himself let it pass in 1939 into the hands of a reliable member of the élite, Manuel Prado y Ugarteche (1939–45).

Prado proved stronger in office than had been expected. Strengthened by the prosperity engendered by the war, he pursued a domestic policy of anti-militarism in the *Civilista* tradition. He was succeeded, again in a free election, by the liberal José Luis Bustamante y Rivero. Bustamante (1945–8) proved unsatisfactory to the Army and lacked his predecessor's prestige; he was overthrown by the military in 1948.

Once again the military had panicked at the remote chance of Aprista gains, and once again they sought to meet change by dictatorship. Manuel A. Odría (1948–56) set out to create what he called a regeneration of the fatherland – on a conservative basis. So little was accomplished that it was once again necessary to find a face-saving successor. One became available when required in the person of Manuel Prado, President for a second time 1956–62.

As already noted, the revolt of 1948 had been touched off by the progress Apra had been making during its brief period of legalisation. Following it, however, Haya had had to take refuge in the Colombian Embassy, and (in violation of the Latin American custom of safe-conduct for exiles) he was kept there by military guards for the space of five years. From this experience he emerged a broken man. At the end of the dictatorship the Prado administration was able to consider him returning, though not to contest an election. In a volte-face of startling cynicism, Apra announced its support for the candidature of no less a person than Odría himself. The Left predictably charged that Haya had sold out to the forces of United States imperialism and Wall Street capitalism.

The military, however, remained consistent. If Haya was for Odría, they were against him. A military *coup* installed a provisional régime under General Ricardo Pérez Godoy (1962–3).[18] In defiance of predictions, this short government distinguished itself by its vigorous espousal of social reform. It had made some dramatic gains before new elections returned a progressive candidate whom the military were prepared to accept. Fernando Belaúnde Terry (1963–) also was in a position to offer an effective programme through his command of an organised political following among civilians, Acción Popular. Belaúnde spoke of self-help as the only certain road to economic betterment. This theme, so much in tune with that expressed by President Kennedy in the Alliance for Progress, meant that (for example) the government would supply the main roads if the local villages built the connecting roads to make their link to the market a reality.[19] The Belaúnde administration markedly advanced Peruvian economic development, and the local version of the guerrillas of the 1960s were conspicuously unsuccessful. Unfortunately, suspicion grew in nationalist circles that in the process it was becoming too closely tied to the United States, and it was overthrown by the military under General Velasco Alvarado (1968–).

In Ecuador, on the other hand, the situation is both more anomalous and more unstable. Twelve presidents held office in the decade 1931–40, the most durable of whom, Federico Páez (1935–7), survived for just over two years. The sequence of military *coups* that they represented did nothing for Ecuador, while intellectuals toyed with curiously irrelevant Socialism and demagogic appeals to the small urbanised *élite*. C. Alberto Enríquez Gallo (1937–8), on the other hand, called a Constitutional Assembly, and the rule of Aurelio Mosquero Narváez (1938–9) showed that aspirations to civil rule remained. Unfortunately he died in office.

Hardly had his constitutional successor, Carlos Arroyo del Río (1940–4), come into office than the long-standing dispute with Peru over the boundary in the Marañón region came to a head. The civil régime of the Peruvian Manuel Prado had to concede a strong policy to the military in the area, since on the one hand there was no option and on the other the facts of Peruvian presence and Ecuadorian absence were indisputable. Though the Ecuadorian claim was in all other respects legalistically sounder, their attempt to maintain it was doomed to failure. The United States was preoccupied and no other power was prepared to intervene in what by this time was one of the last remaining undefined boundary problems in the continent. In 1943 Arroyo del Río agreed under pressure to the loss of all the disputed area and in the following year he was toppled by a revolution at Guayaquil which brought back José Mariá Velasco Ibarra to the presidency (1944–7).[20]

Velasco Ibarra, whose first brief reforming term (1934–5) was cut short by Páez, proposed a new broad programme. He was speedily deposed by the military. His temporary successor, Carlos Mancheno, tried to impose a dictatorship, and in reaction the military under the leadership of a junior officer overthrew Mancheno in a counter-revolution that divided the country under the nominal rule of Mariano Suárez Veintimilla. Ultimately it was left to Congress to choose the new President, and after the interim government of the elder Carlos Arosemena (1947–8) they installed Galo Plaza Lasso (1948–52), son of Leónidas Plaza and a diplomatist without party affiliations.

Galo Plaza canalised the forces of Conservatism behind civilian rule. He was a man of more than ordinary ability in politics and subsequently received the high honour of being elected President of the General Assembly of the United Nations. But as President his diplomatic ability achieved the more immediate aim of establishing orderly government, among the principal achievements of which was to establish a trunk road network that initiated a long period of economic growth.

Velasco Ibarra (1952–6) in his own words, needed only 'a balcony' to rally popular support and returned to the presidency peacefully, continuing the policies of his predecessor in most respects. He was re-elected for a fourth term after the administration of Camilo Ponce Enríquez (1956–1960). Meanwhile investment flowed into the country, and led by the important fishmeal industry Ecuador's economy continued to boom.[21] Velasco Ibarra fell from power in 1961 at the hands of the military, not because he had failed as

President, but because of his sympathy for the aims of the Cuban régime of Fidel Castro. Part of the balance of his term was served out by the younger Carlos Julio Arosemena (1961–3) before he too fell foul of the military, right-wing elements of which had been strengthened by the 1961 *coup*.[22]

Power was vested in a three-man junta displaying an abnormal degree of equality. At elections held in 1968 Velasco Ibarra became President for the fifth time. This reflected the balance between the Air Force of the 1961 *coup*, and the Army of that of 1963. They fell as a trio to a new revolt in 1966, leaving Clemente Yerovi Indaburu as provisional President, subsequently succeeded by Dr Otto Arosemena Gómez (1966–8).

Like Peru, Ecuador's system was challenged in the early 1960s by a guerrilla movement on the Cuban model. Again, it has not proved particularly successful, which suggests that such movements in the Andean countries may not even require the pre-emption of social reform in order to fail.

To the east, anyway, there remains always the giant of the continent, Brazil. Fortunate in the possession at once of mineral resources, population and men of vision and good will, the dominant fact of the post-war years for Brazil has been the opening up of communications.[23]

Under Enrico Gaspar Dutra (1946–50), Vargas's definitive successor and nominee, economic development was fostered by the SALTE Plan – *Saude* (health), *Alimentação* (food), *Transporte*, and *Energia* (power). An influx of capital and immigrants were absorbed into the national life. The programme of Vargas seemed to have achieved justification, and Vargas himself was peacefully returned to office by election in 1950. In his second term of office the dictatorship and the trappings of Fascism were missing, but so too was the vigour and the sense of political realities. Corruption multiplied among his associates until in the words of Carlos Lacerda 'a river of mud' flowed through the

Presidential Palace. Evidence of the charges was brought to him in 1954 by a group of top military leaders who demanded his resignation. In despair, he signed it and shot himself, leaving a political testament which to many Brazilians acted as a painful reminder of the benefits they had gained under his rule.[24]

The interim presidencies of João Cafe Filho (1954), Carlos Coimbra da Luz (1954) and Nereu Ramos (1954–6) reflected the inability of the army to stabilise the situation in the politically emotive atmosphere of the time. Then elections returned a new leader, Juscelino Kubitschek (1956–61), who was to stamp his mark on Brazilian history with remarkable speed.

Kubitschek inherited an overheated economy and a staggeringly disoriented government set in a city where not a square centimetre of land remained for building. The increasing crush of immigrants from other states crowded into slum shanties (favelas) second in poverty only to Caracas. His solution was to let the economy go, and make use of the proceeds of inflation to finance the building of the long-projected new capital inland in the State of Goias. At last technology was equal to such a feat, but this is not to minimise the boldness of the concept. Furthermore, the design of Brasília was entrusted to one man, Oscar Niemayer, who made it an inspiration to a generation of architects. Significantly enough the first building to be completed was the new Presidential Palace.

Brasília was still unfinished; a megalithic monument surrounded by huts and cleared ground, when Kubitschek's successor was inaugurated and went to live there. Jânio Quadros (1961) had made his reputation as a dynamic governor of São Paulo and was chosen to put an end to the inflation.[25] After seven months he resigned, blaming conservative elements for his inability to continue. Since he stood ideologically on the Left and was sympathetic to Castro, blame for his fall was heaped on the figure of Carlos

Lacerda, who had accused him of seeking a dictatorship. His successor as President, João Goulart (1961–4), had served as Vice-President under both Kubitschek and Quadros. It was well known that he stood even further to the Left within the old Vargas formula. The military therefore refused to allow him to succeed without tempering his power with a parliamentary system which was scrapped by general agreement after only two years.

The result was that little was done about inflation. Goulart took the return to presidential government as a mandate for drastic reform, by then generally acknowledged as necessary. Unfortunately for him, before making it good, he tried to divide the military by infiltrating the Navy with his own supporters, and when the Army learnt about this, they reluctantly intervened once more and overthrew him.[26] Marshal Humberto Castello Branco (1964–7) carried out an extensive programme of changes in governmental personnel down to district level, and achieved by rigid control some success in stabilising the economy, before holding elections at which Marshal Arturo Costa e Silva became President for the term starting in 1967. It is the Costa e Silva Administration that will have to cope, not only with the urban legacy of inflation, but also with the rural unrest of the north-east and the continued challenge of Brazil's future. And the future of Brazil is in some sense that of the continent as a whole.

To summarise, therefore, the pressures to respond to the outside world have brought to South America a definite trend towards executive centralisation. South American, like Central American states, now live in a world of Great Powers, and Great Powers expect speedy responses and precise positions. Both are alien to the subtle and time-consuming legalism of traditional Latin American diplomacy, developed out of the delicate balance of survival in the conditions of Latin American internal politics. Where the authoritarian tradition is strong, the result has been conservative strengthening of the system, in the traditional guise of the military acting as guardians of the state. Elsewhere there has been a search for those rare personalities who can assemble a personal following of sufficient strength to defeat alternative coalitions. Aspirants are easy to find, if only because radical reformers, like army officers, expect immediate results.

The strains upon the state system and the changes they have brought about have in each case very readily been transmitted to neighbouring states. Neighbours give governments, and their measures, legitimacy by recognising them as being legitimate. They are therefore encouraged to do so, preferably signalling their acceptance to others by following similar courses. Failing that, they may be called upon as a test of their sincerity to join in a common external campaign, whether against American landlords, British investors or Communist agitators. The best scapegoats are the objects that are least vital and most externalised, since they cause the fewest impulses towards internal dissent. Thus military leaders found Communism a safe target when it was almost unheard of in the Western Hemisphere. Now that Cuba has a communist government they take refuge in safer objects of hostility, such as reputedly blasphemous remarks by the Beatles.

Since South American states are large they have some influence in the world because of their influence with their fellows. It is useful that this influence has been cast so consistently on the side of peace, co-operation and cultural self-expression, even if this does result primarily from their own instability and the inadvisability of subjecting it to a strain of a clearly defined policy. The Caribbean states that have been drawn along in the wake of the United States for the past half-century, including two world wars, have paid the price in the alienation of the intellectuals and their consequent tendency to seek the rival ideology in a bi-polar world. In the last analysis, however, the division between

South America and the Caribbean must not be drawn too sharply, though it does have value as an organising concept. The fact is that the politics of violence is seen in both areas, and is recognised as basic to human organisation. The way to control it is by acceptance and administration of a common code of law through an organisation intended for such a purpose. Within the state such an organisation already exists, so if violence is manifest within the state and is contained there, it becomes relatively controllable. In the international sphere it is very dangerous indeed.

Now as the events of the same period in Europe, Asia and Africa have shown, the Latin American concern to eliminate the smallest causes of violence in the international sphere has a great deal of point. The world, therefore, has much to learn from their sophistication and experience in handling it; indeed we have seen that it already has done so in trying to develop organs of international co-operation. Yet one cannot say that Latin America has received anything like the attention it merits, even from its nearest neighbour, the United States. That it has not done so is to a surprising extent due to quite an irrelevant factor. That is the current Great Power preoccupation – obsession, rather – with technology. For in economic terms Latin America as a whole is regarded as 'underdeveloped'.

In fact Latin Americans as people, living and going about their daily business, have not been notably slow to adopt technological innovations. It is true that difficulties of communication must have handicapped diffusion of technical knowledge considerably. The form of modern society is largely determined by the current kind of public surface transport and the distribution of public utilities. Both are hampered by the mountainous and volcanic terrain. Yet obstacles bring challenge. It is true that few Latin Americans are credited with contributions to the history of science and invention, though a Brazilian – Alberto Santos-Dumont – was a pioneer of aeronautics and several distinguished names in physiology and medicine (including one Nobel prize-winner) originated there. But this does not mean that Latin Americans have not made important scientific contributions, given the chronic nationalist tinge of such claims and the habitual ignorance among political leaders and writers on such matters. Such developments often remain latent for decades or even centuries.

It is true that Latin American countries have been slow to develop heavy industry. This, however, as others have found, is not a matter wholly in human hands. It is an unfortunate fact that natural resources in the area, though often incredibly rich, are very irregularly distributed. For example, only in Mexico do large deposits of coal and iron ore lie in the same country, and there they occur on opposite sides of the Sierra Madre. Latin America is big. Even in the world's present richest countries, only small areas are heavily industrialised, and the consequences are not all good. Certainly the plight of many of the inhabitants of those areas, whether in Mannheim, Magnitogorsk, Liverpool or Gary, Indiana, leaves much to be desired.

It is doubtful if the slum-dweller in Mexico, after all, is really worse off than his counterpart in Harlem or the Gorbals. The climate is better, so he has less need for visible protection against it, though this is still not to say that his condition is not grim. And the comparison with the United States strengthens the conclusion that the real problem for Latin America remains rural rather than urban poverty. Projects for bettering the peasants' lot have fallen short of success where they have been more concerned with collectivisation or distribution than with the plain necessities of clean water, a guaranteed daily meal, a roof over the family's head and a kerosene lantern to see by, and – most important of all – that they should feel that someone cares. It is the ability to supply the last that is the hallmark of the great reformers.

Economic development and social security in the modern

age are alike too expensive for anything less than the State. The State has not been slow to recognise this in Latin America. Chile had unemployment insurance years before the United States, and Costa Rica universal education long before the USSR. The Mexican system of state planning, introduced in the 1930s, was not the first, even in the Western hemisphere, but unlike that of Great Britain it has actually aided economic growth, and phenomenally so. The centralisation although it accentuates rural poverty by draining off the young into the swollen capital cities, does give some hope for their future betterment. But centralisation necessitates a consciousness of national, as opposed to the old regional identity. This generates the political turbulence which, when used as the vehicle for the cry for social reform, leads to absolute rejection of the only cure by those who, one way or another, will eventually have to pay for it.

Paradoxically, the very strength of nationalism in this sharp and undiffused state is the reason why these societies accept material constructs from the outside world but remain largely impervious to the ideas that accompany them. Thus Latin Americans accept artificial means of birth-control without rejecting the Church's teaching that the use of them is sinful. Under the leadership of priest-revolutionaries, moreover, men are even now fighting for Christian ideals with Chinese weapons. The turbulence of Latin America is the surest sign that no part of it is likely to stand still indefinitely. But it does suggest that much of it may do so for a long time, while individual countries and their inhabitants work for indigenous solutions, to the point of rejecting (if they feel it necessary) all external ideologies and aid.

With these conclusions in mind, some guesses about the future can be hazarded. It has recently been suggested that there is a cyclical pattern in the incidence of Latin American violence, with a periodicity of about twenty years.[27] If this is right, it is now on the decline. The authoritarian régimes of the early sixties then, may well endure for some time to come, particularly since the best prospects for economic growth (and hence for some equalisation of wealth) outside Brazil, lie in Chile, Venezuela, Colombia and Mexico – countries with relatively open societies and quite stable political systems. Brazil's centralisation is likely to generate even more remarkable growth than any previous boom, with the consolidation of the Amazon region, perhaps with the aid of the hovercraft. Natural catastrophe, however, could upset any of these trends. There is a warning in the case of Costa Rica. There the economy is under stress as the result of damage caused by a series of volcanic eruptions such as affect all of Central America from time to time. But these eruptions also hit at the basis of Costa Rica's political stability, for they affect the area where most of her small landholdings cluster.

No predictions can really be made for the whole of an area so vast. One can, however, expect the habit of co-operation – both internal and external – to be extended. It is as well that it should, since human beings have made little progress in any field without it. There are three types of simplistic attitude towards Latin America which are particularly unhelpful. One, common among its own intellectuals, is that of gloom about the future, seen as one of growing poverty and misery, only to be averted by social revolution and the destruction of life that accompanies it. Another, represented by the military, is that future benefits are best secured by the return to past simplicities. A third, widely held in the United States, is that democratic government is desirable, but cannot be secured without the basic ingredient of foreign aid. In each case, some see the alternative as status quo; for others it is that the area will 'go Communist'.

Yet observation of the sort of solutions actually achieved under most forms of political process does not suggest that any of these is a likely outcome. Most political problems do not so much get solved as get lost. Something else intervenes, and the new question supersedes the old, at the point at which the situation has progressed beyond the wish of any substantial number of people to change it.

The future of Latin America will be mixed. It has great handicaps to overcome. But after all, its countries are not as crowded as China and India, as poor as Tanzania or as inaccessible as Nepal. So far they have not lain across the great battle routes of the world, like Czechoslovakia or Finland; and many of them share a common language. It is this last that makes Latin America a unique laboratory for the study of the human condition.

If one final prediction may be ventured, therefore, it is that the rest of the world will increasingly recognise the importance of Latin America and its contribution. In the 'one world' of the not very remote future, it will in its idiosyncratic way play a vital role: one at the same time moderating, dignifying and inspiring.

1. Lieuwen, *Venezuela*, pp. 51–89. Rómulo Gallegos, *Doña Bárbara* in *Obras completas* (Madrid, Aguilar, 1958).

2. Robert A. Alexander, *The Venezuelan Democratic Revolution. A Profile of the Regime of Rómulo Betancourt* (New Brunswick, N.J., Rutgers University Press, 1964), gives a detailed account of the rise and fall of the Pérez Jiménez régime and it successor.

3. John D. Martz, *Colombia, A Contemporary Political Survey*, pp. 33 ff.

4. Jules Dubois, *Freedom is my Beat* (New York, The Bobbs-Merrill Co., 1959) pp. 81 ff.; Martz, *Colombia*, pp. 55–68.

5. Pat M. Holt, *Colombia today – and tomorrow* (New York, Praeger, 1964); Martz, *Colombia*, pp. 162–9; Alan Angell, 'Co-operation and Conflict in Colombian Party Politics', *Political Studies*, xiv, 1 (February 1966) 53.

6. Richard S. Weinert, 'Violence in pre-modern societies: rural Colombia', *A.P.S.R.* lx, 2 (June 1966) 340; Orlando Fals Borda, 'Violence and the Break-Up of Tradition in Colombia', in Claudio Veliz, ed., *Obstacles to Change in Latin America* (London, Oxford University Press, 1965).

7. Robert J. Alexander, *The Perón Era* (London, Gollancz, 1952); George I. Blanksten, *Perón's Argentina* (Chicago, University of Chicago Press, 1953); Albert Conil Paz and Gustavo Ferrari, *Argentina's Foreign Policy, 1930–1962* (Notre Dame, Ind., University of Notre Dame Press, 1966).

8. Arthur P. Whitaker, *Argentine Upheaval: Perón's fall and the new regime* (London, Atlántic Press, 1956).

9. James W. Rowe, 'Whither the Peronists?', in Robert D. Tomasek, ed., *Latin American Politics; studies of the contemporary scene* (Garden City, N.Y., Doubleday Anchor, 1966) p. 429.

10. *The Times*, 29 and 30 June 1966.

11. Pendle, *Paraguay*, cited above, but cf. Leo B. Lott, 'Paraguay' in Needler, *Political Systems of Latin America*, p. 381.

12. Taylor, *Government and Politics of Uruguay*, pp. 33–8.

13. Philip B. Taylor, Jr., 'Interests and Institutional Dysfunction in Uruguay', *A.P.S.R.* lvii, 1 (March 1963) 62.

14. *The Times*, 3 March 1967; Richard Wigg, 'Uruguay fights inflation', *The Times*, 4 March 1968.

15. Gil, op. cit.; see also the same author's *Genesis and modernization of political parties in Chile* (Gainesville, University of Florida Press, 1962).

16. Richard Wigg, 'Why social tension has reached explosion point in Chile', *The Times*, 6 December 1967.

17. Pike, *Peru*, pp. 266; see also James C. Carey, *Peru and the United States, 1900–1962* (Notre Dame, Ind., University of Notre Dame Press, 1964).

18. Lieuwen, *Generals versus Presidents*, pp. 25–36.

19. Richard W. Patch, 'The Peruvian Elections of 1963', in Tomasek, *Latin American Politics*, p. 498.

20. Wood, *The United States and Latin American Wars*, pp. 255 ff.

21. Blanksten, *Ecuador*, pp. 42–57.

22. Martin C. Needler, *Anatomy of a Coup d'État: Ecuador, 1963* (Washington, Institute for the Comparative Study of Political Systems, 1964).

23. See the lively if unconventional work of John Dos Passos, *Brazil on the Move* (London, Sidgwick & Jackson, 1963).

24. J. V. D. Saunders, 'A Revolution of Agreement Among Friends; The End of the Vargas Era', *H.A.H.R.* xliv, 2 (May 1964) 197.

25. Frank Bonilla, 'Jânio Vem Ai: Brazil Elects a President', in Tomasek, *Latin American Politics*, p. 468.

26. Lieuwen, *Generals versus Presidents*, pp. 69–85.

27. Frank H. Denton and Warren Philips, 'Some Patterns in the History of Violence', *Journal of Conflict Resolution*, xii, 2 (June 1968) 182.

Chronological Table

1900		Publication of José Enrique Rodó's *Ariel*
	14 May	Mexico: first strike of oil
1901	12 June	Cuba: the Platt Amendment
	22 October–	Second Inter-American Conference,
1902	31 January	Mexico, D.F.
1902		Publication of Euclides da Cunha's *Os Sertões*
	12 December	Venezuela: naval blockade by Germany, France and Great Britain brings agreement to arbitration
1903	22 January	Colombia and the U.S. sign Hay–Herrán Treaty on Panama Canal, not ratified by Colombia
	3 November	Independence of Panama proclaimed; recognised by U.S., 6 November.
	18 November	By the Hay–Bunau–Varilla Treaty Panama grants the U.S. the right to build and fortify an inter-oceanic canal.
	17 November	Treaty of Petrópolis: Bolivia cedes Acré region to Brazil in return for railway concession
1904	6 May	Ecuador cedes rights in Caquetá region to Brazil
	20 October	Bolivia cedes Tacna, Arica and Tarapacá to Chile
	12 December	Paraguay: Pilcomayo Agreement puts Liberals in power
1905	31 March	U.S. appoints customs' receiver in the Dominican Republic
	5 November	Roosevelt states corollary to Monroe doctrine

1906	29 June	U.S. Congress passes Panama Canal Act
	23 July– 27 August	Third Inter-American Conference, Rio de Janeiro
	26 September	Second intervention by U.S. Government in Cuba; forces withdrawn 1 February 1909
1907	8 February	Dominican Republic cedes control of customs to U.S. by Treaty
	24 April	Colombia cedes Caquetá and Río Negro region to Brazil
	15 June	Second Hague Peace Conference
	13 November– 20 December	Conference of Central American States
1909	8 July	Colombia: Reyes overthrown after signing convention with U.S.
	16 December	Fall of Zelaya in Nicaragua
	19 December	Venezuela: *coup* of Juan Vicente Gómez (1909–35)
1910	12 July– 30 August	Fourth Inter-American Conference, Buenos Aires
	20 November	Outbreak of Mexican Revolution
1911	25 May	Mexico: resignation of Díaz
1912		Argentina: passage of Sáenz Peña Law
	9 January	Honduras; U.S. marines landed to protect Bonilla government
1913	18 February	Mexico: fall of Madero and dictatorship of Huerta (1913–14)
1914	21 April	Mexico: U.S. marines occupy Vera Cruz after Tampico Incident (9 April)
	5 August	Nicaragua and United States sign Bryan-Chamorro Treaty
	15 August	Panama Canal opened to traffic
1915	28 July	Haiti: U.S. forces landed after assassination of Guillaume Sam
	16 September	Haiti: U.S. protectorate established by Treaty

1916		Publication of Mariano Azuela's *Los de Abajo*
		Death of Rubén Dario
	15 March	U.S. dispatches Pershing expedition in search of 'Pancho' Villa in Mexico (troops withdrawn 5 February 1917)
1917	16 January	Dispatch of the Zimmermann Telegram
	27 January	Costa Rica: Tinoco dictatorship (1917–19)
	31 January	Mexico: Adoption of the Constitution of 1917
	8 March	Cuba: U.S. forces landed to safeguard elections; Menocal re-elected
	6 April	U.S. enters Great War
	26 October	Brazil declares war on Germany
1918	10 March	Dissolution of Central American Court
1919		Publication of Alcides Argüedas's *Raza de Bronce*, Rómulo Gallegos's *Doña Bárbara* and Laureano Valenilla Lanz's *Cesarismo Democrático*
	1 March	Uruguay: creation of National Council
	4 June	Costa Rica: U.S. intervention on fall of Tinoco (6 May)
	4 July	Peru: fall of Pardo and rise of Leguía (1919–30)
	11 September	Honduras: U.S. intervention on fall of Bertrand
1920	8 April	Guatemala: deposition by Congress of Estrada Cabrera (1898–1920)
	21 May	Carranza murdered at Tlaxcalantongo, Mexico: rise of the 'Sonora dynasty' (1920–35)
1921	19 January	Central American Pact of Union signed at San José, Costa Rica
	20 April	U.S. Senate ratifies Thomson–Urrutia Treaty between U.S. and Colombia

	18 August	Panama cedes Coto district to Costa Rica
1923	25 March–3 May	Fifth Inter-American Conference, Santiago de Chile
	3 May	Treaty to Avoid or Prevent Conflicts between the American States (Gondra Treaty)
1924	5 July	Brazil: revolt in São Paulo
	5 September	Chile: fall of Alessandri and end of the 'Parliamentary Republic'
1925		Publication of José Vasconcelos's *La Raza Cósmica*
1926	2 May	Nicaragua: Sandino's revolt
	14 June	Brazil withdraws from League of Nations
	28 July	Unratified Treaty between Panama and U.S. signed
1927	11 February	Mexico: nationalisation of Church property by Calles; outbreak of Cristero revolt
	6 May	Chile: dictatorship of Ibáñez (1927–1930)
1928		Publication of José Carlos Mariátegui's *Siete ensayos de interpretación de la realidad peruana*
	16 January–20 February	Sixth Inter-American Conference, La Habana
1929	5 January	General Treaty of Inter-American Arbitration
	3 June	By Treaty of Lima Chile cedes Tacna to Peru together with indemnity for Arica
1930	23 February	Dominican Republic: Trujillo seizes power (1930–61)
	7 August	Inauguration of Olaya Herrera and return of Liberals to power (1930–46) in Colombia

	6 September	Argentina: fall of Irigoyen and beginning of military rule 1930–45
	30 October	Brazil: revolt in Rio Grande do Sul brings Getúlio Vargas to power (1930–45)
1931	14 February	Guatemala: Jorge Ubico elected President (1931–44)
	2 December	El Salvador: Maximilano Hernández Martínez becomes President (1931–1944)
1932	4 June–13 September	Chile: the 'Socialist Republic'
	15 June	Incident at Fortín Carlos Antonio López leads to outbreak of Chaco War between Paraguay and Bolivia
	31 August	Peruvian troops capture Colombian town of Leticia
1933		Publication of Gilberto Freyre's *Casa-Grande e Senzala* ('Masters and Slaves')
	1 February	Honduras: Carías Andino President (1933–48)
	4 March	Roosevelt proclaims the 'Good Neighbor' policy of the United States
	31 March	Uruguay: Terra dissolves Congress, proclaims emergency dictatorship
	12 August	Cuba: Machado overthrown by student revolt
	3–26 December	Seventh Inter-American Conference, Montevideo
1934	29 May	Cuba: U.S. abrogation of Platt Amendment
	6 August	Haiti: Withdrawal of U.S. forces
	1 December	Mexico: Lázaro Cárdenas becomes President (1934–40)
1935	14 June	Truce in Chaco War between Paraguay and Bolivia
	27 September	Peru and Colombia settle Leticia dispute by ratification of Protocol of Rio de Janeiro (1935)

	18 December	Venezuela: death of Gómez
1936		Carlos Saavedra Lamas (Argentina) awarded Nobel Prize for Peace
	17 February	Paraguay: Franco dictatorship established
	2 March	Panama and United States sign Treaty modifying status of Canal
	17 May	Bolivia: Toro dictatorship established
	2 June	Nicaragua: Sacasa overthrown by National Guard under Anastasio Somoza (1936–56)
	1–23 December	Inter-American Conference for the Maintenance of Peace, Buenos Aires
1937	March	Bolivia: nationalisation of oil property
	23 June	Mexico: railways put under workers' control
	10 November	Brazil: *Estado Novo* proclaimed by Vargas
1938	18 March	Mexico: expropriation of foreign oil companies
	21 July	Paraguay and Bolivia sign peace treaty ending Chaco War
	9–27 December	Eighth Inter-American Conference, Lima
	24 December	Declaration of Lima on resistance to outside subversion
	24 December	Chile: inauguration of 'Popular Front' government of Aguirre Cerda (1938–42)
1939	23 September	First Meeting of Consultation of American Foreign Ministers, Panama
1940	21 July	Second Meeting of Consultation, Havana
	4 December	Inter-American Peace Committee established
1941	5 July	Outbreak of fighting in Marañón region between Peru and Ecuador
	7 December	U.S. enters Second World War

1942	1 January	Declaration of the United Nations
	31 March	Ratification of Protocol of Rio de Janeiro (1942) ends temporarily dispute between Peru and Ecuador
1943	19 December	Bolivia: fall of Peñaranda and emergence of MNR
1944	8 May	El Salvador: fall of Hernández Martínez
	1 July	Guatemala: Fall of Ubico
1945		Gabriela Mistral (Chile) awarded Nobel Prize for Literature
	21 February– 8 March	Inter-American Conference on Problems of War and Peace, Mexico D.F. (Act of Chapultepec)
		Argentina: election of Perón (1945–55)
1946		Publication of Miguel Angel Asturias's *El Señor Presidente*
	7 August	Colombia: inauguration of Ospina Pérez, return to Conservative rule 1946–53
1947		B. A. Houssay (Argentina) awarded Nobel Prize for Physiology and Medicine
	2 September	Signature of Rio Pact
1948	February	Establishment of United Nations Economic Commission for Latin America (ECLA)
	30 March– 2 May	Ninth Inter-American Conference, Bogotá
	9 April	Colombia: assassination of Gaitán; the *Bogotazo*
	19 April	Costa Rica: fall of Picado and establishment of 'Second Republic'
	December	Costa Rica invaded by Nicaragua
1949		Publication of Raul Prebisch's *Economic Development of Latin America and its Principal Problems*

1950	25 June	Outbreak of Korean War; Colombia sends troops
1951	10 May	Panama: dictatorship of Remón (1951–55)
1952	1 March	Uruguay: abolition of presidency and installation of Conciliar government (1952–67)
	10 March	Cuba: Batista seizes power (1952–1959) in own name
	October	Bolivia: nationalisation of tin mines
	30 November	Venezuela: dictatorship of Pérez Jiménez
1953		Colombia: Dictatorship of Rojas Pinilla (1963–57)
1954	1–28 March	Tenth Inter-American Conference, Caracas
	27 June	Guatemala: resignation of Arbenz
	24 August	Brazil: suicide of Getúlio Vargas
1955	January	Costa Rica and Nicaragua boundary dispute
		Publication of Juan José Avévalo's *Fabula del Tiburón y las Sardinas*
1956	29 September	Nicaragua: assassination of Somoza
1957	May	Honduras invaded by Nicaragua
1958	8 May	Peru: U.S. Vice-President Nixon stoned at San Marcos University; mobbed in Caracas on 13 May
	7 August	Colombia: restoration of constitutional government under Pact of Sitges
1959	1 January	Cuba: fall of Batista
1960	21 April	Brazil: capital transferred to Brasília
1961		Publication of Ernesto ('Ché') Guevara's *La Guerra de Guerrillas*
	16 March	United States: President Kennedy announces Alliance for Progress
	17 April	The Bay of Pigs
	30 May	Dominican Republic: assassination of Trujillo

	5–17 August	Punta del Este Conference on economic development
	25 August	Brazil: resignation of Quadros
	18 November	Dominican Republic: U.S. forces dispatched to eliminate Trujillos
	20 December	Cuba: Castro proclaims himself a Marxist-Leninist
1962	22 January	Eighth Meeting of Consultation, Punta del Este
1962	29 March	Argentina: military overthrow Frondizi
	18 July	Peru: military seize power
	22 October	President Kennedy makes public statement on Cuban missile crisis
1964	2 April	Brazil: military overthrow Goulart
	4 November	Bolivia: Air Force seize power from Paz Estenssoro
1965	25 April	Dominican Republic: outbreak of civil war, followed by U.S. intervention
1966	2 March	Uruguay returns to Presidential rule
	29 June	Argentina: military seize power
		Miguel Ángel Asturias (Guatemala) awarded Nobel Prize for Literature
1967	15 February	Third Special Inter-American Conference, Buenos Aires
	9 October	Bolivia: 'Ché' Guevara killed near Camiri
1968	12 October	XIX Olympic Games opened, Mexico

Bibliography

THE historian of recent Latin America faces a serious shortage of sources. Official documents are scare, inaccessible and singularly uninformative. Memoirs are rare because few people can write them and continue to live in their own countries, and the same consideration extends in many places to historians of the twentieth century in general. The great Latin American historians – Jorge Basadre of Peru, Francisco Antonio Encina of Chile, Daniel Cosío Villegas of Mexico – have produced works of the first rank, but they stop short of the period covered by this book. Scholarly journals, too, concentrate on the colonial and early national period. Periodicals and ephemera are beyond the reach of anyone except the local specialist.

It is for these reasons (and not just for the convenience of readers) that so many references here are made to English language works, especially from the United States. There both the inclination and the freedom to publish are extensive and universities have been quick to translate major works of literary and social significance. Translations, where available, have been cited here in preference to the originals, for which translations, however good, are no real substitute.

I. INTRODUCTORY

The following deal with Latin America in general and in various aspects:

BENHAM F., and HOLLEY, H. A., *A Short Introduction to the Economy of Latin America*. (London, O.U.P. for R.I.I.A., 1960). Deals with the period since 1930.

BLAKEMORE, Harold, *Latin America* (London, O.U.P., 1966). Excellent brief review.

CLISSOLD, Stephen, *Latin America, A Cultural Outline* (London, Hutchinson Univ. Library, 1965). Attractive and informative.

DOZER, Donald M., *Latin America, an Interpretive History* (New York, McGraw-Hill, 1962). Panoramic view; full of insight but difficult to place events.

HUELIN, David, 'Economic Integration in Latin America: Progress and Problems', *International Affairs*, xl, 3 (July 1964) 430. Useful overview.

HUMPHREYS, R. A., *The Evolution of Modern Latin America* (Oxford, Clarendon Press, 1946). The classical introduction to Latin American history.

JAMES, Preston E., *Latin America*, 2nd ed. (New York, Odyssey Press, 1950). Geography of Latin America; a necessary reference work.

LIEUWEN, Edwin, *Generals versus Presidents: Neomilitarism in Latin America* (London, Pall Mall Press, 1964). A *pièce d'occasion*: useful for facts but its thesis that a new kind of militarism has emerged is disputable.

NEEDLER, Martin C., ed., *Political Systems of Latin America* (Princeton, Van Nostrand, 1964). Country by country studies: that of C. A. M. Hennessy on Cuba is particularly worth reading.

PENDLE, George, *A History of Latin America* (London, Penguin Books, 1964). A delightful and lively study.

STOETZER, O. Carlos, *The Organisation of American States, An Introduction* (New York, Praeger, 1965). Wholly factual.

STOKES, William S., *Latin American Politics*. New York, Thomas Y. Crowell. 1959. The best introduction; somewhat unfinished treatment reflects uncertainty of scholars as a whole on what the field includes.

TOMASEK, Robert D., ed., *Latin American Politics: studies of the contemporary scene* (Garden City, N.Y., Doubleday Anchor, 1966). Valuable collection of articles reprinted from various learned journals.

On the history of Spain and Portugal the following are essential:

CARR, Raymond, *Spain, 1808–1939* (Oxford, Clarendon Press, 1966).

LIVERMORE, H. V., *A New History of Portugal* (Cambridge, C.U.P., 1966).

LYNCH, John, *Spain under the Habsburgs*, 2 vols (Oxford, Blackwell, 1964–   ).

The individual states of Latin America are being covered by a unique Chatham House series which combines historical, geographical and economic information under one cover. Variations in treatment are considerable but all are very useful.

BUTLAND, Gilbert J., *Chile, an Outline of its Geography, Economics and Politics*, 3rd ed. (London, O.U.P. for R.I.I.A., 1956).

CLINE, Howard F., *Mexico, Revolution to Evolution 1940–1960* (London, O.U.P. for R.I.I.A., 1962).

GALBRAITH, W. O., *Colombia, a general survey* (London, O.U.P. for R.I.I.A., 1953).

LIEUWEN, Edwin, *Venezuela* (London, O.U.P. for R.I.I.A., 1961).

LINKE, Lilo, *Ecuador, Country of Contrasts*, 2nd ed. (London, O.U.P. for R.I.I.A., 1955).

OSBORNE, Harold, *Bolivia, a land divided*, 3rd ed. (London, O.U.P. for R.I.I.A., 1963).

PARKER, Franklin D., *The Central American Republics* (London, O.U.P. for R.I.I.A., 1964).

PENDLE, George, *Argentina*, 2nd ed. (London, O.U.P. for R.I.I.A., 1961).

— *Paraguay, a riverside nation* (London, O.U.P. for R.I.I.A., 1956).

2. WRITINGS BY LATIN AMERICAN AUTHORS

The following are works by Latin American authors which have a particular significance to the history of political thought in the continent. The list is by no means exhaustive. Characteristically, some are severely factual and others convey their message in fictional form.

ARÉVALO, Juan José, *Fábula del Tiburón y las Sardinas*, *América Latina estrangulada*, 3rd ed. (Mexico, Editorial América Nueva, 1956).

ARGÜEDAS, Alcides, *Raza de bronce* (La Paz, González y Medina, 1919).

ASTURIAS, Miguel Ángel, *The President*, trans. Frances Partridge (London, Gollancz, 1963).

AZUELA, Mariano, *Los de abajo* (Mexico, Fondo de Cultura Económica, 1958).

da CUNHA, Euclides, *Rebellion in the Backlands* (*Os Sertões*), trans. Samuel Putnam (Chicago, Univ. of Chicago Press, Phoenix Books, 1944).

FREYRE, Gilberto, *Masters and Slaves*, trans. Samuel Putnam (New York, Knopf, 1946).

GALLEGOS, Rómulo, *Dõna Bárbara*, in *Obras completas* (Madrid, Aguilar, 1958).

GUEVARA, Ernesto ('Ché'), *Guerrilla Warfare* (New York, Monthly Review Press, 1961).

MARIÁTEGUI, José Carlos, *Siete ensayos de interpretación de la realidad peruana* (Santiago de Chile, Ed. Universitaria, 1955).

VALENILLA LANZ, Laureano, *Cesarismo democrático, estudios sobre las bases sociólogicas de la constitución efectiva de Venezuela* (Caracas, Empresas Cojo, 1919).

VASCONCELOS, José, *La raza cósmica, misión de la raza Iberoamericana* (Madrid, Aguilar, 1967).

3. MEMOIRS

In a survey like this which strives to present a picture of a whole continent and twenty different states, the major sources of references are necessarily the works of numerous historians and other descriptive writers. Some memoirs, however, do have direct relevance to the main themes. Among them are:

ARCE de VAZQUEZ, Margot, *Gabriela Mistral, the Poet and her work*, trans. Helene Masslo Anderson (New York, New York U.P., 1964). Most accessible source for first woman and first Latin American to win Nobel Prize for Literature.

BATISTA Y ZALDIVAR, Fulgencio, *Cuba Betrayed* (New York, Vantage Press, 1962). Apologies for dictatorship, mainly economic.

BUNAU-VARILLA, Philippe, *Panama: the creation, destruction and resurrection* (London, Constable, 1913). Account of the creation of Panama by the big figure in its twilight diplomacy.

DEBRAY, Régis, *Revolution in the Revolution?* (London, Monthly Review Press, 1967). Advocate for continental guerrilla warfare more honoured in Europe than in Latin America.

EISENHOWER, Dwight D., *The White House Years, Waging Peace, 1956–1961* (Garden City, N.Y., Doubleday, 1965). Reminds the reader that the U.S. has other problems and preoccupations.

GUEVARA, Ernesto ('Ché'), *Reminiscences of the Cuban Revolutionary War*, trans. Victoria Ortiz (London, Allen & Unwin and Monthly Review Press, 1968). Includes post-1959 letters, of businesslike brevity.

HOHLER, Sir Thomas Beaumont, *Diplomatic Petrel* (London, Murray, 1942). Covers Mexico 1911–17.

HOOVER, Herbert, *The Memoirs of Herbert Hoover: The Cabinet and the Presidency, 1920–1933* (London, Hollis & Carter, 1952). Dull.

HULL, Cordell, *The Memoirs of Cordell Hull* (London, Hodder & Stoughton, 1948). Little of relevance; significant coming from FDR's Secretary of State, the longest serving holder of that office in history.

LOPEZ-FRESQUET, Rufo, *My 14 months with Castro* (Cleveland & New York, The World Publishing Co, 1966). Title misleading. By the Finance Minister of the interim government 1959–60 and an opponent of Castro.

MORRISON, De Lesseps S., *Latin American Mission, An Adventure in Hemisphere Diplomacy*, ed. and intro. Gerold Frank (New York, Simon & Schuster, 1965). Posthumous fragment with much value for Kennedy diplomacy.

PORTES GIL, Emilio, *Quince Años de Política Mexicana* (Mexico, Ediciones Botas, 1941). By the big figure in the institutionalisation of the Revolution, 1928–36.

SCHLESINGER, Arthur M., Jr., *A Thousand Days: John F. Kennedy in the White House* (London, André Deutsch, 1965). An account by a peripheral member of the Kennedy Administration, though a historian of great distinction.

SORENSON, Theodore C., *Kennedy* (London, Hodder & Stoughton, 1965). The definitive memoir by the President's speechwriter.

VASCONCELOS, José, *A Mexican Ulysses, an autobiography*, trans. and ed. W. Rex Crawford (Bloomington, Indiana U.P., 1963). Unexpurgated reminiscences of celebrated thinker, Minister of Education 1920–4, and unsuccessful presidential candidate.

WILSON, Hugh, *The Education of a Diplomat* (London, Longmans, 1938). Unique description of Guatemala under Estrada Cabrera.

YDIGORAS FUENTES, Miguel, *My War with Communism* 'as told to' Mario Rosenthal (Englewood Cliffs, N.J., Prentice-Hall, 1963).

YNSFRAN, P. M., ed., *The Epic of the Chaco: Marshal Estigarribia's memoirs of the Chaco War, 1932–1935* (Austin, Univ. of Texas Press, 1950).

4. CONTEMPORARY STUDIES

The main sources in all periods for all dubious events are files of newspapers, and in particular here those of *The Times*, *The Guardian*, *The New York Times*, *Le Monde* and *The Economist*, which have not in general been cited separately. Accounts by visitors and travellers are relatively commonplace nowadays. Some of the earlier ones, however, are indispensable, and some more recent ones have value where nothing else is easily accessible.

DENIS, Pierre, *Brazil* (London, Fisher Unwin, 1911).

DOS PASSOS, John, *Brazil on the move* (London, Sidgwick & Jackson, 1963).

DUBOIS, Jules, *Danger over Panama* (New York, The Bobbs-Merrill Co., 1964).

— *Freedom is my Beat* (New York, The Bobbs-Merrill Co., 1959).

GUNTHER, John, *Inside Latin America* (New York and London, Harper Bros, 1940).

HOLT, Pat M., *Colombia today – and tomorrow* (New York, Praeger, 1964).

INMAN, Samuel Guy, *A New Day in Guatemala, a study of the present social revolution* (Wilton, Conn., Worldover Press, 1951).

JAMES, H. G., *Brazil after a Century of Independence* (New York, Macmillan, 1925).

KELSEY, Vera, and OSBORNE, Lily de Jongh, *Four Keys to Guatemala*, 2nd ed. (New York, Funk & Wagnalls, 1945).

KOEBEL, W. H., *Central America: Guatemala, Nicaragua, Costa Rica, Honduras, Panama and Salvador* (London, Fisher Unwin, 1917).

— *Modern Chile* (London, Bell, 1913).

— *Uruguay* (London, Fisher Unwin, 1911).

MAUDSLAY, Anne Cary and Alfred Percival, *A Glimpse at Guatemala and some notes on the ancient monuments of Central America* (London, J. Murray, 1899).

MUNRO, Dana Gardner, *The Five Republics of Central America. Their political and economic development and their relations with the United States* (New York, O.U.P., 1918).

OSBORNE, Lily de Jongh, *Four Keys to El Salvador* (New York, Funk & Wagnalls, 1956).

PRICHARD, H. Hesketh, *Where Black rules White: A Journey Across and About Hayti* (London, Thomas Nelson, 1910).

WALLE, Paul, *Bolivia, its people and its resources . . .* (London, Fisher Unwin, 1914).

5. SECONDARY SOURCES

The following cover aspects common to all or several Latin American countries:

ALBA, Víctor, *Politics and the Labor Movement in Latin America* (Stanford, Stanford U.P., 1968).

CASTILLO, C. M., *Growth and Integration in Central America* (London, Pall Mall, 1967).

HANKE, Lewis H., *Aristotle and the American Indians: A Study in Race Prejudice in the Modern World* (London, Hollis & Carter, 1959).

HARING, C. H., *The Spanish Empire in America* (New York, O.U.P., 1952, revd.).

HUDSON, M. O., 'The Central American Court of Justice', *American Journal of International Law*, xxvi (1932) 759.

HUMPHREYS, R. A., 'Latin America, The Caudillo Tradition', in Michael Howard, ed., *Soldiers and Governments. Nine studies in civil-military relations* (London, Eyre & Spottiswoode. 1957).

SIMON, S. Fanny, 'Anarchism and Anarcho-Syndicalism in South America', *H.A.H.R.* xxvi, 1 (February 1946) 38.

WILGUS, A. Curtis, *South American Dictators during the First Century of Independence* (New York, Russell & Russell, 1963).

WIONCZEC, Miguel S., *Latin American Integration: Experiences and Prospects* (New York, Praeger, 1966).

Under the same heading come a selection of the large number of works dealing with the relations between Latin American countries and the United States. Those dealing with the United States as such (with only occasional references to Latin America) have been omitted.

BEMIS, Samuel Flagg, *The Latin American Policy of the United States, An Historical Interpretation* (New York, Harcourt Brace, 1943). The classical history.

BORCHARD, Edwin M., 'Calvo and Drago Doctrines', in *Encyclopedia of the Social Sciences* (New York, Macmillan, 1930).

CONNELL-SMITH, Gordon, *The Inter-American System* (London, O.U.P. for R.I.I.A., 1966). Most comprehensive account.

DECONDE, Alexander, *Herbert Hoover's Latin American Policy* (Stanford, Stanford U.P., 1951). The crucial period for the abandonment of intervention.

DUGGAN, Lawrence, *The Americas. The search for hemispheric security* (New York, Holt, 1949).

MARTZ, John D., *Central America, the crisis and the challenge* (Chapel Hill, Univ. of North Carolina Press, 1959). Good on individual countries; rather alarmist in context of 'Cold War'.

MUNRO, Dana Gardner, *Intervention and Dollar Diplomacy in the Caribbean 1900–1921* (Princeton, Princeton U.P., 1964). Of great value, as is nearest and most reliable source on big events in Central American history.

NETTLES, H. Edward, 'The Drago Doctrine in International Law and Politics', *H.A.H.R.* viii (May 1928) 204.

PERKINS, Dexter, *A History of the Monroe Doctrine* (London, Longmans, 1960, revised edition). Authoritative study; not, however, the Doctrine as seen by Latin Americans.

SANDS, W. F., *Our Jungle Diplomacy* (Chapel Hill, Univ. of North Carolina Press, 1944). Refers to Caribbean.

SHEA, D. R., *The Calvo Clause. A problem of inter-American and international law and diplomacy* (Minneapolis, Univ. of Minnesota Press, 1955). A small but important aspect given full critical treatment.

WILLIAMS, M. W., *Anglo-American Isthmian Diplomacy, 1815–1915* (Washington, American Historical Association, 1915).

WHITAKER, Arthur P., *The Western Hemisphere Idea: its rise and decline* (Ithaca, Cornell U.P., 1954). Vital and interesting; complements Connell-Smith above.

WISE, David, and ROSS, Thomas B., *The invisible government* (London, Cape, 1965). Journalistic work on the U.S. Central Intelligence Agency, highly coloured.

WOOD, Bryce, *The Making of the Good Neighbor Policy* (New York, Columbia U.P., 1961). Its evolution, 1933–9.

— *The United States and Latin American Wars, 1932–1942* (New York, Columbia U.P., 1966). Essential.

A few works deal with relations between Latin American states:

BOX, P. H., *The Origins of the Paraguayan War*, Studies in the Social Sciences, 15 (Urbana, Univ. of Illinois Press, 1929).

DENNIS, W. J., *Tacna and Arica. An account of the Chile Peruvian boundary dispute and of its arbitration by the United States* (New Haven, Yale U.P., 1931).

GANZERT, F. W., 'The Boundary Controversy in the Upper Amazon between Brazil, Bolivia and Peru, 1903-8', *H.A.H.R.* xiv, 4 (November 1934) 427.

MARKHAM, Clements R., *The War between Peru and Chile, 1879-1882* (London, Sampson Law, Marston & Co. n.d.).

TAMBS, Lewis A., 'Geopolitical factors in Latin America', Norman A. Bailey, ed., *Latin America, Politics, Economics, and Hemispheric Security* (New York, Frederick A. Praeger for the Center for Strategic Studies, 1965) p. 31.

On individual countries, the following are listed in alphabetical order of country. Sources dealing wholly with events before 1900 are cited where appropriate, but not listed here.

Argentina

ALEXANDER, Robert J., *The Perón Era* (London, Gollancz, 1952).

BLANKSTEN, George I., *Perón's Argentina* (Chicago, Univ. of Chicago Press, 1953).

GREENUP, Ruth and Leonard, *Revolution before Breakfast: Argentina 1941-1946* (Chapel Hill, Univ. of North Carolina Press, 1947).

HASBROUCK, Alfred, 'The Argentine Revolution of 1930', *H.A.H.R.* xviii, 3 (August 1938) 285.

McGANN, Thomas F., *Argentina, the United States and the Inter-American System, 1880-1914* (Cambridge, Mass., Harvard Univ. Press, 1957).

PAZ, Albert Conil, and FERRARI, Gustavo, *Argentina's Foreign Policy, 1930-1962* (Notre Dame, Ind., Univ. of Notre Dame Press, 1966).

PHELPS, V. L., *The International Economic Position of Argentina* (Philadelphia, Univ. of Pennsylvania Press, 1938).

ROMERO, José Luis, *A history of Argentine political thought*, intro. and trans. Thomas F. McGann (Stanford, Stanford U.P., 1963).

WHITAKER, Arthur P., *Argentina* (Englewood Cliffs, N.J., Prentice-Hall, 1964).
— *Argentine Upheaval: Perón's fall and the new regime* (London, Atlantic Press, 1956).

Bolivia

ALEXANDER, Robert J., *The Bolivian National Revolution* (New Brunswick, N.J., Rutgers U.P., 1958).
FINOT, Enrique, *Nueva Historia de Bolivia. Ensayo de Interpretación Sociólogica* (Buenos Aires, Imprenta López, 1946).
JAMES, Daniel, ed, *The Complete Bolivian Diaries of Ché Guevara and other captured documents* (London, Allen & Unwin, 1968).
KLEIN, Herbert S., 'American oil companies in Latin America: the Bolivian experience', *Inter-American Economic Affairs*, xviii, 2 (Autumn 1964) 47.
— 'David Toro and the Establishment of "Military Socialism" in Bolivia', *H.A.H.R.* xlv, 1 (February 1965) 25.
PATCH, Richard W., 'Bolivia: U.S. Assistance in a Revolution Setting', in Richard N. Adams, ed., *Social Change in Latin America Today* (New York, Harper & Row for Council on Foreign Relations, 1960) p. 108.

Brazil

BELLO, José María, *A History of Modern Brazil, 1889–1964* (Stanford, Stanford U.P., 1966).
LOEWENSTEIN, Kurt, *Brazil under Vargas* (New York, Macmillan, 1942).
MELBY, John, 'Rubber River: An Account of the Rise and Collapse of the Amazon Boom', *H.A.H.R.* xxii, 3 (August 1942) 452.
SAUNDERS, J. V. D., 'A Revolution of Agreement Among Friends: The End of the Vargas Era', *H.A.H.R.* xliv, 2 (May 1964) 197.
SKIDMORE, Thomas E., *Politics in Brazil, 1930–1964; an Experiment in Democracy* (New York, O.U.P., 1967).
WIRTH, John D., 'Tenentismo in the Brazilian Revolution of 1930', *H.A.H.R.* xliv, 2 (May 1964) 161.

YOUNG, Jordan M., *The Brazilian Revolution of 1930 and the Aftermath* (New Brunswick, N.J., Rutgers U.P., 1967).
— 'Military Aspects of the 1930 Brazilian Revolution', *H.A.H.R.* xliv, 2 (May 1964) 180.

Chile

BLAKEMORE, Harold, 'The Chilean Revolution of 1891 and its historiography', *H.A.H.R.* xlv, 2 (August 1965) 393.
GALDAMES, Luis, *A history of Chile*, trans. and ed. I. J. Cox (New York, Russell & Russell 1964).
GIL, Federico, *Genesis and modernisation of political parties in Chile* (Gainesville, Univ. of Florida Press, 1962).
— *The Political System of Chile* (Boston, Houghton Mifflin, 1966).
HARING, Clarence Henry, 'Chilean Politics, 1920–1928', *H.A.H.R.* xi, 1 (February 1931) 1.
— 'The Chilean Revolution of 1931', *H.A.H.R.* xlii, 2 (May 1933) 197.
NUNN, Frederick M., 'Military Rule in Chile, The Revolutions of September 5, 1924, and January 23, 1925', *H.A.H.R.* xlvii,1 (February 1967) 1.
PIKE, Frederick B., *Chile and the United States, 1800–1962; the emergence of Chile's social crisis and the challenge to United States diplomacy* (Notre Dame, Ind., Univ. of Notre Dame Press, 1963).
PINTO SANTA CRUZ, Aníbal, *Chile, un caso de desarrollo frustrado* (Santiago, Editorial Universitaria, 1962).
STEVENSON, J. R., *The Chilean Popular Front* (Philadelphia, Univ. of Pennsylvania Press, 1942).
THOMAS, Jack Ray, 'The socialist republic of Chile', *J.I.A.S.* vi, 2 (April 1964) 203.

Colombia

ANGELL, Alan, 'Co-operation and Conflict in Colombian Party Politics', *Political Studies*, xiv, 1 (February 1966).
CALVERT, Peter A. R., 'The Murray Contract: An Episode in International Finance and Diplomacy', *P.H.R.* xxxv, 2 (May 1966) 203.

FALS BORDA, Orlando, 'Violence and the Break-Up of Tradition in Colombia', in Claudio Veliz, ed., *Obstacles to Change in Latin America* (London, O.U.P., 1965).

FLUHARTY, Vernon Lee, *Dance of the Millions: Military Rule and the Social Revolution in Colombia, 1930–1956* (Pittsburgh, Univ. of Pittsburgh Press, 1957).

HENAO, J. M., and ARRUBLA, G., *History of Colombia*, trans. and e.d J. F. Rippy. (Chapel Hill, Univ. of North Carolina Press, 1938.)

MARTZ, John D., *Colombia, A Contemporary Political Survey* (Chapel Hill, Univ. of North Carolina Press, 1962).

MINER, D. C., *The Fight for the Panama Route, The story of the Spooner Act and the Hay-Herrán Treaty* (New York, Columbia U.P., 1940).

RIPPY, J. F., *The Capitalists and Colombia* (New York, Vanguard Press, 1931).

WEINERT, Richard S., 'Violence in pre-modern societies: rural Colombia', *A.P.S.R.* lx, 2 (June 1966) 340.

Costa Rica

BUSEY, James L., 'Foundations of Political Contrast: Costa Rica and Nicaragua', *Western Political Quarterly*, xi, 3 (September 1958) 627.

— *Notes on Costa Rican democracy* (Boulder, Univ. of Colorado Press, 1962).

JONES, Chester Lloyd, *Costa Rica and civilisation in the Caribbean* (Madison, Univ. of Wisconsin Press, 1935).

MAY, Stacy, *et al.*, *Costa Rica, a study in economic development* (New York, Twentieth Century Fund, 1952).

STEPHENSON, Paul G., ed., *Costa Rica Election Factbook February 6, 1966* (Washington, Institute for the Comparative Study of Political Systems, 1966).

Cuba

BUELL, R. L., *et al.*, *Problems of the new Cuba* (New York, Foreign Policy Association, 1935).

CHESTER, Edmund A., *A Sergeant Named Batista* (New York, Holt, 1954).

CRONON, E. David, 'Interpreting the New Good Neighbor Policy, Cuban Crisis of 1933', *H.A.H.R.* xxxix, 4 (November 1959) 538.

DRAPER, Theodore, *Castro's Revolution, Myths and Realities* (New York, Praeger, 1962).

FITZGIBBON, Russell H., *Cuba and the United States, 1900–1935* (New York, Russell & Russell, 1964).

— 'The Revolution Next Door: Cuba', *Annals of the American Academy of Political and Social Science*, cccxxxiv (March 1961) 113.

GOLDENBERG, Boris, *The Cuban Revolution and Latin America* (London, Allen & Unwin, 1965).

GRAY, Richard Butler, *José Martí, Cuban Patriot* (Gainesville, Univ. of Florida Press, 1962).

HAGEDORN, Hermann, *Leonard Wood, a biography* (New York, Harper Bros, 1938).

HEALY, David, *The United States in Cuba, 1898–1902; Generals, Politicians and the Search for Policy* (Madison, Univ. of Wisconsin Press, 1963).

HUBERMAN, Leo, and SWEEZY, Paul, *Cuba: Anatomy of a Revolution* (New York, Monthly Review Press, 1960).

MAYER, Leo J., 'The United States and the Cuban Revolution of 1917', *H.A.H.R.* x, 2 (May 1930) 138.

MILLET, Allan Read, *The Politics of Intervention; the military occupation of Cuba 1906–1909* (Columbus, Ohio State U.P., 1968).

PACHTER, Henry M., *Collision Course: The Cuban Missile Crisis and Coexistence* (London, Pall, Mall, 1963).

RAUCH, Basil, *American Interest in Cuba, 1848–1855* (New York, Columbia U.P., 1948).

STOKES, William S., 'The Cuban Parliamentary System in Action, 1940–47', *Journal of Politics*, xi (1949) 335.

— 'Parliamentary Government in Latin America', *A.P.S.R.* xxxix, 2 (June 1945) 522.

Dominican Republic

BOSCH, Juan, *The Unfinished Experiment, Democracy in the Dominican Republic* (London, Pall Mall, 1966).

KELSEY, Carl, 'The American Intervention in Haiti and the Dominican Republic.' *Annals of the American Academy of Political and Social Science*, c (March 1922) 109.

ORNES, Germán E., *Trujillo: Little Caesar of the Caribbean* (New York, Nelson, 1958).

RIPPY, J. F., 'The Initiation of the Customs Receivership in the Dominican Republic', *H.A.H.R.* xvii, 4 (November 1937) 419.

WELLES, Sumner, *Naboth's Vineyard: the Dominican Republic, 1844-1924* (New York, Payson & Clarke, 1928).

Ecuador

BLANKSTEN, George I., *Ecuador: Constitutions and Caudillos* (New York, Russell & Russell, 1964).

NEEDLER, Martin C., *Anatomy of a Coup d'État: Ecuador, 1963* (Washington, Institute for the Comparative Study of Political Systems, 1964).

PARKS, Lois F., and NUEREMBERGER, Gustave A., 'The Sanitation of Guayaquil', *H.A.H.R.* xxiii, 2 (May 1943) 197.

REYES, Oscar Efren, *Historia de la República, Esquema de ideas y hechos del Ecuador a partir de la Emancipación* (Quito, Imprenta Nacional, 1931).

Guatemala

JOHNSON, Kenneth F., *The Guatemalan Presidential Election of March 6, 1966; an analysis* (Washington, Institute for the Comparative Study of Political Systems, n.d.).

JONES, Chester Lloyd, *Guatemala, past and present* (Minneapolis, Univ. of Minnesota Press, 1940; New York, Russell & Russell, 1966).

ROSENTHAL, Mario, *Guatemala, the Story of an Emergent Latin American Democracy* (New York, Twayne, 1963).

SCHNEIDER, Ronald M., *Communism in Guatemala 1944-1954* (New York, Praeger, 1959).

SILVERT, Kalman H., *A Study in Government: Guatemala* (New Orleans, Middle American Research Institute, Tulane Univ., Publication No. 21, 1954).

Haiti

LEYBURN, J. G., *The Haitian People* (New Haven, Yale U.P., 1941).

MILLSPAUGH, A. C., *Haiti under American Control, 1915–30* (Boston, World Peace Foundation, 1931).

Honduras

STOKES, William S., *Honduras, an area study in government* (Madison, Univ. of Wisconsin Press, 1950).

WRIGHT, Theodore P., Jr., 'Honduras, a Case Study of United States Support of Free Elections in Central America', *H.A.H.R.* xl, 2 (May 1960) 212.

Mexico

BEALS, Carleton, *Porfirio Díaz, dictator of Mexico* (Philadelphia and London, Lippincott, 1932).

BRANDENBURG, Frank R., *The Making of Modern Mexico* (Englewood Cliffs, N.J., Prentice-Hall, 1964).

CALCOTT, Wilfrid Hardy, *Liberalism in Mexico, 1857–1929* (Stanford, Stanford U.P., 1931).

CALVERT, Peter, 'The Mexican Political System, a case study in political development', *Journal of Development Studies*, iv, 4 (October 1968) 464.

— *The Mexican Revolution, 1910–1914; the diplomacy of Anglo-American conflict* (Cambridge, C.U.P., 1968).

CLINE, Howard F., *The United States and Mexico* (Cambridge, Mass., Harvard U.P., 1953).

COSIO VILLEGAS, Daniel, *Historia Moderna de Mexico* (Mexico, Editorial Hermes, 1955–).

CUMBERLAND, Charles Curtis, *The Mexican Revolution, Genesis under Madero* (Austin, Univ. of Texas Press, 1952).

DULLES, John W. F., *Yesterday in Mexico, a Chronicle of the Revolution, 1919–1936* (Austin, Univ. of Texas Press, 1961).

QUIRK, Robert E., *An Affair of Honor: Woodrow Wilson and the Occupation of Vera Cruz* (New York, McGraw-Hill, 1964).

— *The Mexican Revolution, 1914–1915; the Convention of Aguascalientes* (Bloomington, Indiana U.P., 1960).

Ross, Stanley Robert, *Francisco I. Madero, Apostle of Mexican Democracy* (New York, Columbia U.P., 1955).

Scott, Robert E., *Mexican Government in Transition* (Urbana, Univ. of Illinois Press, 1959).

Tannenbaum, Frank, *Peace by Revolution: an interpretation of Mexico* (New York, Columbia U.P., 1933).

Townsend, William Cameron, *Lázaro Cárdenas, Mexican democrat* (Ann Arbor, George Wahr, 1952).

Tucker, William P., *The Mexican Government Today* (Minneapolis, Univ. of Minnesota Press, 1957).

Weyl, Nathaniel and Sylvia, *The Re-Conquest of Mexico: the years of Lázaro Cárdenas* (New York, O.U.P., 1939).

Nicaragua

Bailey, Thomas A., 'Interest in a Nicaragua Canal, 1903–1931', *H.A.H.R.* xvi, 1 (February 1936) 2.

Baylen, Joseph O., 'Sandino: Patriot or Bandit?', *H.A.H.R.* xxxi, 3 (August 1951) 445.

Cox, I. J., *Nicaragua and the United States, 1909–1927* (Boston, World Peace Foundation, 1927).

Panama

American University, Washington, D.C., *Special warfare area handbook for Panama*, Special Operations Research Office (Washington, U.S.G.P.O., 1962).

Biesance, John, and Smith, Luke M., 'Panamanian Politics', *Journal of Politics*, xiv (August 1952) 386.

DuVal, Miles P., *And the Mountains Will Move; the story of the building of the Panama Canal* (Stanford, Stanford U.P., 1947).

Ealy, L. O., *The Republic of Panama in World Affairs, 1903–1950* (Philadelphia, Univ. of Penn. Press, 1951).

Pippin, Larry LaRae, *The Remón Era, an analysis of a decade of events in Panama, 1947–1957* (Stanford, Stanford Univ. Inst. of Hispanic American and Luso-Brazilian Studies, 1964).

Paraguay

CARDOZO, Efraim, *Paraguay Independiente* (Barcelona, Salvat Editores, 1949).

WARREN, Harris Gaylord, *Paraguay, an Informal History* (Norman, Univ. of Oklahoma Press, 1949).

— 'Political Aspects of the Paraguayan Revolution, 1936–1940'. *H.A.H.R.* xxx, 1 (Feb. 1950) 2.

Peru

CAREY, James C., *Peru and the United States, 1900–1962* (Notre Dame, Ind., Univ. of Notre Dame Press, 1964).

KANTOR, Harry, *The Ideology and Program of the Peruvian Aprista Movement* (Berkeley, Univ. of California Press, 1953).

PIKE, Frederick, B., *The Modern History of Peru* (London, Weidenfeld & Nicolson, 1967).

Uruguay

FITZGIBBON, Russell H., *Uruguay, portrait of a democracy* (New Brunswick, N.J., Rutgers Univ. Press, 1954).

LINDAHL, Göran G., *Uruguay's New Path, a study in politics during the first colegiado, 1919–33* (Stockholm, Library and Institute of Ibero-American Studies, 1962).

MARTIN, P. A., 'The Career of José Batlle y Ordóñez', *H.A.H.R.* x, 4 (Nov. 1930) 413.

TAYLOR, Philip B. Jr., *Government and Politics of Uruguay* Tulane Studies in Political Science, VII (New Orleans, Tulane Univ. Press, 1960).

— 'Interests and Institutional Dysfunction in Uruguay', *A.P.S.R.* lvii, 1 (March 1963) 62.

— 'The Uruguayan Coup d'Etat of 1933', *H.A.H.R.* xxxii, 3 (August 1952) 301.

VANGER, Milton I., *José Batlle y Ordóñez of Uruguay, the Creator of his Times, 1902–1907* (Cambridge Mass., Harvard U.P., 1963).

Venezuela

ALEXANDER, Robert A., *The Venezuelan Democratic Revolution. A Profile of the Regime of Rómulo Betancourt* (New Brunswick, N.J., Rutgers U.P., 1964).

MORÓN, Guillermo, *A History of Venezuela*, trans. John Street (London, Allen & Unwin, 1964).

PLATT, D. C. M., 'The Allied Coercion of Venezuela, 1902–3 – A Reassessment', *Inter-American Economic Affairs*, xv, 4 (Spring 1962), 2.

'ROURKE, Thomas' (D.J. Clinton), *Gómez, Tyrant of the Andes* (London, Joseph, 1937).

Index

224   INDEX